Effie Mae

By

Patty Mitchell

Copyright © 2016 Patty Mitchell

All rights reserved.

ISBN-10: 0692998349
ISBN-13: 978-0692998342

Acknowledgements

In most instances we have people who encourage us in some form or fashion. It is with sincere gratitude that I'd like to thank Articia Johnson-Hunter, for the support she provided to me in reading my manuscript, during which time she was preparing for motherhood.

I also give thanks to my daughter Ashley for the valuable input she provided in designing the jacket cover of *Effie Mae*, formatting, and completing the necessary legwork that allowed me to combine all the pieces to the puzzle of publishing and ensuring the professional print of my novel.

I would also like to thank Tanisha Morgan-Pinex, for taking time out of her busy schedule as a photographer, to create the beautiful author's photo noted on the back cover of this novel.

Thanks, also goes to my own baby sister, Darnell Lewis-Mathis for having the courage to critique my writing with honesty and sincerity, increasing my confidence as a writer.

And last, but by no means the least, I thank God for anointing me with the gift of writing. To be able to see a story in my head, then bring it to life, by way of ink to paper.

Contents

Chapter One 1

Chapter Two 16

Chapter Three 32

Chapter Four 61

Chapter Five 75

Chapter Six 93

Chapter Seven 104

Chapter Eight 112

Chapter Nine 120

Chapter Ten 129

Chapter Eleven 145

Chapter Twelve 153

Chapter Thirteen 161

Chapter Fourteen 166

Chapter Fifteen 170

Chapter Sixteen 183

Chapter Seventeen 198

Chapter Eighteen 208

Chapter Nineteen 215

Chapter Twenty 218

Chapter Twenty-One 226

Chapter Twenty-Two 235

Chapter Twenty-Three 249

Chapter Twenty-Four 267

Chapter Twenty-Five 278

Chapter Twenty-Six 283

Chapter Twenty-Seven 289

Chapter Twenty-Eight 298

Chapter Twenty-Nine 315

Chapter Thirty 331

Chapter Thirty-One 335

Chapter Thirty-Two 346

Chapter Thirty-Three 352

Chapter Thirty-Four 362

Chapter Thirty-Five 368

Chapter Thirty-Six 386

Chapter Thirty-Seven 398

Chapter Thirty-Eight 400

Chapter Thirty-Nine 407

Chapter Forty 412

Chapter Forty-One 416

Chapter Forty-Two 419

Chapter One

It's midnight. The brand new 1959 white Ford Thunderbird turned onto the highway, its whitewall tires rolled as it accelerated to the 60 mph speed limit. Inside, sat forty-five year old David Reed, his wife, forty year old Helen, and their only child, eighteen year old Willie Lee.

David adjusted his rear end on the cushioned seat, then reached over and turned the radio on, seeking a local station. Little Richard's—"Long Tall Sally" screamed from the speakers, as the family prepared to make their 637 mile, nine and a half hour journey from Jacksonville, Florida to Yazoo City, Mississippi. A trip they'd planned for the last year, to visit David's late cousin Frank Reed's widow, Millie and their two daughters, sixteen year old Effie Mae and fifteen year old Annie Mae.

"That's too loud David. Turn it down some."Helen said, irritated by the earsplitting sound.

"Naw! That's not too loud. It's Little Richard! That's how you play his music!" Helen leaned forward and turned the knob lowering the volume." Come on now

Helen!" He looked over at her. "Just let me listen to "Long Tall Sally" then I'll turn it down." David reached over and twisted the knob and increased the volume. He shifted his eyes to Helen and awaited her response.

"I'm trying to get some sleep David! We have a long road ahead of us." She threw her sweater over her head. David glanced at her then laughed to himself. Helen tossed and turned as she tried to get comfortable then stopped. She pulled the sweater from over her head and glared at him. She gripped the dial and decreased the volume level to low. David looked over at her.

"Come on now Helen! It's "Long Tall Sally!"

"I don't care if it's Short, Fat Fannie, it's too loud!" He decelerated to 50 mph then gazed at her. She stared at him briefly.

"Go ahead David! Listen to "Long Tall Sally" then turn it down! Or else, you'll be picking that radio up from off the highway!" She threw her sweater back over her head. David chuckled then began singing along with Little Richard. Helen peered at him from underneath the sweater then turned her body towards the door. She said nothing further. David glimpsed in the backseat at Willie Lee. He observed his oversized son already sleep and snoring. He accelerated his speed to 70 mph then proceeded to sing off key to his favorite Rock and Roll artist.

...

Millie Reed, a forty year old, dark complexioned, full figured woman, woke up at five-thirty a.m. She climbed out of bed, picked up the basin that sat on her dresser then headed into the bathroom that consisted of only a sink and tub. She turned on the faucet, let the water run until warm, then filled the basin partway. She returned to her bedroom and removed a towel wrapped around a white bar of soap from a dresser drawer. Immersing the combo into the water, she removed the soap then wrung out the towel. She washed her face and underarms while still wearing her sleeveless blue nightgown.

After a complete sponge bath, she slipped on the taupe, short sleeve duster that lay across the foot of her bed. She went back into the bathroom and brushed her teeth, then robotically spit the mint flavored paste from her mouth and into the sink. Millie retreated from the bathroom and again returned to her bedroom. She grabbed a brush from off the dresser and vigorously brushed her hair, twisting a rubber band around it, she concluded the process by placing a ponytail mid-center on the back of her head. Millie hurried from the room. She walked through the kitchen and exited through the back door, entering into the midsized outhouse where she promptly relieved herself. Returning back inside the home, she washed her hands at the kitchen sink then headed in the direction of her daughter's bedroom. She entered into the room and observed her two teenagers still sleeping. She walked over to the window and opened the leaf patterned curtains revealing the sky which displayed an orange-yellowish tint as the sun's rays shined under the clouds and prepared to rise.

"Effie Mae! Annie Mae! It's time to get up!" she stated, loudly. "David and Helen and their boy Willie Lee's on their way here from Florida. And I want to make sure we got lots of hot food ready, when they get here." Millie turned and prepared to exit from the room. Annie Mae threw the cover over her head.

"Momma I don't know them people!"

"You don't need to know them. All you need to know is they your daddy's kinfolk."

"I didn't know *him* either." She said. Hearing no reply from Millie, Annie Mae peered from underneath the covers. She locked eyes with her glaring mother.

"Don't, you ever let me hear you say nothing like that again! Do you understand me Annie Mae Reed?" Millie said, incensed. "Now get out of that bed!"

Annie Mae slowly climbed out of bed and walked cautiously pass her Momma. Millie watched as her young daughter strolled from the bedroom into the kitchen, walking over to the sink. Annie Mae turned on the faucet then splashed her face with water. With her eyes still shut, she grabbed a kitchen towel, using it to dry her face. She exited through the screened back door, allowing it slam shut behind her. She swung open the door to the old outhouse and went inside being seated on the square wooden box consisting of a toilet seat, neatly situated over a round hole. She left the door open and gazed around the backyard as she peed.

"Effie Mae! Get up now, child. Your daddy's cousin David, his wife Helen and their boy Willie Lee, gon be here soon."

"Willie Lee?" Have I ever seen him before Momma?" Millie smiled as she reminisced. "The last time they were here—you were just a lil' girl and Annie Mae was a baby. It's sure gon be good seeing them again."

Effie Mae pulled the covers from over her head and rolled onto her back and lay there. Millie stared at her.

"And, the next time I tell you to get out of that bed; it's gone be with a glass of cold water."

"Okay Momma, I'm getting up." Effie Mae sat up.

"And make sure your sister wash up and brush her teeth. I know how she is when it comes to cleaning herself."

"Momma, she ain't gon listen to me." Effie Mae got out of the bed and stood. Her floor length, over-sized, cotton nightgown flowed down covering her feet.

"I'm gon see you and your sister in the kitchen." Millie said, heading towards the door. She stopped and turned. "In twenty minutes!" She stated firmly, exiting the room.

...

The white Thunderbird crossed into the state of Mississippi. David rode pass the sign that read "Yazoo City—189 miles. He looked on the dashboard to check the speedometer and gas gauge. It dawned on him that it had been a while since he'd last filled-up. He tried to remember the last sign directing drivers to upcoming gas stations. His attention suddenly drew to the fizzled out radio. David reached over and turned the dial as he searched for another station. His search ended when he heard Little Richard's "Tutti Frutti." He cranked up the volume and sang along, wildly. As his voice heightened, he looked over at Helen, still asleep, her back turned to him. He glanced back at Willie Lee, snoring, sounding much like a growing bear. David gradually increased his speed to 75 mph as he continued traveling. The radio blared as he once again combined his un-tuned vocals with Little Richard's.

"What you cooking Momma?" Effie Mae asked as Millie hurried about the kitchen, a white bib apron covering the entire front of the duster.

"I got ham; I'm frying chicken, fried potatoes and onions; smothering some collard greens, fried corn and crackling cornbread." Millie stated as she stood at the sink running cold water over several pieces of raw chicken.

"For breakfast?" Annie Mae said, frowning.

"For all day." Millie replied. "I'm gon cook enough for them to eat breakfast, lunch, and if they want it — dinner."

"I don't think I want all that for breakfast Momma." Annie Mae said.

"Good! That mean it's gon be for more for David, Helen and Willie Lee." Millie shook salt and pepper onto the raw chicken then tossed it into the bowl of seasoned flour. "I heard that Willie Lee was as big as a bear!" She said, chuckling.

"What you need me to do Momma?" Effie Mae asked.

"You can start shucking them ears of corn on that table."

Effie Mae removed the waist apron from across a kitchen chair and put it on then sat down and began pulling the green husk and golden silk strands from the corn.

"And what's Annie Mae gon do Momma?"

"She gon get over here and pick these collard greens. Come on over here to this table child and sit down." Millie said, as she retrieved a large black pot from the cupboard, sitting it onto the table. She again walked over to the cabinets where she retrieved two large, brown paper bags filled with large leaves of collard greens from the countertop. Returning to the table, she sat the bags onto the floor, just left of Effie

Mae then shifted her eyes over to Annie Mae. She raised an eyebrow.

"If you don't get your behind over here and sit it in this chair . . . .

"Momma, I don't know how to pick no greens!" Annie Mae said as she plopped down into one of the four chairs situated around the rectangular table.

"It ain't that hard. All you got to do is take any bugs you see on there—off. After that you gon pull the leaf off the stem, and put it in that pot." Annie Mae leapt up from the table.

"Bugs?" Momma, I ain't picking bugs off of them things!" She abruptly stood. "I'm going back to bed."

"Get on child." Millie said, shaking her head and chuckling, humored by her young daughter's fear of bugs. "I'm gon have your sister pick them. But, soon as she done, I'm gon have her come and get you, so you can wash them!"

"Wash them?" Annie Mae pouted. "Momma, knowing Effie Mae, she's probably gon leave some bugs on there on purpose." Millie laughed. Annie Mae grimaced as she walked away and entered into her bedroom.

"You can do that much, can't you Annie Mae?" Effie Mae teased. Annie Mae slammed the bedroom door. Millie and Effie Mae looked one to the other then burst into laughter. For the next three and a half hours they prepared the huge, country meal for their impending out of town guests.

Annie Mae sat out front on the porch and talked with her best friend Anita from school.

"I think Pete Parker is so cute." Annie Mae stated, starry-eyed.

Pete was the younger of the two sons of Ned and Fannie Mae Parker. He was sixteen and quite mature for his age. He was tall, medium build, and his skin, coffee brown. Embedded in his masculine face were two eye-catching dimples.

"He is now. But he didn't look like that last year." Anita stated, with a bitter look on her face.

"Anita, do you ever think about what it's like being with a boy?"

"Nope! And I don't want to think about it."

"Yeah . . . we should probably wait until we get older."

"Uh, yeah!

"Did you hear that Kelly Ann was pregnant?"

"Yeah, the kids at school talked about her like a dog too!"

"And you already know her daddy's gon make her get married."

"And to Ol' funny looking Alfred Lee!"

"Yuk! With them big ears." Annie Mae frowned.

"Yeah—and it looks like the older he got . . . ."

"The bigger those ears got!" Annie Mae joked. The two girls laughed.

"Well let's just agree to save ourselves until we meet the right man."

"And definitely wait until after we married." Annie Mae said.

"Agreed!" The girls said in unison. And this adolescent pledge may have lasted, except that Annie Mae's infatuation for an emerging Pete Parker, and his for her, trumped that vow.

...

The white Thunderbird displaying a green Florida license plate pulled off the road and into the dirt driveway at the Reed's family home then stopped.

"Momma, they're here!" Annie Mae dashed from the porch and into the house. Millie untied the white bib apron from around her neck and waist then hurried out onto the front porch. Quickly untying the apron from around her waist, Effie Mae followed.

The car doors of the white Thunderbird flung open, David and Helen climbed out. David walked in a circle as he stretched his arms and legs. Helen headed in the direction of the house.

"David, Helen! How y'all doing? How was the drive?" Millie asked, stepping down from the porch, onto the steps and into the front yard.

"It was a long one!" David chuckled as he walked toward her. "Millie! It sure is good to see you again." He said, hugging her.

"How are you Millie?" Helen asked. "I sure am hungry. I hope you have something already cooked on the stove." She walked pass Millie. "I'm ready to eat." Helen walked up the stairs and entered into the house through the front door.

"Willie Lee! Get out of the car boy!" David shouted as he approached the rear back door and swung it open.

"I'm hungry." Willie Lee said, rubbing his eyes as he awakened from his nine hour sleep.

"Run on in the house with your mother—get something to eat." Three hundred pound Willie Lee climbed out. He walked pass Millie and his two cousins without acknowledging their presence, then stepped onto the front porch and went inside the house.

"Now, I got plenty of food in there David if you hungry." Millie stated. David looked at Effie Mae and Annie Mae then smiled.

"You know Millie if Frank were still alive—he'd be proud of the job you've done raising his girls." He stated, locking his lustful eyes onto Effie Mae.

Effie Mae was light skinned, moderate in height and had an hour glass figure she'd inherited from her father's side of the family. She had black shoulder length hair that rippled like the waves on the water's surface, complimenting her hazel brown eyes and bright smile.

"Come on over here girls and give your Cousin David a hug!" Effie Mae and Annie Mae gazed at him in silence. Neither girl moved.

"Go on!" Millie urged. "That's your daddy's cousin. Go on now!" The two girls walked towards David. His roaming eyes pored over Effie Mae's physique.

"That's right! Give your cousin David a hug!" He smiled then reached out and took a hold of Annie Mae. He briefly hugged then released her. Annie Mae was equal in looks to her big sister, except for her chestnut brown eyes and curvy figure.

David's smile widened as he held his arms open to Effie Mae, as if requesting, she come to him. Effie Mae stood still as he walked over and embraced her then discretely kissed her on the neck. She pulled away.

"Come on in David!" Millie said as she turned to reenter the house. Annie Mae and Effie Mae followed. David trailed behind. He watched Effie Mae and smiled as he took note of her exposed legs from underneath the plaid knee shorts she wore.

After breakfast Annie Mae sat alone on the front porch. Pete quietly beckoned her from the side of the house. She hurried down the stairs and joined him then the two snuck away. Effie Mae sat out back on the steps with Willie Lee.

"I bet you have a lot of boyfriends?" He asked, sliding closer towards her.

"Nope! Momma don't allow me to date boys yet."

"I don't see why. You're pretty." He put his hand on her thigh. She pushed it away.

"You like boys?" He asked looking at Effie Mae with interest. "Have you ever been with a boy before?" He rubbed her hair.

"No! And I'm not trying to!" She shoved his hand from her head.

"I've been with a girl before. It was fun!" He said as he looked into Effie Mae's eyes. "You want to do it?"

"What? With you? Ain't you my cousin?"

"Daddy said that don't matter."

"Well, it matters to me!"

"My cousin NeNe didn't care about us being cousins."

"I'm going in the house." Effie Mae stood and turned to go inside.

"Will you think about it?"

"Nope!"

"Don't forget that you said you was gon help me dig for night crawlers tonight, so me and daddy can go fishing in the morning.

"I won't forget." Effie Mae entered the house and walked through the living room where Millie, David and Helen talked about the good old days.

"There she is!" David said. "You and Willie Lee talked about anything interesting?" He asked looking at Effie Mae's enticing figure.

"Nope." Effie Mae headed in the direction of her bedroom.

"Well, now before you disappear into your room I have something for you out there in my car."

"No thank you."

"Effie Mae!" Millie yelled. "Your cousin brought you something all the way from Florida, and you ain't even gon go see what it is? Now, go on out there and see what your Cousin David brought you." Effie Mae hesitated. "Go on." Millie urged as David stood and waited for her to join him at the front door. Effie Mae looked at Millie with reluctance. "Go on." Millie smiled as she shooed her on.

Effie Mae followed David out the door, stopping when reaching his car. He opened the door and sat on the seat, his legs dangled outside the car.

"Come on over here." He motioned with his head. "I won't bite you." He smiled then reached out and pulled Effie Mae down onto his lap. He rubbed her thigh then held her tight as she squirmed to get away. She felt the lump that rose in his pants as he laid the side of his head onto the headrest and she continued to struggle. Effie Mae wiggled for five minutes, trying to free herself before she heard David let out an odd noise, squeezing her tightly, moments before his arms and hands went limp. Effie Mae bucked to escape. David quickly caught ahold of her arm, pulling her back towards him.

"Don't you tell Millie about this, because if you do — I'll come back in the middle of the night and take you from your Momma, and she won't ever, see you again!" He glared into her eyes. "You understand me girl!" Effie Mae nodded. David released her arm, and allowed her to run away. He laughed to himself as she ran onto the front porch and disappeared through the door.

Late, that evening Effie Mae entered into the outhouse to use the bathroom. As she finished, the door swung open. She looked into the peering eyes of Willie Lee. He saw her panties still around her ankles and came inside.

"Get out of here Willie Lee! I'll scream!" She yelled.

"There's nobody here. Daddy took Momma, Millie and Annie Mae to go get some ice cream. He told me, you knew how to keep a secret." He grabbed her from behind. She stood helpless to the three hundred pound male determined to do to her as he'd done with his cousin NeNe. Effie Mae fought, but to no avail. Willie Lee closed and locked the door then proceeded to molest her. Effie Mae shrieked.

...

"Well, Millie I want to thank you for all your hospitality. But it looks like we've worn out our welcome." David shifted his eyes over to Effie Mae. "Three days wasn't enough. Next time we'll have to stay longer. Effie Mae . . . Florida's a beautiful place. Maybe you can come spend this summer with us, now that you and Willie Lee have gotten acquainted." He said testing to see if she would reveal her assaults. He turned his attention back to Millie. "It's a long ride back. So we gon go ahead and hit that road, get on out of here." He hugged Millie and Annie Mae.

"It sure was nice seeing y'all again . . . Helen, Willie Lee." Millie said.

"Well one thing I can say Millie, you sure fed us good!" Helen hugged Millie briefly then headed towards the front door. "Come on Willie Lee." She shouted.

Willie Lee looked at Effie Mae and smiled. "Bye Effie Mae." He joined his mother at the door then the two exited the home. Millie escorted David to the front door, then out onto the porch. Effie Mae and Annie Mae watched from inside the house as he and Millie exchanged a final hug goodbye. David glanced in at Effie Mae, smiled and waved.

Effie Mae lay on her bed writing in the old red diary. In it she wrote about her incidents with David and Willie Lee. Millie entered into the room, concerned about her daughter's withdrawn behavior.

"Effie Mae, you feeling alright child?"

"I'm fine Momma." She continued writing.

"You hardly said a word since your cousins left here a week ago. I guess you missing them, is what it is . . . me too." She smiled. "It sure was nice seeing them though."

"Momma is it okay for you to be with your own cousin?" Effie Mae inquired.

"What? Did something happen to you child?" Millie asked, alarmed.

"Nope! I just heard that two cousins had been together. And neither one of them seemed to think it was wrong." Effie Mae looked up from her diary.

"Effie Mae? Did Willie Lee do something to you, child?"

Effie Mae reached underneath the mattress and pulled out a pair of blood stained panties.

"Lord, have mercy!" Millie cried out. "Who done this to you? Was it Willie Lee?" She shouted.

"Both."

"Both? What both?"

"Willie Lee . . . and Cousin David."

Millie rushed over and grabbed Effie Mae, taking her into her arms. Effie Mae showed no emotion.

Chapter Two

Millie moved swiftly down the dusty dirt road on her way home from work. She noticed Annie Mae sitting alone on the old couch kept on the front porch.

"Where's Effie Mae?" Millie asked as she stepped onto the porch.

Annie Mae looked up. She remained silent, her eyes answering her Momma's question.

"Is she in the house?" Annie Mae nodded.

"Is she alone?" Annie Mae shook her head, no. Millie rushed inside and headed directly to Effie Mae's bedroom. She paused momentarily as she stood outside the door. Seconds later Millie burst inside the room where Effie Mae lay in bed, under the covers engaged in intimacy with an unfamiliar young man.

"Effie Mae Reed!" Millie yelled. The male looked up and into the enraged eyes of Millie. He quickly grabbed the bed sheet and covered his naked body as he gathered his clothes from the floor. Effie Mae rolled off the mattress and onto the side of the bed, attempting to cover herself with a pillow.

Millie watched as the young man darted past her and into the living room then scurried out the front door. He continued down the dirt road, still draped in the bed sheet. Millie then turned her attention to Effie Mae. She momentarily glared at her naked daughter as if she were diseased, then turned and walked away. Effie Mae peeked over the mattress and watched as Millie stormed from the room.

Millie stood at the stove preparing supper. Effie Mae meekly entered into the kitchen. She glanced at her Momma, uncertain of what to say.

"Momma, do you need me to help you with something?" Millie cringed at the sound of her voice.

"You can go and get your sister, so she can help me." She avoided looking at Effie Mae.

"I can help you Momma." Effie Mae stated, hoping to divert Millie's anger. "You know Annie Mae can't cook." Millie turned and gazed into her eyes.

"I'd rather have Annie Mae in here messing up something . . . ." She paused. "Truth is, right now Effie Mae, it pains my eyes, just looking at you." Millie again turned her attention to the stove, stirring the contents in one of the large pots on the burners. Effie Mae remained silent. She showed no emotion to Millie's hurtful words.

"I talked to my sister Kathy and her husband Charles. They think I ought to send you to Jackson, stay with them. Think maybe getting you from around this here place, might cure you of whatever's going on in your head." Millie said with her back still turned to her eldest daughter.

"I'll do better Momma!" Effie Mae pleaded. Millie turned and gazed at her through hurtful eyes.

"How many times do that make child—that you done said that untruth? Seems like every week, here comes a new boy; use to be boys living here in the county, now they appear to be coming from who knows where. Do you even know where? Do you even care, Effie Mae?"

"Momma, I don't want to leave you and Annie Mae." She stated as her eyes filled with tears. Millie dismissed her words and her emotions.

"Now, go get your sister—so we can eat supper." Effie Mae turned slowly away, in obedience to her Momma's request. She walked over to the back door then exited the house, in search of her younger sister's whereabouts.

Millie remained silent as she and her two daughters ate supper. Not a single word passed through their lips.

"Effie Mae, a boy driving a red car came to the house yesterday asking for you." Annie Mae stated, breaking the silence. Millie glared at her young daughter with disapproval. Annie Mae swiftly shifted her eyes down onto her plate.

"Red car? Was he cute?" Effie Mae's excitement heightened. "Did he say what his name was?" Annie Mae glanced up at Millie, but said nothing further. Receiving no reply from her younger sister, Effie Mae looked across the table and into the aggravated face of Millie.

"Annie Mae." Millie said, turning her attention away from Effie Mae and onto her less troublesome daughter. "How's Anita's Momma doing? Sissy told me in church on Sunday that she just 'bout ready to birth that child she carrying; said she looked like she's 'bout to bust!" Millie chuckled, as she continued to ignore Effie Mae's presence at the table. Annie Mae shifted her eyes to her big sister, disturbed by their Momma's dismissal of her.

The following day Effie Mae sat on the front porch accompanied by Annie Mae and Anita. A 1958 red and white Chevrolet Bel-Air Convertible with a white top, white wall tires, and mirror chrome plated hubcaps, drove pass the house. It stopped and backed up then pulled into the driveway.

"That's him Effie Mae!" Annie Mae said with enthusiasm. Effie Mae flirted with her eyes as the young man with curly hair and glasses, wearing a white shirt and black bowtie, looked up at her.

"Are you Effie Mae?" He smiled.

"Who wants to know?" She teased.

"Anthony."

"Yeah—I'm Effie Mae. How do you know me Anthony?"

"Well, I . . . uh don't know you, but I heard of you."

"Heard of me? And just what did you hear?" She flirted.

"I heard that you like to have a good time. Well, I like having a good time too. So I figured, since we both like having a good time, we could have a good time together."

Effie Mae stood. She wore black mid-thigh shorts and a pink polka dotted, sleeveless blouse, tied about the waist. She fluffed her hair with her fingers then walked off the porch.

"Effie Mae! If you leave here, Momma's gon send you to go live with Auntie Kathy and Uncle Charles."

"How Momma gon know Annie Mae? You gon tell her?"

"No." Annie Mae said, passively then lowered her head.

"If you don't tell her, then Momma won't know — now will she?" Effie Mae snapped. "Besides I'll be back, way before Momma gets home from work."

Anthony watched with excitement as she walked off the porch and got into his car. He shifted the gears into reverse then backed out of the driveway and onto the road. Effie Mae smiled and waved at Annie Mae and Anita. The two girls watched in awe, their mouths wide open as Anthony cruised down the road with a very willing, Effie Mae.

Anthony pulled into the parking lot of the Cozi-T Motel. A male in his twenties came out of room—11. He walked over to the car and glanced over at Effie Mae. She looked at him and flirted with her smile.

"You owe me six dollars." He said to Anthony, never taking is eyes off of Effie Mae. Anthony leaned forward and took his wallet out of his back pocket. He counted out six one dollar bills then handed them to the male who then dropped the key into Anthony's opened hand.

"You have to be out by eleven o'clock in the morning." He said.

"Eleven o'clock in the morning! I have to be home long before that." Effie Mae shouted.

"Uh, that's just the check out time. I'll have you back home before your Momma gets there." Anthony stated, calmly. "What time does she get home anyway?" He asked as his eyes explored her body.

"Four o'clock! Five, if she stops to talk."

"Let's see." He looked at his watch. "It's one o'clock now . . . we have plenty of time to do whatever it is that we're getting ready to do." He looked up at the man still standing next to the car and smiled. "I guess we need to get in there then." Anthony got out and walked around the car and opened Effie Mae's door. The man watched as they held hands and entered into room 11.

"Effie Mae! Wake up girl!" Anthony said as he shook her shoulder.

"What time is it?" She asked, from underneath the sheet thrown over her head.

"It's check out time!" Anthony hurriedly began putting on his pants.

"What?" Effie Mae threw off the covers and scrambled to gather her clothes. "My Momma's gon kill me." She buttoned her blouse. "I thought you said you would get me home in time?"

"And I thought I would, but . . . ." He quickly put on his shoes.

"But what? How am I gon explain this to Momma?"

"I'll explain it to her."

"You? And just what do you think you can say that my Momma would listen to?"

"I'll think of something." He swiftly kissed Effie Mae on the lips then the two rushed through the motel door and out to Anthony's car. The tires screeched as he threw the car in reverse and sped off at a high rate of speed, thinking of how he would convincingly explain away the intimate night he and Effie Mae spent together.

Anthony turned onto the road leading to the Reed family's home. He decelerated as he approached. Millie stood out front accompanied by Reverend Otis Hill, a middle aged, slightly balding, obese man and his wife Sissy, tall and thin, ten years his junior and snobbish. They watched as Anthony slowly pulled into the driveway. He turned off the engine and slowly climbed out of the car. Rev. Hill looked at him with familiarity, certain that he most likely knew the young man's parents.

"Good morning Rev. Hill." Anthony greeted.

"Isn't that Betsy Lewis' son?" Sissy asked, as she too recognized him. "And he's a good boy—going to college and everything." She stared as Anthony walked around the car and opened Effie Mae's door. "Why in the world would he be with . . .?"

"Ahem!" Rev. Hill cleared his throat, momentarily turning his attention to his outspoken wife.

"You know what I was trying to say Millie." Sissy said, regrettably, trying to recant her thoughtless statement. Millie ignored her words as she gazed at Effie Mae in anger.

"I was just saying . . . ." Sissy continued.

"Sissy." Rev. Hill shushed her.

"Momma—let me explain."

"You get your behind in that house and go straight to your room! And don't you come out until I tell you too!" Millie yelled. "You understand me child?"

"Yes Momma." Effie Mae looked at Anthony and smiled as if thanking him. Millie gazed at her through frustrated eyes as she entered into the house by way of the back door. Millie immediately turned her attention to Anthony. He nervously looked into the faces of Rev. Hill, Sissy and Millie. They glared at him and awaited his explanation.

"I, uh . . . came by yesterday to take Effie Mae for a ride in my new car – and, uh we drove to Jackson." Anthony paused to see if they were convinced, thus far. "And, uh—it got late, so we decided to stay there all night." He shifted his attention to Millie. "We didn't stay in a motel or anything like that. We, uh—just slept in the car."

"That's the best he could do?" Sissy mumbled, as she looked at him through doubtful eyes.

"Where do you know my daughter from young man?" Millie asked as she stared at him with intimidation.

"I, uh—I, uh . . . ." He stuttered.

"That's what I thought." Millie said.

"Young man, I think you should leave now, while Ms. Millie's still calm." Rev. Hill stated.

"Yes Sir." Anthony politely replied.

"I should tell Betsy on him, coming over here lying like that." Sissy said. Anthony hastily walked over to the driver's side of the car and got in. He started the engine, pulled out of the driveway and onto the dirt road and drove away without looking back.

"I don't know what you're going to do with that one, Millie." Sissy said. "They don't get any hotter in the pants than Effie Mae!"

"Sissy." Rev. Hill gestured her with his eyes to go get into the car.

"Well Millie . . . ." Sissy gave a sigh of relief. "I'm glad Effie Mae made it back home in one piece." She hugged Millie, kissing her lightly on the cheek. "I'll see you in church on Sunday." Rev. Hill watched as his opinionated wife walked down the driveway and climbed into the shiny, black 1959 Cadillac parked on the front lawn.

"Is there anything I can do, Ms. Millie?" Rev. Hill took a hold of her hand.

"Unless you can raise the dead, and bring back my Frank—I'm afraid it ain't nothing you can do at this point, Rev. Hill." He listened with sympathetic ears. "My sister Kathy and her husband Charles want me to send Effie Mae to Jackson with them. After last night, I ain't sure what else I can do!" Millie shook her head in despair. "Truth is—I ain't even sure if that would help that child."

"Well Ms. Millie, you know Sissy and I are here, whenever you need us."

"I know Rev. Hill. And I thank you both." Millie smiled.

"I'll see you and your girls in church on Sunday? I guess that may just be the one place, Effie Mae can't get into trouble." He joked then kissed Millie on the cheek.

Millie raised an eyebrow in doubt. "Don't be too sure."

Saturday morning, at six o'clock a.m., Millie abruptly awakened to the sound of continuous pounding on the back door. She scrambled from the bed, grabbed the pink robe hanging from a nail on the back of the bedroom door then scurried through the living room and into the kitchen. She slowed when she recognized the obscured figure through the opaque curtain covering the back door window, as being that of Ned Parker. She narrowly opened the door, minutes before his fist connected again.

"Mr. Parker? It's a bit early for visitor to be calling—ain't it?" Millie asked, shielding herself behind the door.

"I think you need to come on out here Ms. Millie." He looked towards the outhouse.

Millie opened the door and saw Effie Mae standing near the outhouse. Dressed in a baby blue, sheer, sleeveless nightgown; She stood next to twenty-one year old Jimmy Parker, who wore only a pair of white boxers.

Recruited by Effie Mae to scratch the insatiable itch she seemed to have developed after her incestuous assaults, he too stood mute. Millie stormed out of the house and into the yard. She glared at Effie Mae then shook her head in disgust.

"That gal's worse than a rabbit dog." Ned Parker stated.

"I don't see where your boy's much better . . . Now is he?"

"Gal's spreading herself around the county faster than a cold."

"And, you just happen to be out here this time of morning, Mr. Parker? I hear you been spreading pretty fast around here yourself!"

"You stay out of my business Ms. Millie! Don't let me have to put my foot up your . . . ."

"Daddy!" Jimmy yelled. Ned momentarily stared at Millie. He said nothing further. Millie turned her attention back to Effie Mae.

"You get your behind in that house!" She angrily pointed towards the back door. "I'll deal with you when I get in there."

Effie Mae walked pass Millie and cautiously entered into the house. She hurried into her bedroom where she awaited her fate. Pacing repeatedly from one end of the room to the other, she looked out of the window and watched as Millie and Ned Parker continued arguing.

She tried to read the expressions on Millie's face as the minutes passed and her dispute with their ornery neighbor, diminished. Effie Mae tried hard to figure out what her explanation would be this time. She swallowed the lump in her throat becoming nauseated from the butterflies in her stomach. She suddenly heard the back door slam. Three seconds later, Millie appeared in the doorway. Her eyes, filled with disdain as she gawked at Effie Mae in fury.

"Out there acting like a female dog in heat!" She yelled. "You wasn't raised that way. So you got to be sick in the head!"

"I'm sorry Momma."

"When you sorry 'bout something Effie Mae, you don't keep doing it, child!"

"Every since Willie Lee and Cousin David forced me to be with them . . . ." Millie cut her off.

"Well, ain't nobody's forcing you now — is they?" Effie Mae gave no reply. She believed if she tried to explain her uncontrollable urge to her Momma, it would fall upon deaf ears. On the outside, she believed herself to be a normal teen. Inside, she raged with feelings of guilt and shame, as she blamed herself for her cousin's unwanted actions. "You stay your behind in this house for the next week. You better not even darken that doorway." Millie stated, furiously. "Cause if you do . . . ." She paused. "Pack your bags!" Millie turned and walked swiftly away. She entered into her bedroom and vigorously slammed the door. Effie Mae stood mute in the middle of her bedroom, her emotions growing dim.

Forbidden to leave the house, Effie Mae decided to write in her diary instead. She reached under the mattress and retrieved the red book given to her by her Auntie Peaches, now deceased, when Effie Mae was only ten. She sometimes found spending time with her father's baby sister through written words, more comforting than talking to human beings.

Effie Mae wrote about Jimmy Parker, six feet tall with a masculine build, and butterscotch complexion, he was quite handsome. His good looks were surpassed only by his charm and sense of humor. Effie Mae described their intimate episode in the old outhouse, but before she could provide the vivid details, she heard the front door open and close, as Millie arrived home from work.

Effie Mae quickly stuffed the red diary back under the mattress, positioned herself onto the bed and awaited her Momma to enter into the room. A ritual that usually occurred minutes after Millie entered into the house.

Tired from a full week of housekeeping duties, Millie walked towards Effie Mae's bedroom. She stopped in the doorway, a look of disappointment etched across her face, from the most recent gossip she'd heard about her eldest daughter.

"Spoke to Sissy Hill today on my way home from work." Millie arched her right eyebrow. "Said, she talked to Fannie Mae Parker about Jimmy—and you."

"I already know what you gon say Momma." Effie Mae rolled her eyes and looked up at the ceiling.

"Seems, everywhere I go, people talking 'bout my eldest daughter. How she out there, spreading her legs for every young boy in the Yazoo County!"

"It don't bother me none, what people around here say about me Momma."

"But it bothers me Effie Mae!" Millie said. "And if your daddy was alive, it would bother him too. Is that how you want people to see you child?"

"It would suit me just fine Momma, if they didn't see me at all."

"When I married your daddy, I felt like the luckiest girl in this here county. Your Grand Poppa, Reverend George Reed and his family was some of the most respected folks 'round here. And it wasn't easy for my daddy to convince Rev. Reed, that I was the right girl for their boy Frank. Goodness knows I wasn't the prettiest, or the smartest. But I could cook and clean, and that was good enough for them.

Effie Mae again rolled her eyes. "Momma, I'm different from you. I don't care about being nobody's wife – cooking, cleaning, none of that! If a man wants to eat, let him cook it his self. And if he wants his house cleaned, let him clean it." She said, rebelliously. "Besides, I like doing just what it is I'm doing."

"Stop talking like that!" Millie snapped. "You Frank Reed's daughter . . . a good Christian girl. And it's time you started acting like it!" Effie Mae rolled her eyes and ignored her Momma's words, having heard them numerous times before.

"Momma, I'm not doing anything the rest of the girls in this county ain't doing." Millie's agitation increased.

"Well, you ain't everybody else's daughter—you mines!" She shouted. "And I won't be talked about 'cause my daughter can't seem to keep her legs . . . ."

"Okay Momma." Effie Mae interrupted. "I'll try to do better."

Effie Mae gazed out of the bedroom window as she remained banned from the outside. She spotted Annie Mae and Pete lurking around outback. She snickered when seeing her baby sister kissing the Parker's baby boy.

"Looks like Annie Mae ain't no better than me." Effie Mae said to herself. She watched as Annie Mae and Pete passionately hugged and kissed, unaware that they were being observed. Effie Mae ducked her head below the windowsill, whenever Annie Mae looked in the direction of the house. Effie Mae's eyes widened when she saw her young sister and Pete Parker disappear into the old outhouse.

Her attention abruptly diverted, when she noticed Ned Parker as he made his way through the thickness of the trees located throughout the Reed's family property. A fairly good looking man, he bore the reputation of being a womanizer, rumored to have fathered numerous children outside of he and Fannie Mae's marriage.

Ned walked towards the house, an angry look plastered across his face, and a large stick, held tightly in his right hand. He stormed past the outhouse, minutes after Pete had closed the door. He quickly approached the back door of the house and began pounding. Effie Mae hurried from her room. She ran through the living room and into kitchen, stopping when she arrived at the back door, barely opening it, and peered out.

"Have you seen my boy?" He yelled.

"Which one? You got two of 'em."

"Don't get smart with me gal!"

"I'm just answering the question you asked me."

"Pete! I'm looking for Pete. Have you seen him?"

"If you don't know where he is and he's your boy, what make you think I know?" Ned gazed at her, annoyed by her responses.

"I've told you about all that smart talk, gal." He attempted to look through the cracked door. "Where's

Ms. Millie at?" Before Effie Mae could say anything further, Millie entered through the front door.

"Mr. Parker?" She called out, startling both their unwelcome visitor and Effie Mae.

"Where's my boy?" He shouted. Millie touched Effie Mae's shoulder, urging her to move from the doorway so she could deal with Ned Parker.

"Can I help you with something Mr. Parker?"

"I ask if you seen my boy!"

"Which one—you got two of 'em."

"Now I know where that gal got her smart mouth from."

"Since I just got home from work, Mr. Parker, unless I passed your boys on my way in, I ain't seen either one of them. But it would seem to me that the best place for you to be looking for your boys ought to be at your own home." She stated, sarcastically. "That way when they do show up, you be right there when they arrive." Millie flashed him an illegitimate smile. Ned grumbled then turned and walked away. But not before he looked past Millie and directly to Effie Mae who stood just behind her Momma. "Tell Fannie Mae, I say—Hi." Millie stated, politely as she gently closed the door. She chuckled, amused by her evasiveness with the ornery Ned Parker then swiftly turned her attention to Effie Mae. But before she could speak, Effie Mae responded in her defense.

"It ain't me this time Momma. He was looking for Pete."

"Pete?" Now why on earth would he be looking for Pete over here?" She peered at Effie Mae.

"I know people might think I been with every boy in the county, but I swear Momma, I ain't ever been with brothers."

Millie mentally blocked out Effie Mae's candidness. She said nothing further about her promiscuous daughter's inappropriate behavior, or about Ned Parker and his missing boy, Pete.

"Go find your sister so y'all can start cooking supper—where she at anyway?" Millie asked rhetorically, then hurried into the living room, dropped her purse onto the coffee table and plopped down in her rocking chair, falling quickly to sleep.

Effie Mae exited from the back door. She allowed it to slam shut as if sending a warning to Annie Mae and Pete. She walked past the outhouse and wandered towards the rear of the property giving the teenage lovebirds, time to flee. The door of the outhouse suddenly swung open. Annie Mae rushed out and entered into the house through the back door, being careful not to allow it to slam. Pete quickly followed, but walked in the opposite direction, attempting to give the impression that he'd simply been strolling through the neighborhood, in the event he encountered his irate daddy.

Chapter Three

"Good morning Ms. Millie. How are you doing today?" Rev. Hill asked with a smile on his jolly face as she approached the church. Cloaked in a black silk robe spread outwardly by his large belly and wide stature, the talkative Reverend, literally blocked the church's entire entrance.

"Right now Rev. Hill, I'm doing fine, but the day ain't over yet."

"Well, try to remember what I said to you the other day . . . ." Rev. Hill abruptly quieted, his attention being drawn towards the parking lot where he observed Effie Mae and Jimmy in the midst of exchanging coded, non-verbal cues. He shook his head in dismay, certain that they were up to no good, then again turned his attention back to Millie. A look of sympathy covering his round face, "Uh . . . Ms. Millie, uh—we'll, uh . . . ." He said, nervously. "We gon be sure and say an extra prayer for you this morning."

"Thank you, Rev. Hill." Millie paused. "Something tells me that I'm gon need it." She glanced briefly at Effie Mae and Jimmy as they shared a passionate smile, then a kiss. Millie looked at Rev. Hill pessimistically, and entered into the hot, antiquated church, fragranced with the slight smell of mildew.

She strolled down the center aisle of the sanctuary in search of her usual seat. Like every Sunday, she positioned her queen sized derriere onto the creaking, church pew, as close as possible to where Rev. Hill would be delivering his sermon. Effie Mae and Annie Mae nestled themselves on the back pew as though it were a family tradition.

Ned and Fannie Mae Parker entered the church, being seated mid-center, their two sons accompanying them. As the church doors closed and the service began, the choir opened with the song "I'm a Soldier in the Army of the Lord." Jimmy discreetly signaled Effie Mae with a cough. He continued coughing until he drew the attention of his Momma. Taking note of his sudden cough, she leaned to her left and whispered in Ned's ear.

"Ask Jimmy if he feeling alright." Ned leaned to his left towards Pete.

"Ask Jimmy if he sick." Pete leaned left to Jimmy.

"Daddy said…you sick?"

Jimmy smiled. "Yeah, I think I'm gon need to go home and lay down. I think I might be getting a cold."

"You wasn't coughing this morning. And you ate like a horse!" Pete whispered. He suddenly understood the reason behind his older brother's uncontrollable cough. He turned and looked towards the back pew where Effie Mae and Annie Mae were seated, but saw only Annie Mae. Their eyes locked one onto the other as they shared a smiled.

Pete and Annie Mae's intimate moment suddenly ended when Jimmy stepped across him to begin his journey out of the church. Pete looked up at his big brother and cautioned him with his eyes, to be careful. Jimmy continued on. He stepped past his parents, coughing periodically until he gained access to the center aisle. Giving a final cough, he walked towards the rear of the sanctuary then exited through the doors. He hurried through the parking lot and over to his 1954 blue Ford F100 pickup. He opened the door and got in, then looked down at the floor where Effie Mae crouched. They exchanged smiles as Jimmy started the engine and the two drove away.

Fannie Mae and Ned left church early due to Ned's upset stomach. They entered into the house.
"It must be something going around, first Jimmy — now you."
"Shhhhhhhh! You hear that?" Ned asked.
"Hear what? I don't hear nothing Ned." Fannie Mae paused and listened.
"I thought I heard something. Go get the shotgun Fannie Mae."
"What?" She said. "Ned I don't hear nothing." Ned listened without speaking. The sounds ceased.
"You know Jimmy came home."
"Yeah, but this sounded like a woman."
"I guess you would know." She said sarcastically, glaring at him.
"I'm gon go on upstairs and lay down."
"You go ahead on." Fannie Mae laid her purse on the dining room table. "I'm gon make some chicken soup." She went into the kitchen. I'll bring it up when it's done."

Ned walked up the stairs and headed in the direction of their bedrooms, as he prepared to go back to bed. He stopped when approaching Jimmy's bedroom, believing that he'd heard a woman's voice coming from inside. Ned placed his ear quietly against the door then slowly turned the knob. He swung the door open and stood momentarily in the doorway, but saw only his eldest son lying face down in bed, appearing to be asleep.

"Jimmy?" He whispered.

"Huh" Jimmy turned his head in the direction of the doorway, pretending to have been awakened by the sound of his daddy's voice.

"You feel any better boy?"

"Yep . . . a little better." Jimmy coughed a few times then turned his head toward the wall. He shifted his eyes towards Effie Mae, who lay hidden on the side of the bed. He smiled.

The congregation at St. Ebenezer Baptist Church rose to their feet as the Sunday morning service neared its end.

"This is the day that the Lord has made, let us depart from here and rejoice in it." Rev. Hill stated as he dismissed.

Millie apprehensively turned and looked towards the back pew. She hoped to find both of her daughters seated in their usual places. She gave a sigh of relief when seeing Effie Mae, still present at the church. She proudly joined her girls as they prepared to leave for the day, stopping as she approached Rev. Hill who stood perched at the open double doors of the church, where he positioned himself every Sunday to say his final goodbyes to returning members and visiting guests.

Effie Mae and Annie Mae walked past him and waited out front for their Momma.

"Well, Rev. Hill, look like we made it through Sunday morning. Now, just hope we can make it through the remainder of the day."

"Now Ms. Millie, let's try and remain hopeful."

"You gon have to pray for me on that, Rev. Hill, 'cause I'm just 'bout out of hope, with that child."

"Never give up hope Ms. Millie—never give up hope."

"I'm gon try and keep that in mind." She said, unconvinced. "Now, is you and Sissy still gon join us for supper this evening?"

"We'll be there as soon as we finish up here at the church, Ms. Millie." He said, slightly troubled

"I'm making peach cobbler." Millie teased. "I know how much you and Sissy just love my peach cobbler." A large smile formed on Rev. Hill's face.

"Maybe, it'll be alright for us leave some of this stuff for tomorrow. It ain't going nowhere." He chuckled. Millie giggled.

"Bye, Rev. Hill."

"Alright Ms. Millie, We'll be there shortly."

Millie exited the church then proceeded down the dirt road, headed home. Effie Mae and Annie Mae followed as they'd done as children.

After washing the family's laundry in the kitchen inside of the enormous washtub, Millie pushed open the back door with her foot, as she'd done every Saturday morning. In her arms, she held a woven basket full of freshly washed clothes. Her eyes widened in amazement when she saw Effie Mae, standing outback, hanging laundry on the clothesline. Millie smiled when she thought, how it had been a week since Effie Mae's last inappropriate encounter with a boy.

"When you done with that load, I got another one for you right here." Millie said, playfully.

"Just leave it over there by the stairs Momma, and when I'm done with these, I'll grab those."

"If I ain't known better, I think that I had my old Effie Mae back." Millie said, smiling.

"That's right Momma!" Effie Mae removed the clothes pin from her mouth then hung a pair of her red thigh-high short-shorts on the line.

"I guess I'm gon go on in here and take me a short nap before I start supper." Millie yawned and turned, preparing to enter into the house. "If you need help, Annie Mae right there on the front porch running her mouth with Anita as usual." Millie raised an eyebrow. "I swear that child's got to be the laziest thing I ever seen." She laughed to herself then went inside. The screened door slammed shut behind her.

Effie Mae continued hanging clothes. She leaned over to remove another clothing item from the basket. As she stood to pin it to the line, someone placed an unexpected kiss on her lips. Startled, but pleased, Effie Mae opened her eyes as the kiss ended to see its deliverer. A huge smile formed on her face when she saw a white shirt, black bowtie, curly hair and glasses, all unique to Anthony.

"Hey Effie Mae." He kissed her again. "I bet you never thought you'd see me again, did you?"

Effie Mae glanced at the back door. "Boy, are you crazy? She whispered. "What if my Momma was standing there?"

I've been parked up the road for the last twenty minutes watching. I saw your Momma yawning. When she went inside the house and didn't come back out, I figured she was probably asleep." He kissed her again. "I have six dollars." He smiled.

Effie Mae dropped the item back into the basket. She looked towards the back door then she and Anthony hurried from the backyard and over to his car. He again kissed her as they climbed inside. She smiled.

As they cruised past the house, Effie Mae waved at Annie Mae and Anita sitting on the front porch. The two girls looked in awe, their mouths flung open as Anthony revved up his engine and he and Effie Mae drove away, disappearing in the distance.

Millie awakened from her nap. She climbed out of bed, stretched, then walked through the living room and looked out onto the front porch. She saw Annie Mae and Anita still sitting there. She went into the kitchen and glanced out the door and into the backyard. Her eyes immediately drew to the un-hung basket of clothes still sitting there.

"Effie Mae?" She called out. "You out there child?" Millie opened the back door and hurried outside. She walked over to the outhouse. "Effie Mae, you in there?" She knocked on the closed door. Again, she received no answer. She opened it, and noted it was empty. Millie walked swiftly to the front of the house.

"You seen your sister Annie Mae?"

"She's over there hanging up clothes, ain't she Momma?" Annie Mae shifted her eyes to Anita.

"One thing I ain't ever had to worry about with you, Annie Mae . . . you lying to me!" Annie Mae gazed up at her Momma, her chestnut eyes filled with guilt.

"You see your sister leave here?" Annie Mae nodded her head.

"You know who she left here with?" She again nodded.

"Which boy was it?" Annie Mae shifted her eyes to Anita then again looked into the glaring eyes of Millie.

"Anthony."

"The boy, that drives that red car?" Annie Mae nodded. Millie turned and stormed away. She returned to the backyard then continued to hang the basket of wet clothes.

Rev. Hill, Sissy and Millie stood out front of the Reed's family home as Anthony slowly pulled into the driveway early the next morning. Effie Mae gazed rebelliously at Millie, as she sat nestled underneath Anthony's right arm. Millie and the Hill's watched as he climbed out of the car and strolled over to the passenger side. He opened the door and assisted Effie Mae out as she prepared to face the consequences of her actions.

"Before you say anything Momma, Anthony's got something he wants to ask you." Effie Mae said as she and Anthony approached Millie, stopping directly in front of her, as if engaging in a standoff. The teenage lovers briefly looked at one another then smiled. Anthony cleared his throat.

"Uh, Ms. Millie . . . I, uh wanted to ask—ask you, if I could marry Effie Mae?" He reached inside his shirt pocket and took out a 0.60 carat diamond white/gold engagement ring.

"Lord, have mercy." Sissy said. "Does Betsy know what you doing?"

Rev. Hill coughed. "Sissy."

"How long have you known my daughter, Anthony?" Millie asked.

"Uh, it's been about three or four weeks." He glanced at Effie Mae. She smiled.

"You done laid with my daughter, Anthony?"

"Uh, you mean this time or the times before?" He looked at Rev. Hill then again to Millie. Rev. Hill's mouth flung open, shocked by Anthony's response.

"Lord, have mercy." Sissy shook her head.

"How do you know Effie Mae?" Millie asked.

"Uh, I first heard about her . . . ."

"Heard about her?" Sissy said. Rev. Hill coughed, signaling his wife to hush.

"And, what did you hear 'bout my daughter Anthony?" He glanced briefly at Effie Mae, then Rev. Hill, and Sissy. He again positioned his eyes back onto Millie.

"Uh, uh—that she liked to have uh—have a good time."

"Lord, have mercy." Sissy said then turned to her husband. He subtly shook his head, no.

"You have a good time with my daughter, Anthony?" Millie glared into his eyes. Anthony shifted his eyes over to Effie Mae and blushed, then again to Millie.

"Uh, uh—yes Ma'am." Effie Mae likewise blushed.

"You think that might be the reason why you wanting to marry my daughter, Anthony?"

"Uh— uh . . . yes Ma'am." He again looked at Effie Mae.

"Lord, have mercy." Sissy said, starring relentlessly at Anthony.

"Did you know Anthony, that Effie Mae's got a number of young men she like having a good time with?" Millie looked over at Effie Mae then again to Anthony.

"Yes Ma'am." He replied. "But when we're married all of that will stop."

"Effie Mae!" Millie yelled. "Get your behind in that house!" She said as her eyes continued to be fixed on Anthony. Effie Mae stared at Anthony with anticipation. He grasped a hold of her hand as if defying Millie's demand.

"Young man . . . ." Rev. Hill said, calmly. "I know you probably think that you love Effie Mae . . . ."

"Yes sir—I do."

"But, I can assure you that you don't want to stand up against Ms. Millie." Rev. Hill shifted his stare from Anthony to Effie Mae then again to Anthony. "So turn Effie Mae's hand a loose, and let her go in the house like her Momma told her."

Anthony turned to Effie Mae and kissed her quickly on the lips then released her hand. Effie Mae gazed into his eyes as she walked slowly towards the house. Anthony lovingly watched as she stepped onto the porch and entered through the front door.

"Now here's what I want you to do Anthony . . . ." Rev. Hill said, interrupting his gawk from the girl he loved. "I want you to get back in your car, go home to your parents and tell them that you want to marry— Effie Mae Reed." He emphasized." Rev. Hill looked at Millie. His eyes apologized for referencing to Effie Mae as he had. "If your parents say that it's okay for you to marry—Effie Mae Reed, and it's okay with Ms. Millie here, then come Saturday, I'll perform the ceremony myself." A huge smile formed on Anthony's face. He hurried over to his car and got in.

"I'll see you on Saturday Rev. Hill." He said, starting his engine. He sped from the driveway, his wheels spinning as he threw the car in gear and drove away, believing that come Saturday, he would indeed be marrying Effie Mae Reed.

"Thank you, Rev. Hill." Millie said, softly.

"Ms. Millie, I just want to apologize for . . . ." She cut him off.

"It's fine Rev. Hill. I'm sure when his folks hear the name Effie Mae Reed; he won't be coming back out this way no time soon." Millie looked towards the house in defeat.

"What you gon do Millie?" Sissy asked, shaking her head in pity.

"Come tomorrow, Kathy and Charles gon be here to get her."

"Let's hope that a change in location will do the trick." Rev. Hill said as he looked through the front door and took note of Effie Mae defiantly waiting for Millie to enter.

Effie Mae awakened the next morning to the sound of unfamiliar voices coming from the living room. She lay in bed and pretended to be asleep as she listened.

"She's not pregnant is she Millie?" Kathy asked. "I don't run a home for girls in trouble!"

"Naw—she ain't pregnant. And that surprise me." Millie said, puzzled.

"Well, maybe she's barren. That not unheard of in young girls like Effie Mae." Kathy said as she looked at her husband Charles. He nodded his head in agreement. "You know Millie, trying to raise two girls with no man around—well; maybe Effie Mae's looking for a man in her life." She said then glanced at Charles. He nodded.

"Effie Mae been doing just fine until . . . ." Millie stopped.

"Until what Millie?" Kathy asked. "She discovered boys? Ain't that how it usually works?" Millie made no mention of Effie Mae's assaults by her cousins, concerned that the blame for her immoral behavior might somehow be directed towards her. "So where is she? And does she know that we're here to take her back to Jackson with us?" Kathy asked. Charles again nodded.

"She usually up by now. I don't know why she still sleeping." Millie headed in the direction of Effie Mae's bedroom, concerned by her prolonged stay in bed.

"Well, get her up! We need to be leaving here as soon as possible." Kathy yelled. Charles nodded in agreement. Millie entered into the bedroom. She saw Annie Mae sitting on her bed, listening to the grown-up's discussion on Effie Mae.

"Momma, is Effie Mae going away?"

"Right now Annie Mae, I don't know what else I can do with your sister."

"Momma— Effie Mae's not doing anything that a lot of the girls around here, ain't doing." Annie Mae said in her big sister's defense.

"You ain't doing it— is you?" Millie looked her firmly in the eyes and awaited an answer.

"No. but . . . ."

"That's what I thought." Millie again turned her focus back to Effie Mae. "You got to understand Annie Mae, your sister sick in the head." Millie reached over and gently shook Effie Mae's shoulder. "Effie Mae."

Effie Mae threw the sheet from over her head then rolled over onto her back, pretending as though she had just awakened.

"What time is it Momma?"

"Effie Mae, Kathy and Charles is here . . ." She paused. "They come to take you back to Jackson to stay with them."

Millie felt ambiguous about her decision to send Effie Mae away. She rationalized that sending her to the home of her married Auntie would transform her young daughter back into the innocent girl she was before her cousins' visit. On the other hand, she realized that she could no longer endure Effie Mae's distressing behavior.

"Momma, I don't want to live with Auntie Kathy and Uncle Charles. I want to stay here with you and Annie Mae." Effie Mae's eyes pleaded.

"It seems that decision's no longer in your hands or mines." Millie said.

"Millie! What's taking so long? We don't have all day!" Kathy shouted from the living room. "Is she coming or not?"

Millie glared momentarily at Effie Mae then looked away.

"She on her way, Kathy." She again turned her focus to Effie Mae. "All your belongings is packed, and sitting in the living room." Millie shook her head in despair, then turned and walked away. She reentered the living room. "Charles you can go 'head on and take Effie Mae's bag out to the car." Millie stated. He looked at Kathy then picked up the bags after she nodded her head with approval.

"Effie Mae, come on now girl! We don't have all day!" Kathy yelled.

Annie Mae watched as Effie Mae got out of bed and took a hold of the white sheet, pulling it from the bed then wrapping it around herself. Neither girl said one word. Effie Mae slowly walked from the bedroom and entered into the living room. Kathy stared at her with unfamiliarity. "It's been so long since I've seen that child; I'd forgot how pretty she was." She pulled open the sheet to take note of Effie Mae's pregnancy status. She gazed at the yellow thigh-high shorts and white brassiere she wore. "I can see why you having so much trouble with her." Annie Mae rushed into the living room. She looked briefly at Kathy then walked over and wrapped her arms around Effie Mae from behind. Kathy gazed at Annie Mae.

"Millie I didn't realize your girls were so pretty." She shifted her eyes to Charles. "Look just like their daddy." He nodded. "It's been so long, I forgot how good looking Frank Reed was." She chuckled. "Well anyway . . . I guess we'd better head on out of here. Come on Effie Mae!" Kathy walked over and gave Millie a half-hearted hug. She glanced at Annie Mae then turned and exited through the front door.

Effie Mae gazed at Millie, hoping she'd somehow change her mind. Millie stared briefly at her out of control daughter, but gave no indication, that she intended to stop her from leaving. Effie Mae pulled away from Annie Mae's embrace then walked out the front door. She climbed into the back seat of Kathy and Charles' 1956 blue and white Ford Victoria then lay down on the seat in preparation for the hour long drive. She showed no emotion as she covered herself completely with the sheet, throwing it over her head. Charles honked the horn as he backed out of the driveway and pulled onto the road, headed back to Jackson, Mississippi. Millie stood mute in the living room, unable to look at her eldest daughter being driven away. Annie Mae rushed angrily from the living room and back, into her bedroom then briskly slammed the door.

...

Millie sat on the front porch with Rev. Hill and Sissy. The three friends relaxed in the warmth of a soothing, southern breeze as they enjoyed a glass of Millie's slightly tart, homemade lemonade.

"How's Effie Mae doing Millie? It's been three months now. Have you heard anything from her?" Sissy asked as she took a swallow of lemonade.

"To tell the truth Sissy, it's been so peaceful since Kathy and Charles took that child to Jackson, I've just been . . . ." Millie smiled.

"Enjoying the peace and quiet?" Sissy added.

"Well, it sure is good to see you so happy Ms. Millie." Rev. Hill stated. "I know you've been through a lot with Effie Mae."

"Thank you, Rev. Hill."

"Millie! Did I tell you that my baby brother J.R. was coming home to Yazoo City?" Sissy said with excitement.

"No . . . you sure didn't, Sissy."

"It's been about five years since I've seen that boy." Sissy said. "I remember when J.R. was just a baby." Sissy reminisced. "He was a surprise baby, you know?" She shifted her eyes to Rev. Hill. He maintained his silence. "Momma was going through the change when she got pregnant with him—you know." She again glanced at her husband. He continued his silence.

"Yeah, I've known that to happen." Millie said as she took a swallow of lemonade. "Boy moved up north to Boston or somewhere out east, didn't he?" She asked.

"New York City." Rev. Hill answered, breaking his silence.

"Yeah, Millie . . . my baby brother has himself a little church up there somewhere." Sissy said, bragging. "But, you know as a preacher, he can't marry just anything." She shifted her eyes to her husband. "Problem is, he just can't seem to find the right woman to marry, up there in New York City."

"Yeah, it's definitely important that a preacher's wife be an upstanding woman." Millie said, complementing Sissy. A proud look formed on her face.

"And, she also needs to know how to keep her opinion to herself." Rev. Hill stated, glancing over at his wife. She ignored his words.

"I figured him coming back home to Mississippi; my baby brother can find himself a wife with the same southern values, he was raised with." Sissy gloated.

"Before Effie Mae made such a drastic change, she would have made J.R. a good wife." Rev. Hill added. "I never could figure out what happened to that girl to make her change like that." He scratched his head as he pondered over the possibilities.

"I'll tell you what happened, Otis . . ." Sissy said, preparing to give her unsolicited opinion. "She got hot in the pants! And you know, any and everything can and will happen after that." She took another sip of her lemonade. Millie gave no reply as she listened to Sissy's outspoken assumptions.

"I don't know Millie . . ." Rev. Hill rubbed his index finger and thumb alongside of his chin. "Maybe a man like J.R. might be just what Effie Mae need." Sissy's mouth flung open as she gazed at him in disbelief, outraged that he would even make such a statement.

"Well, I guess we don't have to worry about that, now do we, Otis?" Sissy said with satisfaction. "Effie Mae's doing just fine where she is— in Jackson." She stated, dismissing the idea completely. "Now, Sister Davis' daughter Ramona, she would be the perfect wife for my baby brother." She smirked at her husband. "She's what Effie Mae used to be." She quickly turned to Millie when she realized her insulting words might be offensive to her dear friend. "Did I just say that? I'm sorry Millie." She glanced over at her husband. He raised an eyebrow but said nothing. "I guess I need to learn how to keep my thoughts to myself." She said apologetically as she swallowed the newly formed lump in her throat. "Millie, you know I didn't mean no harm . . ." Millie gave no reply.

Sissy's ineffective apology was suddenly interrupted by the sound of a honking horn speeding down the dark road. The threesome peered into the oncoming headlights, attempting to identify the approaching vehicle.

"Now who on earth can that be, keeping up all that fuss." Millie said, trying to recognize the automobile as it drew nearer. "If I ain't known better, I say that was Kathy and Charles car. But what would they be doing back here?" She asked herself, minutes before the vehicle swung into the driveway and came to a screeching halt.

"Get your ass out of my car, you little slut!" Kathy shouted as she swung open the front passenger door and hurried out. She moved swiftly to the back and snatched open the door. Effie Mae scurried out and ran in the direction of the house. Kathy reached inside and grabbed Effie Mae's luggage and threw it onto the front lawn. "Don't you ever send that heifer back my way Millie! Charles may not be much—but he's mines!" she bellowed as she climbed back inside the car.

"Kathy?" Millie called out, confused by what had just happened. She stood to her feet and hurried from the porch and in the direction of the driveway. "What happened? Kathy?" Millie asked as she moved swiftly in the direction of the car.

"Drive, Charles!" Kathy shrieked. The tires spun as Charles thrust the gears into reverse and backed onto the road. Millie watched from the front yard, through the massive dust as he spun off at a high rate of speed then disappeared into the darkness of the old country road. Millie promptly turned her attention to Effie Mae, still standing in the front yard. The Hills looked one to the other in shock.

Effie Mae picked up her suitcase from the front lawn and headed in the direction of the house. She stepped onto the front porch and prepared to enter.

"Is everything alright Effie Mae?" Rev. Hill asked.

"Everything's fine Rev. Hill." She said, pleased to be back home. She opened the door and went inside. Sissy curiously observed, before the reality of Effie Mae's return home, sunk in. She gasped.

"Otis . . . Don't let me forget to call Sister Davis when we get home tonight. I need to talk to her about Ramona." She stared into Rev. Hill's eyes, completely in awe by what had just occurred.

Annie Mae stood over Effie Mae bed and watched as she lay sleeping, the cover thrown over her head.

"Effie Mae. Are you awake?"

"Nope."

"How can you answer me if you ain't woke?"

"What you want Annie Mae?"

"If you get from under the cover I can tell you." Effie Mae threw the cover from over her head and sat up.

"I'm listening."

"Well—well" Annie Mae stuttered.

"Well, what?" Effie Mae stared at her briefly then lay back down, throwing the covers back over her head.

"I'm late."

"Late? Late for what Annie Mae?" Effie Mae asked from underneath the cover.

"My period." Annie Mae whispered.

"Girls are late all the time; that happens."

"For, four months?"

Effie Mae slowly took the cover from over her head and again sat up. She looked at Annie Mae in silence. "That many months late only happen when a girl is pregnant." Annie Mae said.

"Annie Mae, you telling me that you pregnant?"

"Yeah, that's what I'm telling you."

"What you gon do?"

"Pete's gon ask his Momma and Daddy, if he can marry me."

"Pete? How you know its Pete's?"

"Because I'm not you Effie Mae, I haven't been with nobody else but Pete."

"And Momma talked about me. Wait until she finds out "little Ms. Goody two shoes" done got herself pregnant. She gon kill you." Effie Mae thought for a second. "No, she gon send you to Jackson to live with Auntie Kathy and Uncle Charles." She laughed.

"Effie Mae, this is serious." Annie Mae whispered, being seated on Effie Mae's bed.

"Pete got you pregnant, let him figure it out." Effie Mae lay back down and again threw the cover over her head.

The Parkers congregated at the dining room table eating a Sunday dinner of collard greens, ham, fried chicken, cornbread and mashed potatoes and gravy. Fannie Mae watched Ned from the opposite end of the table as he mixed the various cuisines together on his plate.

"You know Ned, when you mix all that food together like that, it looks like garbage." She said.

"Good! Because, that's what it tastes like!" He scraped the meat from his chicken leg with his fork then added it to the mixture.

Jimmy nudged Pete in his left side, urging him to tell their parents of his plan to marry Annie Mae Reed.

"Uh, Momma—Daddy, uh—I have something I want to ask y'all." He said, nervously.

"You look nervous Pete." Fannie Mae stated. "What you got to ask us that would make you so nervous?"

"Don't come in here talking about you done got somebody pregnant either! I don't want to hear it, and I know Fannie Mae don't!" Ned said. Pete shifted his eyes to Jimmy then to his Momma.

"You remember, Annie Mae Reed, don't you Momma?"

"Ain't that Ms. Millie's Ol' whorish daughter?" She asked as she continued watching her husband eat, nonstop.

"Uh, no Momma, that's Effie Mae." Pete glanced at his older brother. Jimmy again nudged him in the side.

"It's only a matter of time. They cut from the same cloth." Ned stated as he shoved spoonfuls of the unusual looking food into his mouth.

"No Daddy, Annie Mae's different. She's a good girl." Pete shifted his eyes to Jimmy then turned to his father.

"You ain't been around that gal no more, have you boy?" Ned asked.

"Who? Annie Mae?" Jimmy joked. Pete gently elbowed him in the stomach.

"That gal's gon rabbit!" Ned stated. "And I don't want you nowhere near her!" He halted eating and momentarily glared at Jimmy. "You hear me boy?" He yelled.

"I hear you Daddy." Jimmy replied then looked briefly at Pete.

"Why you asking us about Annie Mae Reed, Pete?" Fannie Mae asked.

"Uh, uh—uh . . . ." Pete stuttered.

"That's way too many uh's." Ned stated. "You hiding something, boy?" He gazed at his wife. "Fannie Mae . . . that boy's getting ready to make you a Grand Momma! You watch and see."

Ned picked up the jar of water located to the right of his plate. He looked at Pete then to Jimmy and again at his wife, before he drank half of its content. He sat the jar back onto the table and awaited Pete's news.

"Is that right Pete?" Fannie Mae asked. Jimmy laughed, as his young brother squirmed to convey his message.

"Thing is—Momma, I love Annie Mae."

"It's a difference between love and lust, boy!" Ned stated as he continued stuffing food into his mouth. "You think I don't know you been sneaking around here with that gal?"

"Daddy . . ." Pete paused. "I love Annie Mae. And I want to marry her."

"When she due?" Ned asked.

"Now, that ain't what he said Ned." Fannie Mae looked at Pete in question. "Is she pregnant Pete?" Pete shifted his eyes to Jimmy, uncertain if he should answer truthfully.

"That ain't why I want to marry her though, Momma."

"I knew it!" Ned shouted. "That's what all that sneaking got you . . . ain't it boy?" Ned looked over at Jimmy. "You hear that Jimmy? Your baby brother here, done messed around and got Ms. Millie's daughter pregnant!"

"How you know it's love you feel for Annie Mae, Pete?" His Momma asked.

Pete's enthusiasm increased. "Momma, if Annie Mae needed a heart . . . ." He paused then smiled. "I'd give her mines, even if it mean I had to die to do it." His smile grew.

"That boy's got it bad!" Ned turned to Fannie Mae. "Well, it's up to your Momma, boy!"

"Me? I think that's up to Ms. Millie. How old is Annie Mae, Pete?"

"Sixteen." Pete said.

"It don't matter how old she is now!" Ned rationalized. "She's pregnant ain't she?"

"That ain't why you marrying her, is it Pete?"

"Naw Momma. I love Annie Mae."

"Well, if it's okay with Ms. Millie—it's okay with me." She smiled then looked at Ned as he shook his head pessimistically.

"Well if Pete gon get married, I'm gon get married, too." Jimmy teased.

"Married? You Jimmy? I thought you were too good looking to settle down with any woman." Fannie Mae said, puzzled by his announcement. "And who you talking about marrying anyway?"

"Effie Mae." He stated, jokingly. Ned began choking on the food in his mouth. Jimmy leaped from his chair and hurried to his father. He briskly stroked him on the back. Ned grabbed the jar of water and drank the remainder. He suddenly stood to his feet, looked at Fannie Mae without speaking then left the room. She watched as he stormed away then turned her attention back to Jimmy.

"I hope you was just playing boy? If you marry that girl, you better be ready to share your bed with every man in this county—and the next." She chuckled.

Ned hastily returned to the room carrying two black leather sacks. He dropped them onto the floor then gazed into Jimmy's eyes.

"Boy, if I ever hear you say that again, you may as well put all of your belongings in these bags and walk straight out that door!" He shouted. "I wouldn't let that gal marry that Ol' bull I got out there— too loose!" Jimmy chuckled at his Daddy's words then returned to his seat and continued eating, and nudging his baby brother in congratulations.

Annie Mae and Pete stood in the Parker's living room the following Saturday evening as Rev. Hill presided over their nuptials. Effie Mae served as Maid of Honor to her baby sister and Jimmy, the Best Man. During the ceremony, Jimmy kept his eyes glued on Effie Mae. Sitting on the sofa, Millie, Sissy, Ned and Fannie Mae observed the exchange. Ned focused his attention solely on Jimmy, as Pete and Annie Mae were united as husband and wife.

"Well Ms. Millie, I hope we can get along better, now that our kids are married and expecting their first child." Fannie Mae stated.

"I don't see no reason why we can't." Millie said as she rose from the sofa.

"Now you feel free to come see Annie Mae and the baby, anytime you want. You know you always welcome." Millie's mouth flung open.

"Annie Mae gon be staying right there where she at—with me!" She yelled.

"And Pete's gon be right here, with us!" Fannie Mae grabbed Pete by the arm.

"If Pete gon be married to my baby girl, he's gon be living right there, in the Reed family home. My husband Frank built that house with his own hands. And that's where my children and grandchildren gon stay!"

"I don't care if it was built by the seven dwarfs, and Snow White hammered in the nails! My baby boy is living right here on the Parker's family farm—with or without Annie Mae!" Millie grasped a hold of Annie Mae's right arm.

"Come on Annie Mae!" Pete gently took a hold of Annie Mae's left arm.

"Wait a minute, Ms. Millie—Momma, I just made Annie Mae my wife, and this day, is the happiest day in my life." He looked lovingly at Annie Mae and smiled. "Momma, if you and Ms. Millie just let us enjoy this one day, we can decide where we gon be living tomorrow." Fannie Mae and Millie looked one to the other

"Well, I guess Pete's right. It can wait 'til tomorrow." Fannie Mae smiled. "We probably need to be checking on that food anyway . . . ."

". . . And set the table so we can go head on and eat." Millie stated, subtly calling a truce. "I just want my baby to be happy." She turned to Annie Mae. "And, if Pete make her happy, that's all what matters."

In the midst of the "in-law" confusion, Jimmy joined Effie Mae in the living room on the sofa. He stared at her passionately and smiled. She blushed. Ned entered into the living room from the kitchen. Holding a jar of water in his right hand, he glared at Jimmy, then squeezed between he, and Effie Mae.

"I got my eye on you boy." He glanced over at Effie Mae then shook his head. "Loose!"

...

"God loves a cheerful giver." Rev. Hill stated as he stood in the pulpit, and the Deacons passed the collection plate throughout the congregation. The choir director pounded the keys on the black upright piano as the choir sang, "Wade in the Water." The basket passed from person to person and pew to pew. From the rear of the church, a woman's voice suddenly rang out as she burst opened the church doors and entered.

"Ned Parker!" She hollered out. The multitude of members in the congregation turned simultaneously in the direction of the voice. "I need to know, what you plan on doing about this child I'm carrying!" She shouted. The pregnant woman walked down the center aisle of the church, in searched of Ned. She spotted him seated next to Fannie Mae, mid-center of the sanctuary, then strolled over and stood directly above him. Fannie Mae stood quickly to her feet.

"Woman if you don't step away from my husband, I'm gon hit you so hard in your stomach, you gon be delivering that baby through your mouth!"

"Husband? Yours and everybody else's!" The woman stated, sarcastically. "I bet you don't even know how many babies Ned's got out there—do you Fannie Mae?"

Hearing those challenging words, Fannie Mae balled up her fist. She drew back her arm and prepared to strike the unknown pregnant female. Moments before her right hook connected with the woman's mouth, Jimmy intercepted the blow. He threw his right arm up, blocking the impact then lowered his Momma, down onto the wooden pew. Pete angrily glared at his Daddy from the back pew, where he now sat, with his new bride and sister-in-law; angered by his father's dishonorable "womanizing".

"Daddy, you need to handle that." Jimmy said as he held onto his Momma. Ned beckoned a deacon over and whispered in his ear. The deacon waved his hand and another deacon approached. The two men escorted the pregnant woman out as the atmosphere hummed with whispers and endless gossip.

Rev. Hill and Sissy stood in the doorway of the church as they'd customarily done every Sunday, saying their farewell's to the departing members and first time visitors. A 1956 silver and black Buick Roadmaster pulled into the grassy parking area in front of the church and stopped. The passenger's door opened. Sissy watched as the individual stepped out. She saw the smiling face of her twenty four year old baby brother, J.R. Smith, five foot-eleven, thin framed, clean shaven, semi-attractive, and wearing glasses.

"J.R.! There's my baby brother!" Sissy rushed over and the two hugged. "When did you get here?"

"I just arrived. I came straight here." He waved the driver on. "I had my buddy Jeffrey, drop me off. You remember Jeffrey don't you Sissy? We played on the same baseball team in high school."

"Is that him?" She watched as the car drove off. "I haven't seen that boy in years. I heard he just got divorced, too."

"Sissy." J.R. shook his head, urging her to end her gossiping.

"Well, anyway . . . I'm glad you came here to the church."

"I figured you and Rev. Otis would probably still be here. I thought maybe I could come and take a look at some of the young ladies, here." He smiled as he watched the various women exiting through the church doors.

"And, I have just the girl for you J.R." Sissy said with excitement. "Her name is Ramona. She's Sister Davis' daughter and she's a real sweetheart." She shifted her eyes to Rev. Hill, who stood talking to some first time visitors. "I think she may still be in the church, too." She grabbed a hold of J.R.'s arm and led him towards the church entrance where Rev. Hill, now stood speaking with Millie.

"Oh, Millie this is my baby brother J.R." She said interrupting the conversation between her husband and Millie. "Isn't he handsome?"

"Hey! How you doing J.R?" Rev. Hill asked, excited to see him. The two men shook hands and embraced.

Rev. Hill patted him on the back. "Sissy tells me that you here looking for a wife, huh?"

"Yeah, brother-in-law, Sissy seems to think I'll find a better woman down here than in New York City."

"Well, there's plenty to choose from." Rev. Hill grinned.

"Now how would you know that, Otis? You, been looking at the young girls around here?" She stared at him. He glanced at her briefly, but ignored her words.

"Well J.R., good luck to you." Sissy broke her stare, turning her attention again to Millie.

"Whatever young girl's lucky enough to marry my baby brother, can't ask for a better man. And I'm not just saying that because he's my brother, Millie." She said, bragging. "My Momma and Daddy raised this little boy, right!"

J.R. smiled and extended his hand to Millie. "How you doing, Ms. Millie? It's good to meet you." Millie shook his hand and smiled.

"Polite. I like him already Sissy."

"Did you see Sister Davis and Ramona leave out the church yet? I was just getting ready to take J.R. inside to meet Ramona."

"I don't think so. I'm pretty sure I saw Sister Davis talking to Sister Porterfield before I left out." Millie said.

"Let's go Momma! I want to finish this dinner so we can eat early. I got something I need to do this evening." Effie Mae stated as she moved swiftly past Rev. Hill, Millie, Sissy and J.R.

Sissy gazed at Effie Mae and shook her head in disapproval then leaned towards Millie and whispered.

"Did you ever find out what happened at Kathy and Charles place in Jackson? She asked, careful not to let

J.R. hear her inquiring words. Sissy's eyes followed Effie Mae as she walked out into the parking lot and over to Jimmy's truck. She took note as the two spoke through the opened window, nosily wondering what their conversation might entail. J.R. locked his eyes onto Effie Mae, intrigued by her fiery personality. He smiled with interest.

"Whenever I call Kathy, all she do, is hang up." Millie said, as she too, watched her less than honorable daughter from a distance.

"Millie ain't no telling what Effie Mae done when she was down there. And didn't I hear Kathy say something about Charles?" Sissy raised an eyebrow as she continued whispering.

"Sissy, only way I'm gon ever find out what happened, is to ask Effie Mae. And I ain't sure, I even want to know." Millie shook her head in dismay. "I guess if you gon catch Sister Davis and Ramona, you better hurry before they leave."

"Alright Millie, I'll talk to you tomorrow." Sissy again shifted her eyes to Effie Mae. She gazed momentarily as the two lovers intimately grinned at each other. "Girl, I don't know what you gon do with that one." Sissy suddenly noticed J.R.'s eyes fixated on Effie Mae. "J.R., we better get on in here before Sister Davis, leaves. I'm just dying for you to meet Ramona!" She stated, determined to break his unrelenting stare. She yanked him by the arm, literally pulling him inside the church.

Rev. Hill smiled as he too had taken note of J.R.'s reaction to Effie Mae. He then continued chatting with exiting members as Millie departed on foot for her long journey home.

Chapter Four

Rev. Hill and Sissy joined Millie on her front porch the following, Saturday evening. The three chatted as they each enjoyed a bowl of Millie's freshly baked peach cobbler.

"Millie, girl this peach cobbler is delicious! You know, you gon have to give me the recipe." Sissy swallowed the spoonful she'd just put into her mouth.

"Yeah, Ms. Millie you put your foot in this! But don't waste your time giving the recipe to Sissy. She wouldn't do nothing but burn it." He glanced over at his wife and shook his head. "Burn everything! I told her about talking on that phone while she cooking." Sissy ignored his words as she slid another spoon of peach cobbler inside her mouth.

"I meant to ask you Sissy, how things work out for J.R. and Ramona?" Millie asked.

"It didn't." Rev. Hill said, chuckling. Sissy glanced at him then turned her attention to Millie.

"I guess you can't ever really know people—now can you?" Sissy said, regrettably.

"Well, hush your mouth."

"Here all this time Millie, I thought Ramona was a really sweet girl"

"It turns out, she crazier than a *Betsy bug*." Rev. Hill said, laughing.

"Show you, that you can't always tell what's going on in somebody's head just by looking at them." Millie stated. Sissy looked momentarily at Rev. Hill then again to Millie as she prepared to give the specifics.

"J.R. said, he decided on taking Ramona to get some ice cream. She agreed—and even told him that she liked chocolate. So naturally, he bought her what she asked for …."

"Turns out . . . girl's allergic to chocolate." Rev. Hill interrupted, bursting into laughter.

"Do you want to finish telling the story, Otis?" Sissy snapped. "Because, now, if you do, I'll let you!"

"Noooo! I'm gon let you finish telling it." He chuckled.

"So, anyway Millie, J.R. bought that girl, chocolate ice cream just like she asked—and she ate it!"

"Hush your mouth." Milled said, intrigued.

"That poor child broke out so bad her face looked like raw chicken skin …." Rev. Hill again interrupted.

"Yeah, when J.R. took Frankenstein's monster, home— Sister Davis had a fit!" He stated, unable to control his laughter.

"Why don't you just go ahead and tell the story, Otis—gon!" Sissy yelled, annoyed by his constant interruptions.

"No—I told you, it's your story, your brother—you go ahead on."

"Millie that girl knew she was allergic to chocolate! Ain't that crazy? Do you know that crazy Sister Davis called the Sheriff?"

"She done what?" Millie said, surprised.

"She sure did. And to make it worse, both her, and Ramona told the Sheriff, that J.R. had done poisoned that child! Millie, they were gon to take my baby brother to jail!" She shouted.

"But, he had them to call me—and I vouched for him. Everything worked out fine." Rev. Hill said, calmly.

"And it's a good thing that he did. Girl, the whole thing was just crazy!" Sissy said, frustrated. "Now, how I'm supposed to look that woman and her crazy daughter in the face in church tomorrow." She turned to Rev. Hill. "We should just throw them out of the church. Can we throw them out the church, Otis?"

"Now Sissy, you know we can't do that." He stated, chuckling.

"I guess folks all got they shortcomings." Millie said.

"Speaking of shortcomings, where's Effie Mae tonight?" Sissy asked.

"She slipped out of here earlier today, and I ain't seen her since." Millie shook her head in pity. "Why can't she meet a nice boy like Pete and get married?"

"Speaking of a nice boy, J.R.'s been steady asking about Effie Mae, Millie." Rev. Hill stated. "After seeing her at the church last Sunday, and he ain't stopped talking about her yet."

"I've told you now, Otis!" Sissy said, displeased. "I don't mean you no disrespect Millie, but Effie Mae ain't exactly what I want for my baby brother." She momentarily stared at

Rev. Hill then continued speaking. "J.R. ain't had that much experience with women, if any. And Effie

Mae, well . . . what J.R. lacks in experience, you can multiply that by a hundred, with that child. That's not all bad, Sissy." Rev. Hill stated, raising an eyebrow.

"Otis! Shame on you! Talking like that in front of Millie."

"Maybe having a woman with a little more experience than him is a good thing." He grinned.

"Well Sissy, it's my daughter he talking 'bout." Millie chuckled. "But Rev. Hill, I got to agree with Sissy. Effie Mae is way too much for that boy."

"He's definitely interested Ms. Millie. And when a man's has his eye on a woman, there ain't much you can do about it."

"Well, I bet I'm gon do something about it!" Sissy stated with insistence.

"I say we give it a chance and let J.R. decide." Rev. Hill replied.

"How's Pete and Annie Mae coming along living here with you Millie?" Sissy asked, abruptly switching topics. "I'm sure Fannie Mae ain't taking too kind to that?"

"We still trying to get the sleeping arrangements figured out. But . . ." Millie hushed when she noticed Sissy's mouth fly open and her eyes locked onto the road. Curious as to what could have grasped a hold of her old friend's attention; Millie turned and looked in the direction of Sissy's relentless stare. Her eyes widened as she watched Anthony's red convertible cruising towards the house.

"I know that's not Anthony?" Sissy stated as she looked on in awe. "And look who's behind the wheel. Otis, remind me to call Betsy Lewis when we get home."

Effie Mae pulled into the driveway and stopped. Anthony quickly climbed out. He rushed around the front of the car and opened the door then helped Effie Mae out.

"Rev. Hill, Ms. Sissy, Ms. Millie . . . how's everybody doing?" He politely asked.

"Hey Momma." Effie Mae said. "Rev. Hill, Ms. Sissy."

"Anthony . . . is Betsy at home?" Sissy asked.

"Yes Ma'am." He replied as he and Effie Mae stood smiling at one another.

"Son, did you ask your parents what I told you to ask them? Rev. Hill asked, a puzzled looked plastered across his face.

"Yes Sir."

"Can I ask what they said?"

"At first they said no. But when Father talked to me without Mother in the room, he said it was okay for me to keep seeing Effie Mae. I just can't say anything else about marrying her or they'll take my car away. Then he gave me six dollars."

"Six dollars?" Millie asked, confused.

"Uh—Ms. Millie, you don't want to know." Rev. Hill shook his head.

"Ain't that something? That's just like a man." Sissy said, frowning.

"Son, do you still want to marry Effie Mae?" Rev. Hill asked.

"Yes Sir."

Millie looked at Effie Mae.

"How you feel 'bout that Effie Mae?"

"I don't feel nothing Momma. You know I ain't trying to marry nobody!" Sissy turned quickly to Rev. Hill.

"I guess that takes care of that other little issue — now don't it Otis?"

"You tell that to J.R." He replied.

"I sure am — but after I talk to Betsy Lewis." Sissy glared at Anthony.

J. R. picked at the food on his plate. He couldn't think of anything else except for the fiery girl he'd seen again in church that morning. He wondered why she hadn't been introduced to him. Rev. Hill recognized the look in his eyes that indicated his interest in Effie Mae had grown. Sissy ignored her brother's unacceptable preoccupation. She hoped to find a young lady soon, one that she deemed more suitable for her baby brother than Effie Mae Reed.

J. R. suddenly pushed away his plate.

"Tell me about Effie Mae." Sissy's eyes shifted quickly to her husband, as she felt challenged by her brother's demand.

"What do you want to know J.R.?" Rev. Hill asked, briefly glancing at his wife.

"Why hasn't she been introduced to me? That's my first question. Is she married?" Sissy turned to him and tried to think of an answer she hoped would be acceptable.

"Effie Mae already has a young man who wants to marry her." She shifted her eyes to her husband, hoping he'd support her subtle untruth.

"I didn't see an engagement ring on her finger. If she has a fiancé, I haven't seen him in church with her."

His enthusiasm increased. "I want to meet her. Until she's married, she's still available."

"Be careful what you ask for J.R." Sissy said underneath her breath.

"Huh? You say something Sissy?" She rose swiftly from the table and walked away. She pushed opened the front screen door and exited the house, going out onto the porch, disappointed by her baby brother's persistence in meeting Effie Mae.

J.R. watched her ambiguous behavior, perplexed by her reluctance in wanting him to meet a woman of his choosing, since she was the one who encouraged him to come back to Yazoo City in search of a wife.

"Will you excuse me J.R.? Let me go talk to my wife." Rev. Hill got up from the table and joined Sissy outside on the front porch. He sat next to her on the porch swing. "I've always heard that the heart wants what it wants. And if J.R. wants Effie Mae, well then Sissy it ain't much you or I can do about it." He calmly stated.

"Otis, you know what kind of girl Effie Mae is. If we had a daughter would you want her to be like Effie Mae?"

"If only it was that simple. Do you think that Ms. Millie wanted Effie Mae to turn out the way she did? Something happened to that girl. I know it — and Ms. Millie knows it."

"You think so, Otis? I figured she was just hot in the pants."

"If that was the case Sissy, why wait so long?" He contemplated.

"Otis, you know how girls can get when they start dating."

"Was Effie Mae dating? Up until the time she seemed to have gon wild, I had never even seen her with a boy. Plus, Ms. Millie hadn't allowed her or Annie Mae to date yet."

"Now that you mention it, Otis, I remember how proud Millie was that her girls, was so different from a lot of the girls at the church."

"Like I said, let's just give it a chance. J.R. might be just what Effie Mae need. And— she may be just what he need." Rev. Hill put his arm around his wife and gently kissed her on the cheek.

"Thank you Otis." She said, smiling.

"For the kiss?" He teased.

"No. For making me see that even Effie Mae deserve a chance at having a good man in her life. And not just those boys out there, only wanting to take advantage of whatever's going on with her." She placed a gentle kiss on his lips. He smiled.

Millie looked out when she heard the sound of a running engine pull into the driveway. She saw Effie Mae passionately kissing Jimmy inside of his truck as he dropped her off following an intimate evening. Millie shook her head as she thought of the young men who had violated her daughter's body, and how she willingly allowed it. She watched as Effie Mae entered into the house.

Aware of J.R.'s insistence on meeting her much sought after daughter, Millie promised Rev. Hill that she would at least speak to Effie Mae about it. Sissy gave her promise that she would not interfere, convinced that J.R would never find Effie Mae to be a suitable mate, once meeting her.

"Was that Jimmy, who dropped you off?" Millie asked.

"Yep." Effie Mae opened the refrigerator and took out the pitcher of lemonade then went in search of a glass in the cupboard.

"I talked to Sissy today." Millie hesitated. "Said her baby brother J.R. saw you in church and thought he might want to meet you."

"Meet me, for what Momma? Ain't he a Preacher?" Effie Mae poured lemonade into the glass then looked at Millie. "Momma, you think I don't know what Ms. Sissy thinks of me? That woman probably thinks I ain't even good enough to say hi— to her Ol' plain looking brother. Do you know she talked to Anthony's Momma? Now he can't drive his car no more." Effie Mae took a sip of the lemonade. "And, Momma I really liked being with Anthony." Millie looked away, shamed by her daughter's candidness. "I like being with Jimmy too, but it's different." Millie stared at her without saying a word. Effie Mae put the pitcher of lemonade back into the refrigerator. Millie sighed.

"What Momma? Now you gon tell me how you wish I was more like Annie Mae, so I could find a nice boy like Pete and get married?"

"Would it matter one bit, if I did?"

"Nope!"

"I ain't asking you to marry Sissy's brother, Effie Mae. All he asking to do, is meet you child." Millie knew that J.R. setting his sights on Effie Mae would be the beginning of unending trouble—for him. Effie Mae glanced out the kitchen window.

"And besides, Momma, I ain't exactly what people around here see as being a preacher's wife."

"I don't see why not!" Millie said closing her eyes to the truth. "You just as worthy as any other girl 'round here. Better! You Frank Reed's daughter."

"Momma!" Effie Mae looked at her with doubtful eyes. "But that don't matter no way, because I ain't marrying that man." She said, again looking out the kitchen window. Millie ignored her words.

"Well, he gon be here this coming Sunday after church. Promise me Effie Mae, you gon stay 'round here long enough to meet him." She suddenly took note of Effie Mae repeated glances out of the window. "You expecting somebody, child?"

"Okay Momma. I'll meet him, but only if you talk to Anthony's Momma about letting him get his car back."

Millie looked up at the ceiling then again to Effie Mae. She now understood her daughter's anxious behavior.

"And just what you want me to say to Betsy Lewis?"

"If you want me to meet Ms. Sissy's brother bad enough Momma, you'll think of something." Effie Mae hesitated. "I know Momma. Tell her that Ms. Sissy thinks I'm good enough to marry her brother — The Preacher." She chuckled. "Momma, how long Annie Mae and Pete, gon be staying here? I'm tired of sleeping on that couch." She paused. "And besides, Jimmy is too tall to be lying on . . . ."

Millie interrupted. "Jimmy? What cause Jimmy got to be lying in here on the couch?" She stared at Effie Mae in disappointment. Effie Mae ignored her question.

"Momma, can't you let Annie Mae have your room, then we can share me and Annie Mae's old room? I promise I won't have any boys coming through the window." She joked. "Not even Jimmy." Effie Mae set the empty glass in the sink then walked into the living room. She picked up the folded blanket lying on the couch and began unfolding it. Her short, thin strapped, pink night gown fell out and onto the sofa. Millie watched in disgust, but made no comment. Effie Mae grabbed it and threw it across her shoulder. She picked her pillow from up off the floor then laid it on the couch. She began undressing. Millie cleared her throat.

"Don't forget there's a man living in this house now. I'm sure Annie Mae don't want her husband seeing you in your birthday suit. You can do that in my room."

"Momma, Pete ain't trying to see me, and I ain't trying to see him." Effie Mae walked in the direction of Millie's room then entered. She left the door open.

"Close that door." Millie said. Effie Mae looked at her as if being clueless as to why the door needed to be shut then closed it. Millie wondered if her daughter's disgraceful behavior would ever change. Minutes later, Effie Mae returned to the living room wearing the seductive gown. She lay on the couch then covered herself completely with the blanket. Millie shook her head in hopelessness then walked away. She entered into her bedroom and quietly closed the door.

Millie walked briskly down the dirt road as she headed home from work. She stepped onto the front porch then entered into the house, going directly into her bedroom. She tossed her small black purse onto the bed and took off the white sweater she wore, hanging it inside of the closet. Unusually quiet, she walked out of her room and entered into the kitchen. She opened the bottom drawer on the old gas oven and prepared to light the pilot.

"Effie Mae!" Millie called out as she retrieved the box of wooden matches from on top of the stove. She struck a match then leaned down and ignited the flame inside. She again closed the oven drawer just as Effie Mae entered into the kitchen.

"You called me Momma?"

"Where your sister and Pete?" Millie asked; her mind seemingly preoccupied.

"Oh, they went over to see Ms. Fannie Mae. I think Pete said they were staying over there, tonight."

"What so happen, you home this evening?" Millie removed a tin container of flour from a bottom cabinet. "Now that Anthony's Momma done gave him his car back, I thought for sure you'd be with him."

"Momma, this is my week off!"

"Week off?"

"You know what I mean. Even though it's more like three days, I still take the week off, sometimes."

Millie reached inside of the tin can and scooped out a handful of flour. She sprinkled it onto the wooden cutting board she'd just placed onto the kitchen table, draped with a plaid yellow tablecloth. She went to the refrigerator and grabbed a large, red bowl covered with cellophane, containing a lump of dough. She turned the bowl over and dropped the dough onto the wooden board and began kneading it.

"I see this is turning into a who's who in Yazoo County." Millie said. Effie Mae watched in silence as her Momma ground her fingers and palms into the defenseless lump of dough. "Seems like they think my daughter ain't good enough!"

"Who think I'm not good enough Momma— and good enough for what?" Effie Mae asked certain that she was the daughter Millie spoke of.

"I guess it take something like this to find out just what folks think of you— now don't it?" Millie seized a rolling pin from on top of the refrigerator. She dusted it with flour then rolled it across the dough. "It seems folks round here think their doo-doo, don't stink!" She took a glass out of the cupboard and dipped it into a small pile of flour next to the dough. And without measuring, she collected the exact amount of flour on the glass's rim, then pressed it down into the dough, forming perfectly round, buttermilk biscuits.

Effie Mae suddenly broke her silence. "Momma, are you gon tell me what you talking about? Or do I need to walk up the road to the Parker's, and ask Ms. Fannie Mae what's going on in this county?" She teased.

"You stay your behind away from that woman." Creases formed in Millie's forehead. "And I especially want you to stay away from Jimmy Parker!" She snapped, then walked over to the sink and washed the flour from her hands. Effie Mae assumed Millie's unexplained frustrations had a direct link to her reputation.

"One of these days Momma you gon realize that the people who demand the most respect, are the ones, least deserving of it."

Millie glared at her briefly then lessened her fury. "Will you promise me child, that you gon wear something descent and respectable when you meet with J.R., tomorrow?"

"What's respectable and descent Momma?"

Millie walked out of the kitchen without saying another word. Effie Mae watched as she entered into her bedroom and briskly shut the door.

"I guess I'll find out when he gets here—now won't I?" Effie Mae smiled, cleverly as she began arranging the biscuits onto an aluminum pan.

Chapter Five

Effie Mae entered into Annie Mae's bedroom as she lay in bed resting. She looked at her young sister and smiled.

"Look at my baby sister." Effie Mae leaned forward and rubbed Annie Mae's round belly. "I wonder if I'll have a niece or nephew. What you think Annie Mae?"

"Pete and Ms. Fannie Mae say I'm having a boy. Mr. Ned and Jimmy say I'm having a girl. And I say whatever it is, I'll just be glad when it gets here." Annie Mae looked at Effie Mae with concern.

"Effie Mae, do you think you gon ever get married?" Effie Mae sat down onto the bed.

"I'm not blind Annie Mae. I know men only see me as somebody to satisfy themselves with. And you know . . . sometimes I feel like that's all I'm good for." She said.

"I know you don't mean that Effie Mae."

"Little girl, it's so many men out there—Effie Mae Reed just seem to want them all!" She joked, attempting to conceal the emptiness she felt inside.

"Well, I don't believe that Effie Mae. Whatever happened to make you change, one day, you gon get over it." Annie Mae's eyes revealed that she knew.

"You know don't you?" Effie Mae felt ashamed.

"Yeah, I heard when you told Momma. And I saw you when you put those panties under your mattress." Annie Mae sat up and hugged her big sister, tears now streamed down her teenage face. "I wish I could've done something to help you Effie Mae."

Effie Mae gazed at her through pained eyes as she momentarily remembered the incident with David and Willie Lee.

"It ain't no help for me Annie Mae. I tried to change, but something inside of me, just won't let me." She stared into nothingness. "Maybe, marrying that preacher is just what I need."

"What? Who's marrying a preacher?" Annie Mae asked, astonished by the words. Suddenly realizing what she'd said, Effie Mae tried to redirect the focus back onto her younger sister. "Have you and Pete picked out a name if it's a girl? Because we already know if it's a boy, his name's gon be Pete." Effie Mae laughed. "But if it's a girl, please don't name her Millie. And for sure don't name her Fannie Mae!"

Annie Mae momentarily chuckled then gazed at Effie Mae in silence. She knew her big sister well enough to know that she harbored a juicy secret. In addition, her interest had now been piqued.

"What is it that you tryin' not to tell me Effie Mae Reed?" She asked. "Is Momma trying to marry you to J.R.? Pete told me that Ms. Sissy's told his Momma, that her brother was here looking for a wife." Effie Mae listened, but gave no reply, uncertain if she should reveal Millie's questionable command. She knew in her heart, that if she married Sissy's baby brother, it would end in disaster. No longer able to keep the secret, words erupted from Effie Mae's mouth.

"Ms. Sissy's brother told Rev. Hill, he wants to meet me. I guess he's thinking he might want to marry me." Annie Mae's mouth flung opened. Her jaws appeared to be stuck. "Why you looking like that Annie Mae?"

"Effie Mae, I know you my sister and all . . . and I love you, but … you?"

"Were you listening to me Annie Mae? I said Ms. Sissy brother thinks he might want to marry me. I didn't say that I was gon do it!"

"Effie Mae Reed, if you step your loose behind in that church talking about marrying a preacher, people are gon run out of there so fast, you'd think the building was on fire." Annie Mae laughed hysterically. "And if you do let Ms. Sissy talk you into marrying her baby brother, don't you dare wear a white wedding gown!" Annie Mae suddenly placed her hand on her belly. "Even my baby had to kick behind that." She laughed.

"Annie Mae, you can stop all that laughing, because I ain't marrying that man! I ain't marrying nobody." Effie Mae paused. A serious look formed on her face. "I ain't like you Annie Mae." She stared into Annie Mae's eyes. "You and Pete— y'all were meant for one another. Effie Mae Reed ain't meant to be with nobody, at least not for more than a night, day, whenever!" She laughed then reached over and again touched Annie Mae's belly. "Do you here that, Pete Jr.?" She quietly laughed.

"Effie Mae!" Millie shook her sleeping daughter, caped beneath a blanket on the couch. She momentarily gazed at Effie Mae as she thought how innocent she looked while asleep. For a second, Millie hoped that when her eldest daughter opened her eyes, she would again be the respectable young girl that was once, the apple of her eye.

Effie Mae peeked from underneath the blanket covering her head and opened her eyes in response to Millie's touch.

"What time is it Momma?"

"It's almost seven thirty. Why?" Millie asked, curious. Effie Mae threw the cover off.

"Momma, why you wait so late to wake me up? Anthony's gon be here in thirty minutes!" Effie Mae leaped up from the couch and hurried into the kitchen. She snatched open the back door then ran swiftly outside and into the old outhouse.

Millie's hopes diminished as she accepted the realization that her eldest daughter's return to her old self wouldn't be today.

Effie Mae rushed back into the house and into Millie's room where she washed, using the basin of warm water Millie had prepared for her own morning bath. She changed into a pair of yellow thigh-high shorts and a yellow button down shirt with black polka dots.

Millie watched with disappointment as Effie Mae stood in the kitchen and looked out of the window, anxiously awaiting Anthony's arrival.

"Child do you ever give your body a rest?" She asked as Effie Mae poured herself a glass of orange juice.

"From what Momma?" She again looked out the window.

"So, I guess you didn't plan on coming to church? Millie looked at her hot to trot daughter and thought about what a mismatch she would be for J.R.

"Yeah, I'll be there. I might be a little late though." Effie Mae blushed.

"Well, make sure you clean yourself up before you walk through the doors of the church." Millie said, shaking her head at her daughter's shamelessness. Effie Mae walked over and opened the front door.

"Oh, here come Anthony—I will. I'll see you at church Momma." She darted out the door and off the porch then stood on the passenger's side of the car and waited. Anthony climbed out and walked around to the other side. He opened the door and Effie Mae got in. He kissed her on the lips then gently closed the door. Anthony hurried back over to the driver's side and again got in. Millie watched from the kitchen window as he backed out of the driveway and pulled onto the road. Effie Mae waved as she and Anthony drove away—on their way to the Cozi-T Motel. Millie glanced up at the ceiling as if she'd prepared to speak to God. And, for a fleeting moment she appeared as if somehow she knew that the assault on her first born daughter had changed her life forever.

"Morning Ms. Millie. How are you feeling today?" Rev. Hill observed the troubled look on her face.

"I guess I'm doing as best as I can Rev. Hill."

"I see that Effie Mae's not with you. Is everything alright?"

"Alright— for Effie Mae; Anthony got his car back."

"I heard." Rev. Hill raised an eyebrow. "Ms. Millie, don't tell me she's with that young man on a Sunday morning?" He said disturbed by the thought.

"Then I won't tell you." She raised an eyebrow. "But she said she gon be here this morning." She paused. "Late, but she gon be here."

"Is she gon be alright this evening to meet J.R.?"

"Rev. Hill, we already had that talk." Millie suddenly became overwrought with grief. She began to cry. Rev. Hill placed her head onto his chest and comforted her.

"I wish I could tell you everything's gon be alright Ms. Millie, but I just don't know; only thing we can do is just keep praying for Effie Mae." He gently wiped away Millie's tears.

The members of St. Ebenezer Missionary Baptist Church turned and stared in the direction of the door when they unexpectedly heard it open, then close, an hour into the service. The entire congregation took note as Effie Mae strolled through the sanctuary flaunting a button down navy blue dress accented with a patent leather white belt, fastened around her narrow waist, complimented by the pair of white patent leather, high-heel shoes on her feet. On her hands, a set of white gloves; highlighting her fashionable attire, and attractively placed on top of her head sat, a white flying saucer hat.

Millie's mouth flung open as she watched Effie Mae stroll through the church, appearing as a window ready store mannequin. J.R. smiled with delight. He decided at that moment, he would ask Effie Mae to be his wife.

Rev. Hill looked at Millie and nodded, impressed by Effie Mae's respectable presentation. She also caught the eye of Jimmy Parker. He fixated on the girl he routinely spent intimate evenings with.

"If I hadn't seen it with my own eyes Rev. Hill, I never would've believed it!" Millie said following the morning service as she stood on the cement platform directly outside of the front doors of the church. Rev. Hill remained silent as he exhibited a smile equal to one seen on the face of a *father of the bride*.

"Don't ever give up hope Ms. Millie" He stated.

"I know they only clothes, but . . . ."

Rev. Hill interrupted. "Take one step at a time Ms. Millie, one step at a time." He smiled.

Sissy stood face to face with Effie Mae inside the church, admiring her reputable, but uncharacteristic look. J.R. watched anxiously in the distance and waited for the introductions.

"Effie Mae? Child, I didn't even recognize you when you walked into the church. You look so pretty — respectable!" Sissy said as she gazed at the expensive apparel Effie Mae wore. J.R. cleared his throat in anticipation of Sissy's acknowledgement of his presence. She shifted her eyes to her overly anxious younger brother.

"Oh, Effie Mae . . . that's my baby brother J.R." She said, reluctant to introduce him to the town's harlot. He hurried over. "And, J.R. this is Ms. Millie's daughter Effie Mae." He reached over and clasped Effie Mae's hands into his own. He stared helplessly, captivated by her beauty.

"It's a pleasure to meet you Effie Mae." He said with an unbreakable smile on his face.

"It's a pleasure to meet you too J.R." Effie Mae smiled. She thought to herself that this just might be her opportunity to once again, gain Millie's love and respect. J.R. held onto her hand, momentarily speechless.

"Uh, I guess—I'll see you later on." He said.

"I guess you will." Effie Mae said, gently sliding her hand from his grasp. J.R. turned and walked away as he prepared to exit the church.

Although Sissy felt pleased by Effie Mae's effort to present herself as a lady, she thought of the many young men she'd availed herself too. She also wondered if introducing her baby brother to Effie Mae could somehow be her biggest mistake ever.

"Effie Mae, it looks like you just might become Mrs. J.R. Smith." Sissy stated as she took note of the smiled plastered across her brother's face as he walked down the center aisle of the church, repeatedly glancing back at Effie Mae.

Effie Mae entered into the kitchen and walked over to the stove. Curious about dinner, she began lifting the tops from the various pots simmering on the burners.

"Momma—when are we gon eat?"

Millie remained silent as she proudly admired Effie Mae. She knew deep down inside, that her daughter's prim and proper persona wouldn't last long. She inhaled, then exhaled and waited for the bubble to burst.

"What Momma?" Effie Mae said when she noticed Millie's persistent stare. "I guess you want to know where I got these clothes from."

"The question had crossed my mind." Millie stated, not really wanting to know the answer, for fear that it would be less than honorable.

"Anthony took me shopping this morning." Millie smiled, relieved by Effie Mae's unexpected, acceptable response. Effie Mae removed the glove from her right hand and quickly dipped her finger inside the pot of greens that sat on the right front burner. She tasted the liquid from the tip of her finger. "After, we had done doing what we were doing at the Cozi-T." Millie frowned. "Momma you need to put more salt in these greens!" Effie Mae placed the top back onto the pot, then hurried from the kitchen and entered into Millie's bedroom, gently closing the door shut behind her. Millie laughed to herself. A skill she'd learned to use in place of anger and aggravation.

Effie Mae emerged from the room minutes later. She now wore a pair of white thigh-high shorts and a white polka-dotted, button down shirt tied mid-waist. Millie glared, shocked by her unexpected transformation.

"What Momma?" She yelled.

"Is that what you wearing for your evening with J.R.?"

"What's wrong with this Momma? Anthony likes it! And I know Jimmy do! He bought it for me!"

"Effie Mae can't you for once . . . ." Millie let out a disappointing sigh. "I knew this was gon be a mistake. Let me call Sissy and tell her to just keep looking for J.R. a wife."

"Momma, I told you I didn't want to meet that man in the first place." Effie Mae yelled. She took note of the disappointed look on Millie's face then glanced down at the clothes she now wore. She suddenly remembered the glow in her Momma's eyes that morning in church.

"I'll go change Momma."

Effie Mae and J.R. sat on the front porch. Her thoughts were ambiguous. On the one hand, she thought about how good it would be to once again gain the love and respect her Momma once had for her. On the other hand, she wondered how long J.R. would be hanging around, in that she had an impending date with Jimmy that evening.

"So…uh, I hear you already have a marriage proposal on the table." J.R. asked.

"Who? Anthony? Nope!"

"So, are you seeing anybody special?

"Special? Nope!"

"Did Sissy tell you that I was looking for a wife?"

"Yep."

"So, what do you think about that?'

Effie Mae remembered how Millie looked at her before she became something her Momma despised.

"I think that you seem like a nice man, but . . . ."

"But what?" He asked, curiously.

Effie Mae glanced briefly through the living room window. She saw the worried look on Millie's face as she waited in anticipation of what her less than honorable daughter would say if indeed J.R. asked her to be his wife.

"I don't really know you—and you don't really know me."

"I'm aware that we don't really know one another . . . ." He gazed into her eyes. "I don't know what it is, but I feel something for you Effie Mae, that I've never felt for any other woman." He took a hold of her hand. "I've only courted a few women, but . . . ."

"But what J.R.?" Effie Mae blushed.

"I see us married, with lots of children—" She interrupted.

"Lots? How many children are you talking about?" They both chuckled.

"I see me loving you and you loving me." He moved his lips close to her cheek. "Marry me Effie Mae." He said, softly. Effie Mae shifted her eyes inside the house and momentarily looked at Millie. Her attention was abruptly diverted when she heard the familiar sound of Jimmy's truck motor as he slowly cruised down the road. They briefly made eye contact then Effie Mae quickly looked away. She thought of how, although she never seriously considered marrying Jimmy, their relationship had slightly advanced from being simply, physical. She again turned her attention to J.R. She gazed into his eyes and smiled.

"Okay." She said.

"Huh?"

"I said, okay!"

"I promise you Effie Mae that no matter what, I'll always be there for you." J.R. closed his eyes and gently kissed her on the lips. Effie Mae glanced at Jimmy from the corner of her eyes. She watched as he turned in the driveway, backed out onto the road then slowly drove away. With his eyes tightly shut, J.R. kissed Effie Mae again.

Millie climbed out of bed the following Saturday morning. Still dressed in her light purple nightgown, she rushed from her bedroom and into the kitchen. One by one she began opening the bottom cabinet doors. When she got to the very last door, she reached inside and pulled out a steel-blade, table fan. She sat it on the kitchen counter, plugged it in and turned it on.

Millie plopped down at the table then leaned her head slightly back as she allowed the breeze from the fan to dry the beads of sweat on her face. Her lips pursed as she blew out, relieved by the steady flow of warm air. All alone at the kitchen table, she quietly talked to herself.

"Feel like it's hot enough to fry an egg on the sidewalk. It may even be hot enough to cook the chickens in the coop." She chuckled. "It looks like my daughter just might become her old self again." A huge smile formed on her face. "Now the only talk I'm gon be hearing 'bout my Effie Mae— is how respectable she is. And the only thing Fannie Mae gon be saying, is how beautiful my grandbabies is." Millie giggled.

Her prideful moment ended when she suddenly realized time was winding down. And the wedding ceremony planned by Sissy and J.R. would be taking place in only five hours. Millie rose from the chair and hurried into the living room where Effie Mae slept.

"Effie Mae! Wake up, now! We need to be heading over to the church." Millie pulled the blanket from over Effie Mae's head.

"What time is it Momma?" She turned her body away from the sound of Millie's voice and again covered her head.

"It's time for you to wake up— and get up! You getting married today, child!" Millie said with excitement. "We don't want to keep folks waiting at the church . . . Now do we?" Millie walked over to the closed bedroom door occupied by Annie Mae and Pete. She knocked. "Annie Mae, Pete!" Millie called through the door. It suddenly opened and Pete, still half asleep stood on the other side. He nodded his head.

"We getting up Ms. Millie." He said wiping his eyes. "Annie Mae didn't sleep to good last night. This baby's already giving her trouble and he ain't even here yet." He chuckled.

"He?" Millie raised an eyebrow.

"Yeah Ms. Millie, it's a big head boy; too hardheaded to be a girl." He lightly chuckled. "I'm gon have Annie Mae ready in time." Pete assured, and closed the door. Millie walked away and again over to Effie Mae to make another attempt at awakening her. She pulled back the covers from over the impending bride's head.

"Momma!"

"Don't Momma me! I ain't wanting to be late, for my wedding Effie Mae!" Millie snapped.

"Your wedding?" Effie Mae turned over and glared into Millie's eyes. "I didn't know you were getting married Momma. I thought it was my wedding."

"With all the mess you done put me through . . ." Millie stopped when she saw Effie Mae's eyes growing dim. Effie Mae shook her head, displeased by Millie's words.

"Momma—don't."

Millie gave no reply. She turned and vigorously walked away. She gave no further thought to the bride who still lay on the couch.

Annie Mae exited the bedroom wearing a lilac chiffon dress. Her belly protruded as her due date fast approached. She entered into the kitchen and watched as Millie combed Effie's Mae hair into a fashionable bun.

"I still can't believe my big sister getting married— and to a preacher!" She chuckled. "Now when Rev. Hill says repeat after me, and he tell you to say—I, Effie Mae Reed, take . . ." Annie Mae's laughter increased. "Make sure you remember which man is standing next to you. Now as your baby sister, I might understand that slip . .

." She paused. "But I can tell you now, Ms. Millie Reed right there, won't." Annie Mae quickly glanced at her Momma. "Neither will Rev. Otis T. Hill, and I know for sure—Ms. Sissy Hill, definitely won't!" She burst into laughter.

Effie Mae humored by her younger sister's teasing, joined in.

"Yeah. When Rev. Hill ask me to repeat after him, and ask me if I take, Rev. J.R. Smith to be my husband— I just might say—Now, Rev. Hill before I can say, I do . . . I might need to check with Anthony Lewis and Jimmy Parker, before I answer that question." The two sisters playfully laughed, humored by Effie Mae's words. Millie remained solemn. She found her daughters' teasing less than amusing.

"Effie Mae, you must want Momma to leave St. Ebenezer Missionary Baptist Church and never go back!" Annie Mae laughed uncontrollably.

"The church? Annie Mae, Momma's gon leave all of Yazoo County!"

As Millie's adolescent daughters laughed hysterically, Millie's anger grew.

"Your laughter would sound a whole lot better coming from inside the church—it's getting late!"

The sanctuary at St. Ebenezer Missionary Baptist Church flourished with white and lilac flowers. Matching sheers were draped at the ends of each pew. The altar was surrounded by several large corresponding floral arrangements. Displayed on top of the wooden table, centered at the front of the church, were two large white candles, a lilac ribbon tied across the middle of them each.

Millie stood in the overcrowded dressing room where green choir robes hung on both sides. She tightened the laces attached to the back of Effie Mae's floral, white wedding gown as Annie Mae placed a band of white baby breaths onto Effie Mae's hair. Several church members and friends moved busily throughout the small room. All helped Effie Mae as she prepared for a woman's most treasured and memorable occasion—her wedding day.

Without warning, Sissy pushed her way through the crowded room. She approached Effie Mae, where she stood face to face.

"I want everybody out of here! I need to talk to Effie Mae!" She ordered. Millie peered from behind Effie Mae as she tightened the last of the laces.

"Sissy? Everything alright?

"This don't involve you Millie! This here's between me and Effie Mae." She stated.

"Well, I ain't going nowhere 'til I know what it is you want to talk to my daughter about." Millie said, stepping from behind Effie Mae. "And why you think, folks need to stop what they doing and leave."

"I don't want any trouble with you Millie . . . ." Sissy said.

Effie Mae interrupted. She stared Sissy in the eyes then looked quickly over at Millie. "It's alright Momma. If Ms. Sissy wants to talk to me, I guess she has a right to say her peace. J.R. is her brother." Millie glanced around the room and into the faces of the other women, all awaiting her response.

"If it be what you want Effie Mae then I'm gon leave as Sissy ordered me to do. But I'm gon be standing right outside that door." Millie looked at Sissy in astonishment, surprised by her friend's conduct. She turned to Effie Mae and kissed her on the cheek then smiled. Millie took one last gaze at Sissy before exiting the room, along with all the other women, Annie Mae included.

"You know, I never wanted my baby brother to meet you in the first place, let alone marry you. But I guess he saw in you what every man in Yazoo County—that's had you, seen. That smile, those hazel brown eyes and that body that's been used more than toilet paper. I cried all night thinking how I talked J.R. into coming back here to look for a wife. At the time, I never even saw you as a possibility." Sissy paused when Millie glimpsed inside the room.

"I'm alright Momma."

"I'm just checking."

"But since it wasn't my choice to make—I guess you must be what he wants. I don't know how you did it. I know my brother, and it definitely wasn't from . . ." Effie Mae cut her off.

"Ms. Sissy, you done said your peace, now you let me say mine." Effie Mae demanded. "I was okay with doing just what I was doing. And I don't care what you or nobody else think about it! I can't help it if your brother liked what he seen." She paused. "Maybe I'll make your brother a good wife, and maybe I won't. But if marrying your brother, makes my Momma look at me like I'm a human being, and not a dog in heat, then it looks like I'm gon be marrying your preacher brother, whether you like it or not."

Rev. Hill quickly entered into the room, a puzzled look on his face.

"Sissy! Everything alright in here?" He stared impatiently at her. "We're ready to start." He momentarily stood waiting for his wife to break her angry stare at Effie Mae then escorted her from the room. Millie hurried back inside.

"Now, what in the world was all that about?"

"Nothing Momma— it wasn't about nothing."

"I now pronounce you husband and wife." Rev. Hill said as Effie Mae and J.R. stood front and center at the altar. "You may kiss your bride." J.R. looked into Effie Mae's eyes through the veil, slightly obscuring her face. He smiled then raised it over her head as he wrapped his arms around her. He placed a gentle kiss onto her lips. He gazed into her eyes then took a deep breath and exhaled. He closed his eyes and romantically embraced her then passionately kissed her. Sissy's jaws dropped at his actions. Millie smiled, pleased by her eldest daughter becoming the wife of a preacher. Jimmy sat mid-center in the sanctuary and watched with ambiguity. He knew that Fannie Mae and Ned would never accept Effie Mae as his wife. But, despite her tarnished reputation, he was in love with her.

Ned shook his head in disgust as he watched the bride and groom kiss. Fannie Mae felt relieved that somebody else's male family member had married Effie Mae Reed, eliminating the possibility of Jimmy ever making her his wife.

Wearing his white shirt and black bowtie, Anthony watched through tearful eyes from the very back pew. His heart ached as the girl he longed to marry committed herself to another. The crowd looked on as the prolonged kiss appeared to be never-ending.

"Uhm! Rev. Hill said, clearing his throat. J.R. slowly opened his eyes then released the mouth to mouth suction he and his new bride shared. He looked around the church at all the gazing eyes and quietly chuckled. He took a hold of Effie Mae's hand then Mr. and Mrs. J.R. Smith turned to face their many guests. Congratulations echoed throughout the sanctuary as the couple strolled down the center aisle and prepared to depart from the church.

Jimmy stared at Effie Mae as she walked hand and hand with her new husband. He lowered his head when his eyes filled with tears. Effie Mae noticed Anthony seated in the rear as she and J.R. neared the open church doors. She glanced subtly over at him, her eyes apologized. They momentarily stared into one another's eyes before Anthony looked away. He understood that his parents would never allow him to marry Effie Mae Reed, but hoped that one day their opinion of the girl he loved would change.

Walking through the sanctuary, Effie Mae wondered if she was actually capable of possessing true love. She rationalized that if she were, it would have definitely been for Anthony. As the bride and groom continued down the aisle, Anthony for a split second contemplated nabbing the girl he believed to be rightfully his. He stood to his feet. Unable to move, he took no action as Effie Mae and her new husband exited the church, stepped off the cement platform and climbed into the back seat of Rev. Hill and Sissy's black Cadillac. Millie watched with joy as she convinced herself that the worst was finally over. Rev. Hill comforted his sobbing wife as she shed endless tears for the heartbreaking fate she knew her brother would one day endure.

Chapter Six

Effie Mae and J.R. lay in bed at the Cozi-T Motel. She envisioned herself waking up with Anthony as she had so many times before. Then, remembered that just yesterday, she'd married J.R. She dismissed the thought when reminded of the look of acceptance on Millie's face as she walked down the aisle with Sissy Hill's baby brother.

J.R. gazed at Effie Mae as she lay in his arms. He smiled and considered himself, truly blessed to have captured her.

"I think you really gonna like New York." He stated then gently kissed her on the lips.

"New York." She smiled. "For the honeymoon?"

"No." J.R. kissed her again. "To live."

"Live? I ain't living in New York! Why would I leave Yazoo County and move to New York?"

"That's where I live. And you my wife." Effie Mae turned her head when he again attempted to kiss her. J.R. sat up. "What's wrong?"

"What's wrong? Momma didn't tell me that I'd be moving to New York!"

"Where did you think we would be living?"

"Here! I thought you were gon be living here!"

"No. I just came here to look for a wife."

"Well, it looks like you need to keep looking, because I ain't leaving my Momma and baby sister!"

"You can always come back and visit." He gently took a hold of her arm. "Effie Mae, you my wife . . . ."

She jerked away from his hold then climbed out of bed wearing a lavender lace trimmed, thigh-high, nylon gown.

"Take me home! I'm going back to my Momma's house, and that's where I'm staying!"

J.R watched as she walked over to her suitcase, sitting in a chair, and opened it. She took out a pair of red short-shorts and white brassiere then slipped them on while still wearing the lingerie.

"Wait! Can we talk?" He asked. Effie Mae looked at him and rolled her eyes. She pulled the gown over her head and stuffed it inside the luggage.

"Talk about what?" She yelled as she retrieved her sleeveless, red polka-dotted, button down blouse.

"Where are you going?"

Effie Mae stared at him as she put the seductive blouse on, tying it at her waist. "I'm going home— with my Momma and Annie Mae!" She loosened the bun on top of her head. Her rippling, black hair fell down onto her shoulders. She combed through it with her fingers then grabbed a hold of the handle on her suitcase. Effie Mae walked over to the door and stopped. J.R. watched in awe, shocked by her less than respectable attire.

"Is that what you wearing?" Effie Mae gave no reply. He shifted his eyes to the wedding gown thrown over a chair. "Don't forget your wedding dress."

"You keep it! Now take me home!"

Effie Mae slammed the back door as she stormed into the house.

"Momma!" She shouted.

J.R. hurried in behind her. Millie rushed from her bedroom and into the kitchen. She noted Effie Mae pacing back and forth, once again wearing the less than flattering clothes she wore prior to getting married. She cringed.

"You called me, child?"

"Momma, this man talking about moving me to New York …."

"Well, that's where he lives." Millie stated, innocently.

"You didn't tell me that Momma!"

"I thought you knew." Effie Mae shook her head in disbelief, and then stared Millie in the eyes.

"Do you hate me that much Momma?" She shouted. Millie gazed at her in silence then looked away. Annie Mae and Pete hurried from their bedroom, when hearing the loud commotion. They entered into the kitchen and witnessed the standoff between Effie Mae and Millie.

"You hate me too Annie Mae?" Effie Mae yelled walking towards her. Annie Mae began crying, hurt by Effie Mae's harsh words. Pete stepped between the two sisters. He placed his hands on Annie Mae's shoulders and turned her in the direction of their bedroom then looked into Effie Mae's angry eyes.

"Effie Mae—you wrong girl. You know Annie Mae don't hate you. That girl loves you with all her heart. She never judged you, always accepted you for who you was." He shook his head. "You know you wrong." He broke his stare with his sister-in-law then put his arm around his crying wife, and escorted her back into the bedroom. He momentarily glared at Effie Mae, disappointed by her attack on Annie Mae. Pete turned away and entered into the room, slamming the door shut behind him.

"You want me to leave Momma? Okay, I'll go. But don't you ever expect that you gon see me again!" Millie remained silent. Effie Mae brushed past her and entered into the bedroom to retrieve the rest of her clothes. J.R. watched in horror at the bizarre behavior of the girl he'd just wed. Millie flinched as Effie Mae violently slammed the bedroom door. She shifted her guilt-ridden eyes over to J.R. She now questioned if the subtle pressure she placed on Effie Mae to marry Sissy's baby brother would bring him the unbearable grief and shame she'd endured over the past year.

The Hill's black Cadillac pulled into Millie's driveway and parked. Rev. Hill and Sissy accompanied J.R. back to the Reed family home to pick up his new bride.

"Now don't be all day J.R." Sissy stated. "Don't forget we got to drive all the way to Jackson, so you and Effie Mae can catch the train from there."

J.R. retreated from the car. He felt it best, that he not alert Sissy or Rev. Hill of his new bride's temper tantrum that morning. He stepped onto the front porch, uncertain which Effie Mae he would encounter once he'd entered into the house. He gently knocked then opened the door and went inside. He saw only Millie seated at the kitchen table.

"Ms. Millie."

"How you doing J.R.? You here for Effie Mae?"

"Yes Ma'am." Lowering his voice, he said, "Ms. Millie— is she like that all the time?"

"Truth is J.R . . . ."

"Momma! Is that J.R. you talking to?" Effie Mae yelled from inside the bedroom then opened the door. She gawked at him from the distance. "Just let me go say bye to my little sister— if Pete let me." Effie Mae walked out of the bedroom and into the kitchen. She held her luggage in her right hand.

"You need me to get that for you, wife?" J.R. asked as he rushed to her, and removed the luggage from her hands then sat it down onto the floor. He looked at her cautiously and smiled. Effie Mae ignored his kindness, rolling her eyes as an adolescent. She turned and walked away then headed in the direction of Annie Mae's bedroom.

Uncertain if Pete would allow her anywhere near her younger sister, she knocked on the door. It slowly opened. Pete stood on the other side.

"What you want Effie Mae? I ain't gon let you talk to my wife like that no more . . . ." She cut him off.

"I just want to apologize to my baby sister and tell her that I love her. And that I'm gon miss her." Pete hesitated then stepped back and allowed her to enter. Annie Mae sat up at the sound of her big sister's voice.

"I'm sorry Annie Mae. I know you don't hate me."

"You know I love you Effie Mae . . ." She said interrupting.

"I know you do." Effie Mae walked over being seated on the bed. She smiled and hugged her baby sister. Pete watched without intervening.

"Like Pete said, when everybody else around here thought you wasn't good enough to eat dirt off their floors, I was proud of my big sister— and admired you for not letting their ugly words tear you down." Annie Mae's eyes filled with tears as she began to cry. "I'm gon miss you Effie Mae."

"I'm gon miss you too Lil' girl."

Annie Mae stared sympathetically into Effie Mae's eyes. "Momma don't hate you either Effie Mae, she just never learned how to accept the new you." Annie Mae smiled. Effie Mae rose from the bed and prepared to leave.

"You take care now, Effie Mae . . . uh, Mrs. J.R. Smith." Pete said chuckling as he walked over and embraced her.

"I don't know if I can be somebody's wife, Pete."

"Don't worry 'bout it, I think you gon make J.R. a fine wife," Pete looked over at Annie Mae and smiled. "Just like Annie Mae."

"Thank you Pete. But you know I ain't nothing like my baby sister." Pete chuckled as they ended their embrace.

"You know you broke my brother's heart don't you?"

"What?"

"Yeah, after you married J.R., Effie Mae—my big brother sat in his truck and cried most of the evening! He didn't let Daddy see him though."

"I don't believe you Pete. Jimmy Rae Parker didn't like me like that!"

"What you talking about, girl. My brother was in love with your crazy behind."

Effie Mae ruminated on Pete's words then smiled.

"He sure didn't act like it."

"That's because he knew that daddy would shoot his self in the foot, before he'd let Jimmy Rae marry you."

Annie Mae's mouth flung open. "Don't be talking about my big sister like that, Pete Nathanial Parker.

"What? He would've! I'm just telling it like it is!" Pete laughed, light-heartedly.

"Well, I guess your daddy don't have to worry about that now — do he?"

"You always gon be my sister-in-law, though." He shifted his eyes over to Annie Mae and again smiled. She blushed. "I love you Effie Mae." Pete stated. "But only as my sister-in-law." He said, quickly clarifying his statement.

"Don't y'all forget to let me know, when Pete Jr. gets here."

"We sure will." Pete said as he noticed Annie Mae crying. "Now, there she go again." He hurried over and sat down on the bed, taking her into his arms.

"Effie Mae!" Millie yelled from the kitchen. "You ready child? Your husband, been standing here near 'bout twenty minutes. I'm sure he ready to go." Millie said, swallowing the lump in her throat as she tried to fight back her tears.

"I'm coming Momma." She yelled. Effie Mae turned and looked at her sobbing sister being comforted by Pete. She wiped away the single tear that emerged from her right eye, gradually rolling down her face. "Let me go before Momma have a heart attack or something." Effie Mae smiled goodbye then exited the room.

She walked through the living room and entered into the kitchen, ignoring J. R.'s presence. She went over to Millie and leaned down. Effie Mae wrapped her arms around her Momma's plump neck and hugged her. Millie inwardly combated her emotions as a new lump formed in her throat. Her eyes puddled with tears.

"I'm gon miss you, child." She said. Effie Mae showed no emotion as she brought their mother-daughter embrace to an end.

"I wish I could believe that Momma."

J.R. stood mute; baffled by the unpredictable personality of the girl he'd just married. Millie maintained her silence as she struggled with the hard truth, that deep inside, she looked forward to her shameless, rebellious daughter's absence from the Reed family's home.

"You be sure and call when you get there." Millie dabbed her eyes with a small white handkerchief, almost appearing as if trying to wipe away the guilt she now felt— for J.R.

"Well, it looks like we need to be leaving Effie Mae . . . wife." J.R. retrieved her suitcase from the floor, his objective being to load both it and her, into the awaiting car.

"You take care of my daughter, now J.R."

"I plan on doing just that, Ms. Millie."

Effie Mae suddenly thought about Anthony. She remembered the hurt look on his face as she walked down the aisle, married to a man, she neither, knew or loved. She wished at that moment, that he would pull into the driveway and take her away, as he had the first day they met. She reminisced on how they'd overslept the first time they went to the Cozi-T Motel. She blushed.

"Yep—I guess we need to be heading on out. This is it." J.R. said, unknowingly interrupting Effie Mae's thoughts of Anthony. The sound of his voice diminished as Effie Mae's thoughts again drifted. This time she pondered over the spoken words of Pete. She replayed them in her head, flattered by the thought of how Jimmy was actually in love with her. "I guess, I—uh, can go ahead and take this bag out to the car." J.R.'s words fell on deaf ears. He hurried out of the front door and over to the open car trunk. He put Effie Mae's suitcase inside and closed it.

"You and Effie Mae coming J.R.?" Sissy asked, impatiently. "What's taking so long? We don't have all day!"

"We'll be right out Sissy." J.R. assured then reentered the house; this time determined to bring Effie Mae out with him. "I guess we'd better get going and . . ."

Effie Mae rebelliously sat down at the kitchen table. She folded her arms as if refusing to leave. J.R. walked over and lightly took a hold of her arm. She jerked away from his hold. He gently grasped her arm a second time. Effie Mae looked up at him in response to his unwanted action. She focused her attention to the hand that gripped her arm. J.R. quickly released his grip when noting the look of fury forming in her eyes. His mind raced as he thought about what his next move would be. J.R. walked slowly over to Millie, collecting his nerves.

"You take care now, Ms. Millie." He said, giving her one last hug goodbye. He looked silently into her eyes as if requesting her advice. Millie subtly nodded. J.R. again approached his new bride and again, he took a hold of her arm.

Coming to the realization that Anthony would not be coming to the rescue, Effie Mae slowly rose from the chair and allowed her new husband to guide her out the front door of the Reed's family home. Millie stood and watched as they departed. She walked over to the kitchen window and glared out as Effie Mae and J.R. climbed inside of the opened back doors of the Hill's black Cadillac. Tears streamed down her brown cheeks as Rev. Hill backed out of the driveway and onto the road, then drove away with Effie Mae tucked away inside, headed to the train station in Jackson, Mississippi. Millie's mind wandered as she thought to herself how New York City could only bring more trouble for her country-raised, untested daughter.

Effie Mae buried herself in the back seat of the oversized car. She felt abandoned and alone as she listened to Sissy explain the *dos* and *don'ts* of married life, and the many other necessities she believed her young brother needed to hear.

"Remember now, once y'all get to New York City, wait at the train station until Cousin Daniel arrives. He said he was gon pick you and Effie Mae up." Sissy turned her head part-way in the direction of her young sister-in-law. "Effie Mae, I hear Cousin Daniel's got himself a good wife. Name's Geraldine. But that's—Ms. Geraldine to you." She emphasized. "I heard she's a good Christian woman—got a good job too; lives real fancy-like." She boasted. "Now, I know you ain't use to that kind of living, since Millie ain't ever had much. But as long as you listen and do what your husband tells you—you gon, do just fine. Fit right in." Effie Mae gave no reply as she watched Sissy's partially turned head that seemed to reveal only her lips moving, nonstop.

The train's engine roared like a ferocious lion as it made its grand entrance into the crowded Jackson train station.

"I guess we'd better hurry." J.R. said as he swung open the car door and departed from the automobile. Effie Mae reluctantly followed. "It appears that old train calling our names." J.R. said, making an effort at being humorous. Sissy climbed out of the car to exchange her final hugs, kisses, and goodbyes with her younger brother and her new sister-in-law. Rev. Hill watched from inside the vehicle.

"Now remember what I said J.R. Wait at the station until Cousin Daniel gets there." She said, hugging her baby brother goodbye before turning to Effie Mae. "Effie Mae." She whispered. "If you remember that you a married woman now, and give yourself only to your husband, you just might make my baby brother a good wife." Sissy stated, pessimistically then applied a half-hearted kiss to Effie Mae's cheek.

J.R. gave Rev. Hill a final wave goodbye then walked around to the opened trunk. He reached inside and grabbed their luggage then approached Effie Mae and extended his arm, nonverbally requesting that she take a hold. She complied, then without further resistance, the two hurried to board the train. Sissy shouted and waved.

"Y'all take care now!"

J.R. and Effie Mae hurried in the direction of the train. A voice shouted out as they disappeared through the steel doors of the steaming locomotive.

"All aboard" The steaming locomotive gave a final roar as if to say goodbye, then headed due east.

Chapter Seven

Several weeks had passed since J.R. and Effie Mae's move to New York City, and into the home of his Cousin Daniel and wife, Ms. Geraldine. Effie Mae's transitions from the south to the east and from teenager to wife brought chaos and confusion to the entire household.

Ms. Geraldine, an average height, big boned, caramel complexioned woman stood at the stove as she prepared a breakfast of pork sausage, French toast and fried eggs—over easy. She looked up when she saw Effie Mae walking through the dining room.

"Good morning Effie Mae."

Effie Mae ignored her words. She stared down at the floor and kept her head lowered as she continued in the direction of the bathroom, then entered inside, slamming the door shut behind her. Ms. Geraldine shook her head.

"What's wrong with her today?" She said to herself. Daniel hurried into the kitchen from the bedroom in response to the loud noise.

"Now, what the hell was that?" At five-foot eight, pudgy with salt and pepper hair, his handsome face bore a slight resemblance to that of Cab Calloway.

"That was J.R.'s wife." Geraldine said as she placed a piece of French toast onto a plate already stacked with several slices.

"What did you say to her Geraldine?"

"Good morning?"

"Geraldine . . . Leave that girl alone!"

"What? All I said was good morning."

"Well you shouldn't have said that!"

"I can't say good morning in my own house because of that—Daniel I'm not going to be walking on eggshells . . . ." She quieted when J.R. entered into the kitchen from the living room. He looked at Daniel then to Ms. Geraldine.

"Morning Cousin Daniel, Geraldine. What y'all fussing about this early in the morning?" Ms. Geraldine dropped a spoonful of butter on top of the French toast she'd just added to the stack.

"Your wife." She said.

"Effie Mae?" J.R. asked, curiously.

"Yeah—Effie Mae." She said. Daniel looked at J.R. with inquiring eyes.

"Is that where you slept last night J.R.?"

"Uh—I, uh . . ." He stuttered.

The bathroom door suddenly opened. All eyes were on Effie Mae as she stood in the doorway and prepared to return to her bedroom.

"Effie Mae." She stopped at the sound of Ms. Geraldine's voice. "Are you going to eat today? I know you're hungry. You haven't eaten in the last two days."

J.R. looked at Ms. Geraldine then turned to Effie Mae, shocked by the news of her nutritional status. Effie Mae continued her downward stare. She gave no reply.

"Effie Mae? Wife, are you. . . . ." J.R. began. Without warning, Effie Mae darted off in the direction of the bedroom then hurried inside and slammed the door. Geraldine shook her head.

"You see what I mean?"

Daniel looked in the living room and saw the pillow and blanket lying on the couch. He turned to J.R.

"Are you sleeping in the living room J.R.?"

"Uh, yeah." He said then again turned his attention to Ms. Geraldine. "Uh, Geraldine, did I hear you say that Effie Mae hadn't eaten in two days? Is she sick?"

"Yeah, she sick! Sick in the head."

"Geraldine! Now that's just mean." Daniel stated, sharply.

"What Daniel?"

"Now how you just gon say that Ella Mae—is sick in the head?"

J.R. looked quickly to Daniel in response to his mispronunciation of Effie Mae's name.

"Effie Mae, Cousin Daniel."

"Ain't that what I said?' Daniel again looked into the living room and again at J.R. "Now hold on J.R." He said, determined to get the bottom of his cousin's sleeping arrangements. "You want to tell me why you sleeping in my living room?"

"No." J.R. replied, humbly as he directed his attention back to Ms. Geraldine. "Do you know why my wife's not eating, Geraldine?"

"How should I know? You need to ask her that."

"Is everything alright between you and uh . . . ." J.R. interrupted him.

"Later, Cousin Daniel—we can talk later. Right now I need to go talk to my wife."

"You sure do, because there's something wrong with that girl." Ms. Geraldine stated.

"Geraldine!" Daniel yelled.

"What Daniel?"

"There you go again! That's just mean."

J.R. left the kitchen and walked over to the bedroom door. He paused before opening it to a crack. He visually searched the room to locate Effie Mae's whereabouts then entered when he saw her lying motionlessly in bed.

"Good morning, wife." Effie Mae ignored him. "You feeling alright today?"

J.R. lowered himself down onto the bed. He reached over and rubbed her exposed shoulder. She rose in response to his touch.

"Ahhhhhhhh!!!" Effie Mae screamed and swung her arms wildly. J.R. jumped off the bed and watched as his new bride engaged in a yet another temper tantrum.

Ms. Geraldine picked up the two plates of food she'd just set on the dining room table.

"There she goes again." She shook her head. 'I don't see how J.R. can even stand that girl."

Daniel stood deep in thought. His ears deafened to Ms. Geraldine's words.

"Did you know that J.R. was sleeping on the couch, Geraldine?" He asked as she walked towards the back door.

"It looks like we'll be eating breakfast on the porch again." She ignored Daniel's concern about his cousin's possible marital issues.

Daniel relaxed outside on the back porch as he enjoyed his usual nightly smoke of his pipe. Tonight J.R. joined him.

"I'm sorry Cousin Daniel for all the trouble my wife has caused you and Geraldine." Daniel ignited the wood pipe and positioned it in his mouth then took two puffs. Smoke flowed around his face.

"It's not your fault J. R." He shook his head. "You need to do something about that girl." He took two more puffs. "What's her name again—Edna Mae?" J.R. silently chuckled.

"Effie Mae, Cousin Daniel."

"Yeah, well—whatever her name is, you need to do something about her. She around here crying all the time, not eating, screaming like somebody crazy— anytime anybody says anything, to her! Look like you should've left her in Mississippi with her Momma." Daniel shook his head. "I tell you what she need though. . . . J.R. interrupted.

"What she need, is more time to miss her life in Mississippi, time to accept New York City as her new home, and me as her husband."

"Where you get her from anyway? And how old is that girl? I know sometimes these young girls go around looking older than they really are! Next thing you know—here comes her daddy with a shot gun, and you wondering why."

"She's old enough Cousin Daniel." J.R. quietly chuckled.

"That's a good looking woman!" Daniel gazed at J.R. then did a double take. "What's wrong with her? Is she alright in the head?"

"I don't think Sissy would've brought us together if she thought Effie Mae was crazy."

"What? Did she come with a cow — a couple of pigs or something?" J.R. grinned at his cousin's foregone conclusions.

"She's a good woman." J.R. stated. "And besides, Rev. Otis said . . ."

"Rev. Otis — Hill? Sissy's, husband?" Daniel shook his head. "Oh boy! Now I know you're in trouble. Rev. Otis Hill can't see the bad in people! He thinks everybody's a saint."

"Effie Mae's gon be alright, Cousin Daniel. She just needs . . ." Daniel cut him off.

"I know — a little more time? Yeah, I heard you the first time. Well J.R. all I got to say is, time will tell." Daniel relit the fizzled out pipe. Ms. Geraldine suddenly exited from the back, joining the two men on the porch.

"J.R., you need to do something about Effie Mae." She stated. "She has the devil all in her." Daniel shifted his eyes to J.R. and sighed, then turned to his meddling wife. He took two puffs from the pipe.

"Geraldine! Me and J.R. just discussed that. So whatever you were doing in the house, before you came out here, saying something that's already been said — go back in there and finish doing it."

"Well, I was just saying . . . . ." Daniel cut her off.

"Uh-huh. Now go say it, where somebody wants to hear you saying it — nowhere." Daniel shook his head as Geraldine reentered through the back door then slammed it shut. J.R. laughed, humored by his cousin's sharp words. "You know she's right J.R. I don't know about you, but she's getting on my nerves."

"Who? Geraldine?" J.R. joked.

"Her too — but I was talking about Essie Mae.

"Effie Mae." J.R. said, correcting him.

"Yeah, well anyway, you better talk to her. Call her Momma if you have to. But whatever you do . . . . ." J.R. interrupted.

"Time, Cousin Daniel, time."

"Uh-huh." Daniel propped the pipe in his jaw. The back door swung open and Geraldine rushed back out onto the porch with an afterthought.

"J.R., you might need to call her Momma." She said. Daniel turned to Geraldine then to J.R. and shook his head. He pointed his rigid index finger in the direction of the back door and used his eyes to say—*take your butt back in the house.*

The following day, Effie Mae got out of bed and went in search of her old red diary. She walked over to the closet and opened it. She stared inside at the cluttered space then grabbed the handle of her luggage and pulled it out. She placed it on the bed, unzipped it then rummaged through the numerous articles of clothing until she felt it. She removed the diary then slid down onto the multi-colored rug on top of the hardwood floor and began writing.

She wrote about her move to New York and her unfavorable opinion of her new cousin in-laws. Effie Mae's entry ended when she heard the sound of Ms. Geraldine's voice as she entered in from work.

"Effie Mae! Where are you? I need you to come in here and help me with this dinner." Ms. Geraldine yelled. Effie Mae gave no reply. "Effie Mae, do you hear me calling you? You better answer me!" Effie Mae tucked the diary underneath the mattress then rose to her feet. She exited the bedroom and entered into the fifties style kitchen. "And since you're living in my house for free, I shouldn't have to ask you to do anything around here! You hear me Effie Mae?" Ms. Geraldine shouted.

"You call me Ms. Geraldine?"

"Oh . . . . there you are." She said, startled by Effie Mae's sudden presence. "Well, didn't you hear me say Effie Mae? That is your name isn't it? And what kind of name is that anyway? Child, if I were you, I'd get rid of that old country name, and find yourself a new city name. Something like, Evelyn! Yeah, now that sounds much better, more sophisticated than, Effie Mae".

"Ms. Geraldine!" "Effie Mae is the name Millie and Frank Reed gave me, and I'm proud to have it. But, now if you like the name Evelyn so well, I'd be happy to call you that. But when you talking to me—Effie Mae is the only name I'm gon answer to."

"Well excuse me—Effie Mae! I was trying to make you sound like—a somebody, since you married to J.R. But it seems like I'm just wasting my time.

"Yep. So the next time you got something you think's worth saying Ms. Geraldine, maybe you should write it down and let me read if first, that way you can keep from wasting your time and mines." Effie Mae turned and walked away. She returned to her bedroom and slammed the door.

Chapter Eight

J.R. arrived home late Thursday night. He entered quietly into the bedroom carrying a small yellow flashlight in his hand. He used the light's beam to guide him over to the bed.

"Effie Mae. You sleep?" He shined the light in her face then leaned in towards her. Effie Mae turned over, and threw the covers over her head as if she were asleep. She ignored his attempt to awaken her. He took the cover from over her head and rubbed her hair. "Effie Mae. You woke." She remained silent. J.R. stared at her for a few minutes then kissed her on the cheek. He turned off the flashlight and walked away. Effie Mae opened her eyes after hearing the door close then quietly laughed.

J.R. entered into the kitchen. He opened the oven and removed the plate of food Ms. Geraldine routinely put away for him, due to his late night arrivals. He picked up a fried chicken leg and bit into it as he headed towards the back porch. He pushed open the door with his back and exited the house. Ms. Geraldine turned and looked when she heard the door open.

"Did you get that plate I left you in the oven J.R.?" She asked. He held up the half-eaten chicken leg.

"I got it Geraldine. Thank you."

"No problem. Maybe one day your wife will get out of that bed, so I can teach her how to cook"

"How's she doing?" He asked. Ms. Geraldine hesitated before answering. She wondered if Effie Mae had told him about the ongoing verbal altercations between the two women. J.R. took another bite from the chicken leg then perched himself in one of the three wooden chairs on the porch. He awaited her report.

"That one's got a real mouth on her. Always seem to have something sassy to say! Maybe you should teach her — you know as her husband, how to talk to people that are nice enough to let her live under their roof." She stated.

"Aw, Geraldine . . . . There you go. You ain't innocent! You just can't stand anybody who got more mouth than you." Daniel stated.

"What? I haven't said anything to that girl."

"You mean — anything that you'd be willing to admit to." Daniel stuffed his pipe with tobacco. "Geraldine, leave that girl alone! Don't nobody need you talking about how she's living under your roof. That's J.R.'s wife, and they're both welcome to stay here as long as they want." Daniel struck a wooden match on the concrete porch then ignited the pipe and took two quick puffs. Ms. Geraldine turned to J.R.

"Well, have you tried talking to her J.R.?" She asked.

"I guess I could, if she wasn't always sleep by the time I make it in from the church."

"Sleep!" Ms. Geraldine shouted. "That girl's not sleep! She goes in that bedroom about ten minutes before you walk through that door. I'm surprise she even have time to put on her night clothes. Oh— that's right, she never takes those off."

"Geraldine!" Daniel intervened. "Close your mouth. Just close your mouth. J.R. didn't asked you all that!"

"I'm just saying . . . ."

"And now that you've said it—now what?" Daniel asked, staring at her.

"What you mean, now what? I guess J.R. can say something to her about it."

"And when he does—then what?

"What do you mean, then what?"

"You see where I'm going with this Geraldine? I'm telling you woman, one day that big mouth of yours, is gon bring you trouble you can't get out of." He glared at her as a steady flow of smoke streamed from his mouth. Ms. Geraldine rose from her chair, upset by his scolding then prepared to enter into the house.

"Goodnight J.R." She looked at Daniel and rolled her eyes then went inside. Daniel watched as she disappeared through the back door. He removed the pipe from his mouth, turning to J.R.

"I don't know what I'm gon do with that woman J.R." He shook his head. "She's always somewhere running her mouth."

"You were a little hard on her, weren't you Cousin Daniel?"

"Naw, she's gon be alright. It's just that, every now and then, I have to tell her about all that meddling." Daniel paused. "Everything alright between you and Effie Mae, ain't it boy?"

"Uh, we're doing okay. It's gon work itself out."

"Yeah, she looks like she can be a handful." Daniel grinned.

"You don't have your eye on my wife, do you Cousin Daniel?" J.R. joked.

"Naw, but now—I'm gon call it like I see it. If Effie Mae wasn't your wife . . ." Daniel's excitement heightened. "That's a good looking woman! But, you're my cousin and I respect that. Family comes first." Daniel lapsed deep into though—about Effie Mae.

J.R. gazed at Effie Mae as she lay in bed and watched him dress in preparation for his daily to trip to the church.

"Will you wait up for me tonight Effie Mae, please?"

Effie Mae remained silent. J.R. walked over and sat down on the bed. He leaned over and tried to kiss her. She turned away and threw a blanket over her head. J.R. stared momentarily at her draped beneath the cover then leaned in and kissed her on the shoulder. He rose from the bed and walked over to the door, leaving the room. After hearing the door shut, Effie Mae chuckled from underneath the blanket.

Ms. Geraldine prepped dinner in the kitchen prior to leaving for work. Suddenly fed up with Effie Mae's lying around, not helping she walked out of the kitchen and burst into her bedroom.

"I'll be glad when J.R. gets his own place, so he can get your behind out of my house!" She yelled. Effie Mae remained unmoved by the habitual confrontations.

You know what Ms. Geraldine—for the first time since I've been living in your house, looks like we finally agree on something, because I can't wait to get out of here!" Effie Mae screamed.

"I just cooked breakfast for your husband—again! And I don't think that's my job. You're his wife. And in case your Momma didn't teach you, it's a wife's duty to cook for her husband."

"Ms. Geraldine if you believe cooking for Mr. Daniel is your duty as his wife, I guess that's between you and him. But I didn't ask to be nobody's wife!" Ms. Geraldine looked puzzled, unsure exactly what those words meant. "So, if J.R.'s expecting me to cook his meals, then I guess, if you don't feed him, he's gon starve!"

"You're probably all looks anyway. I bet you wouldn't know how to color an egg on Easter Sunday."

"Well Ms. Geraldine I'd rather be coloring the eggs, than to look like I ought to be laying one."

"If it wasn't for the fact that I know it would hurt J.R., I'd throw your country behind out of here!"

"Then it looks like to me Ms. Geraldine—you got yourself a real problem." Effie Mae climbed out of the bed and brushed past her as she stood partially blocking the bedroom doorway.

Ms. Geraldine watched as Effie Mae strolled through the dining room and into the bathroom, slamming the door shut.

"Ol' high yellow heifer!" Ms. Geraldine suddenly glanced at the watch on her left arm and realized the bus would be arriving in five minutes. She hurried out the front door and headed to the bus stop. Effie Mae rebelliously retreated from the bathroom after she heard the front door close.

"I hate this place! And I hate these people!" She yelled. She looked around at her unfamiliar surroundings and wished that she were—back in Yazoo City. "I want to go home!" Effie Mae shouted as she thought about her unhappy life with her unknown husband. Her eyes filled with tears. She returned to her bedroom and slammed the door. She opened it, and again slammed it. Effie Mae opened the door, a third time and slammed it again. She again opened the door for a fourth time and prepared to slam it. She hesitated. She marched down the hall to Daniel and Ms. Geraldine's bedroom and stood outside the door.

"I'm sick of you Ms. Geraldine!" She screamed, as she entered. Effie Mae stood in the center of the room and looked around. She stared at the expensive lamps, bedding, curtains and furniture, crowded into the mid-sized room.

"I should tear all this junk up! See how you like that Ms. Geraldine!" She shouted then turned and rushed from the room.

"I'm getting out of here! I'm gon call Anthony right now, and have him drive up here and get me—that's what I'm gon do!" She swiftly entered into her room and began pulling out each of the dresser drawers. She threw her clothes onto the bed in anticipation of leaving then suddenly stopped. Effie Mae lowered herself onto the bed and began to cry.

"Don't hate me Momma. I'll stay." She remembered the look in Millie's eyes as she walked down the aisle as—Mrs. J.R. Smith. Effie Mae suddenly became angry. She stopped crying and stood to her feet then wiped the tears from her eyes.

"You know what Momma?" She said with defiance. "I ain't gon let you or nobody else, keep me from being me. I'm Effie Mae Reed! And it's time I started acting like it."

She stormed from her room and again entered into the bathroom. She filled the tub with water and climbed inside. Effie Mae scrubbed her body and face, as if washing away the apathetic feelings she'd harbored. She emerged from the bathroom wearing Ms. Geraldine's pink bathrobe that hung from a hook on the back of the bathroom door then returned to her bedroom as . . . Effie Mae Reed. She stood momentarily silent then walked down the hall and again entered into Ms. Geraldine's bedroom. She strolled over to the closed closet door and snatched it open. Effie Mae gazed at the multitude of clothes that hung inside. She sorted through the dresses, blouses and skirts then stopped when she discovered a red negligee. Effie Mae laughed as she removed it from the closet, still on the hanger.

"Ms. Geraldine, Ms. Geraldine." She looked in disgust. "I bet a frog would look better in this than you." Effie Mae laughed then hung it back up. Her eyes were suddenly drawn to the black polka dotted, button down dress. She smiled then removed it from the hanger. "Now, I know you can't get your big boned behind in this." She held the dress up against her shapely physique then noticed a large, white cardboard box sitting inside the closet, on a wooden shelf. Effie Mae opened it and looked in amazement at the numerous belts, gloves, stockings, purses, garter belts and scarves of various colors.

She sifted through the items and assembled the perfect pieces to complement the dress. She tossed the various articles onto the bed then went in search of a pair of shoes. Effie Mae saw a wooden shoe rack with numerous pairs of shoes located just outside of the closet. She picked up a pair of black patent leather high heels and looked inside the shoe for size. "A size seven and a half!" Now, Ms. Geraldine, you know you can't get your big feet in these shoes." She laughed, silently.

Effie Mae gathered everything into her arms then took a final look around the room. She threw her head up in victory then walked out and closed the door.

Effie Mae returned to her room and dressed herself from head to toe in the assortment of clothing. After fastening the last button on the dress, she enveloped her small waist with the shiny black belt. Effie Mae brushed her hair and pinned it up in a bun then clamped a pair of gold colored earrings with a dime sized red circle in the center, onto her ears. She looked at herself in the dresser mirror and concluded that she looked like a movie star. She smiled then slid a pair of black gloves onto her hands, as if putting the icing on the cake. She picked up the black patent leather purse then realized she had no money. She remembered J.R. kept money in the top drawer of the four drawer chest. Effie Mae reached inside and grabbed three dollars in change. She dropped the money inside the purse then shut the drawer. She exited the room and headed in the direction of the front door then paused when she arrived. She took a deep breath, opened the door then stepped out.

Effie Mae headed to the bus stop and waited for its arrival. When the bus pulled up, she climbed on, paid the fare then took a seat, positioning herself on one of the many unoccupied seats. She looked around the bus and let out a deep breath. Effie Mae suddenly felt free as she began her unknown journey through New York City on her own unbeaten path.

Chapter Nine

Effie Mae wandered around the streets of downtown New York City. She gazed at the people filled maze and it's many fascinating sights and sounds. She took note of its every detail like an out of town tourist. Captivated by the uniqueness of the Statue of Liberty, Effie Mae momentarily lost sight of her immediate surroundings as she stared in amazement at the enormous structure.

"Hey girl." The gentle, distracting voice of an unseen man said, capturing her undivided attention. Effie Mae's eyes searched as she turned in the direction from which the unfamiliar voice appeared to have come. She saw only the tall brick buildings encompassing her. Unsure if the voice was real or even if the words were meant for her ears, she stood in silence.

"Now what's a fine thing like you, doing out here all by your lonesome?" The faceless voice asked. Effie Mae glanced around in an effort to locate the male communicating the complementary words. A man suddenly stepped out of a doorway which served as entryway to one of the many tall buildings.

A tailored and well groomed, exceptionally handsome thirtyish Colored gentleman appeared. He wore an ash gray zoot suit and a matching trilby hat on his head.

"Down here minding my own business—and I might suggest that you do the same." She stated. The mysterious man smiled as he approached.

"Girl, don't you know it's dangerous for a sweet, young thing like you to be roaming these streets?" He eyed every inch of her physique. "People might want to bring harm to you." He smiled. "How long you been in this fine city? That is—if you don't mind me asking."

Effie Mae, who'd always been outspoken, stood mute, taken by the debonair male's reverence when speaking to her. "Let me introduce myself to you. Henry Lee White's my name. But most people call me Huck. What should I call you? That is—if you don't mind me asking?"

"Effie . . ." She paused when she remembered Ms. Geraldine's words then without shame, she disclosed her birth name. "Effie Mae." She said, unnerved by the stranger's intent.

"Effie Mae." He hesitated. "I like that—it's, a little country, but I like it." He smiled. "I'll bet you're a Mississippi girl?" He said. "I got family in Mississippi myself." He gazed at Effie Mae and took note of her naivety. "It seems we're almost, family." He stared into her hazel brown eyes. She blushed when noticing him. He smiled. "Where you headed Ms. Effie Mae?" She lowered her guard as the charismatic male effectively lured her in.

"You tell me." She flirted. "I'm just walking around here admiring this fine city of yours." Effie Mae stated, drawn by Huck's irresistible smile.

"I tell you what—Ms. Effie Mae. How about you do me the honor of letting me escort you around this extraordinary place, sort of like your knight in shining armor?" He chuckled. "That is, if you don't mind a gentleman's company." He extended his arm to Effie Mae. She accepted his invitation taking ahold of his arm.

"I'd be pleased to have a gentleman's company." She smiled, seductively. Huck winked. Then he and Effie Mae set out on a journey that would ultimately lead her into a lifestyle unbefitting of a preacher's wife.

Huck entered into the closed jazz club, in that its business hours didn't start until late evening. A man polishing his brass saxophone looked briefly to the door as they entered.

"Who's that you got with you Huck?" asked a tall, dark, bearded man with his eyes hidden behind the beatnik sunglasses he wore. Effie Mae gaped at the nameless man, intrigued by his odd look. She silently admired the beatnik hat that tilted to the right side of his head, and his shiny horn.

The proprietor of Blue's Jazz Club, he turned away from his instrument and took note of the beauty, his old acquaintance had brought into the club.

"Uh, this here's my new friend Ms. Effie Mae." Huck smiled. "Ms. Effie Mae, this here's Blue." Effie Mae's looked perplexed by the bizarre name.

"Blue?" She asked.

"Oh! No—Blue ain't my real name baby girl!" He said when seeing the look of confusion in her hazel brown eyes. "My birth name is Tyrell Jones." he said removing the sunglasses from his eyes. Effie Mae smiled. "Maybe you can bring Baby girl back later, when we open." His eyes shifted from Effie Mae to Huck then back to Effie Mae.

"Yeah, I might do that." Huck glanced at Effie Mae as she focused her attention on Blue."

"Okay, that's cool." Blue glanced at Huck then locked his eyes on Effie Mae and smiled. "It was nice meeting you Ms. Effie Mae."

"It was nice meeting you to Tyrell."

"Uh-uh, Baby girl. Call me Blue!"

"Okay, Blue." Effie Mae blushed. Huck observed the exchange.

"Now Huck, don't do anything to get Baby girl in trouble before she make it back here to Blue's." He and Effie Mae stared at each other.

"Well Blue, I'm gon let you get back to shining that horn, and me and Ms. Effie Mae's gon move on. I have other people I want her to meet." He took a hold of Effie Mae's arm and guided her towards the front entrance. He opened the door like a real gentleman. He shifted his eyes to his saxophone playing buddy and winked as the *victor* then he and Effie Mae departed.

Seated at the bar with their backs turned were Huck's well-known partners in crime, Lawrence aka Buckeye and Gerald aka Gus. Both men looked one to the other. They smiled, impressed by their friend's new young, very attractive companion. They surmised that their old friend had just struck gold.

"Are you going somewhere Effie Mae?" Ms. Geraldine asked when seeing her headed towards the front door.

"You just keep cooking for Mr. Daniel. Don't you worry about what Effie Mae Reed, is getting ready to do." She opened the door and walked out, slamming it shut behind her. Daniel hurried into the kitchen from the back porch.

"I'm about ready to put that damn girl—and J.R. out of here!" He looked out the front door. "Where's she going this time? Did she say?"

"Does she ever?"

"She's doing something she don't have any business doing. Leaving here every night then bringing her butt back in here just before J.R. gets home." Daniel said. "Whatever she's doing, it's gon catch up with her. You mark my words Geraldine." He nodded his head then returned to the back porch.

"Reed? Did she say Reed? Ms. Geraldine said to herself.

Effie Mae walked a block then hurried around the corner to where Huck awaited in his 1959 navy blue and white top Eldorado Cadillac, accented with white wall tires. She opened the front door and climbed in. Huck pulled off.

"I have something for you." He handed her a colorful gift bag. Effie Mae became excited as she looked inside. She removed an aqua blue, polka-dotted, sleeveless dress that strapped around her neck. She kissed Huck on the cheek then retrieved from the bag, a pair of white stiletto heeled pumps. Effie Mae again kissed him on the cheek. She reached inside the bag and removed a white patent leather belt. She placed one hand on each side of Huck's face and turned it towards her own then passionately kissed him on the lips.
"I know you want something for all this stuff." Effie

Mae kissed him again, this time he kissed back. "I never knew a man to give you anything and didn't want something in return." She again kissed him. Huck momentarily lost control of the car. He rode up onto the curb then off.

"Hold on a minute Effie Mae, girl, you gon make me crash!" He diverted his attention back onto the road.

"Then pull over." She gazed at him then slid over next to him, smiling.

"Effie Mae! Hold on girl. Now I'm your friend and I respect our friendship. But, I don't mess with what belongs to another man." He looked at her. "Now, you fine as wine, but . . ."

Effie Mae slid back over towards the door. She stared at him, curious by his rejection of her. She wondered if he might possibly be attracted to men.

"Okay. If that's the way you want it." She said.

"Get dressed."

"What?"

"Get dressed. I want you to put on the clothes I bought you." He smiled.

"Here, in the car?

"Yeah, I promise I won't look."

"Would it matter if you did?"

Huck laughed to himself. "Go ahead. We'll be there soon."

Effie Mae began undressing. "Be where?" She pulled the pink tank top over her head then slid the dress on and tied it around her neck. She reached under the dress and unbuttoned the thigh-high pink shorts and took them off.

"Effie Mae." Huck glanced at her brassiere. "Take that off."

Effie Mae smiled. She thought his words were an indication that he'd changed his mind about her advances. Effie Mae reached behind her back and unclamped the brassiere. Her eyes focused on him as she slipped it off then held it up, trying to entice him.

"Now what?" She teased.

Huck realized she'd heard his words as an invitation.

"Oh! No. It's just that you don't wear a brassiere with that kind of dress." Effie Mae threw it at him. It landed on his head. He took it off and threw it in the back seat. He chuckled.

"Where did you say we were going anyway?"

"I'm taking you to Blue's tonight. You like it there — right?"

"Anything's better than sitting there looking at Ms. Geraldine and Mr. Daniel."

"Well Blue, he kind of like seeing you there." Huck awaited her response.

"Is that right?" She blushed.

"You're blushing — you like Blue or something?"

"Effie Mae Reed likes men, period."

"That's good to hear." Huck smiled then pulled in front of Blue's Jazz Club and parked. He and Effie Mae got out and went inside.

Daniel and Ms. Geraldine sat at the dining room table eating a dinner of mashed potatoes, roast beef, green beans and cornbread.

"Do you think we should tell J.R. about Effie Mae sneaking out of here, Daniel?" She put a spoon of the mashed potatoes in her mouth.

"It ain't that simple Geraldine." Daniel mixed his potatoes and roast beef together.

Ms. Geraldine scowled as his white potatoes turned brown with the mixture of the two foods.

"What do you mean that it's not that simple?"

"Think about it Geraldine. How do you think it would make J.R. feel to know that his wife's tipping out on him?"

"Yeah, I guess he would be pretty hurt." She picked at the roast on her plate and thought about his rationale.

"Pretty, hurt? He'd be plenty hurt!" Daniel tossed a piece of cornbread into his mouth. "I'm not gon say a word. I can't hurt that boy like that. It'll catch up with her! Mark my words Geraldine." He washed the food in his mouth down with a glass of tea.

"I hate to say it Daniel, but I never liked that girl. She just didn't seem like she was right for J.R."

"For J.R.? Geraldine, that girl ain't right for nobody!" Daniel dropped another scoop of potatoes onto his plate and added it to the brown mixture. Ms. Geraldine thought about Daniel's words as she picked at the food on her plate.

Effie Mae watched in astonishment at the multitude of people dancing, drinking and enjoying the sound of the jazz band. Huck poured himself a shot from the bottle of scotch placed in the middle of the table.

"Don't I get any of that?" She asked.

"Uh-uh Effie Mae, you don't want to mess with this stuff.

"Why?"

"You got a husband to go home to."

"That don't mean nothing!"

"Just enjoy the music."

A gentleman that watched Effie Mae from across the room approached Huck's table.

"Hey Huck! Man where you been hiding? I ain't seen you around for a while." He said then shifted his eyes onto Effie Mae.

"I've been around—here and there." Huck observed his gawk at Effie Mae. "What you been up to?"

"Is this your lady?" He asked with interest.

"Who? Oh! Effie Mae." Huck noted Effie Mae flirting. "No. Effie Mae's my friend. You know Huck don't mess with them pretty women. Most of the time they're all looks anyway. If Huck's gon be with a woman, she's has to be worth his while." He laughed. "But, since she seems to find you so interesting, if you want to spend a little time with her—she's all yours?"

"What kind of time?" His excitement heightened.

"Tonight, ah—a little dancing and talking." Huck smiled. "Nothing more, nothing less."

The man extended his hand to Effie Mae. "Ms. Effie Mae would you like to dance?" She glanced at Huck as if asking for permission. He nodded.

"Tonight is your night sweetheart. Have fun. I'll come get you when it's time to go."

The man took a hold of Effie Mae's hand as she stood to her feet. He winked at Huck then escorted her onto the dance floor. Gus watched then hurried over to the table.

"Can I dance with her Huck?" He asked, eagerly.

"Listen to me Gus and listen, good." He stared Gus in the eyes. "Effie Mae is hands off. You understand that Gus?"

"Yeah Huck, I understand." Gus gazed at Effie Mae dancing cheek to cheek with Huck's acquaintance.

Chapter Ten

J.R. and Daniel relaxed on the back porch. Daniel removed the wooden pipe from his shirt pocket and prepared to smoke.

"Hey Cousin Daniel, you think I'm doing something wrong?" J.R. asked from out of the blue.

"Wrong? What you mean J.R.?"

"You see, I been hoping to get Effie Mae pregnant for a while now, since I'm thinking it's about time we started a family." He looked into the gazing eyes of Daniel. "But Effie Mae's sleep six days out of seven, when I get home from the church.

"Sleep huh?" Daniel said as he stared at J.R. with doubting eyes. "As much as I hate to repeat anything Geraldine says, I'm getting ready to do just that." J.R. looked at him with inquiring eyes.

"That girl's not sleep J.R.; she probably gets in here about fifteen minutes before you. And we don't know where she's at, or who she's with." Daniel raised an eyebrow. "But that's what you get for marrying a pretty woman!"

"What?" J.R. said in response to Daniel's candid statement.

"You just have to expect that she's gon, stray."

"Now, Cousin Daniel, I don't believe Effie Mae would do anything like that." He stated, naively.

"Why not? She's a woman ain't she?"

"Cousin Daniel you wrong about that . . . ." Daniel cut him off.

"Was she pure when you married her boy?"

"As far as I know, yeah—she was."

"Who told you that?"

"Well, Sissy said . . . ." Daniel cut him off.

"Oh boy; there you go again listening at something Sissy done told you. I don't see how you can still believe anything she said about that girl, after the way she been carrying on around here."

"My sister wouldn't introduce me to a woman that wasn't . . . ." Daniel again cut him off.

"What? Pure—don't you believe that! I'm telling you J.R., it's something wrong with that girl. Ol' funny color eyes in her head."

"Funny color? Cousin Daniel they're brown."

"Well, they don't look brown to me." Daniel removed the pack of tobacco that bulged inside of his right pocket, and began filling his pipe. He momentary looked at J.R. peculiarly then chuckled at his naïve cousin's trusting nature.

"You know J.R., I didn't find out that Geraldine couldn't have children until after I'd been suckered into marrying her." Daniel paused, shaking his head as he reminisced. "You see just like Sissy, Geraldine's Momma told Big Momma that she was ripe as a thirty day old banana, and fertile as twin rabbits." Daniel flashed his young cousin a look of skepticism. He removed the wooden match from behind his ear then struck it on the heel of his boot. He applied the flame to the pipe then continued speaking. "Said they were just waiting on the right man to come along, somebody who could afford to take care of their daughter, and all them children she was gon be having." Daniel slowly took a drag from the pipe supported by his hand.

"You mean—Geraldine, she can't . . . ."

"Let me put it this way— I would've come out better if I'd married them damn bunny rabbits." Daniel burst into laughter. J.R. chuckled.

"I'm sorry Cousin Daniel. I didn't know that Geraldine couldn't have children."

"Nope, she can't. But, it ain't nothing wrong with me!" He stated, sharply.

"So, I guess you won't ever know what it's like to be a father?"

"Oh, that's right J.R. you haven't met my baby boy or my baby girl, have you?" Smoke flowed from the pipe wedged in Daniel's jaw. J.R. waited for an explanation, astonished by his cousin unexplained mystery. "Me and Geraldine couldn't have children. But now, me and Ms. Sadie Ann could." Daniel stated matter-of-factly, as he raised his left eyebrow at his clueless cousin. J.R.'s mouth flung open, shocked by Daniel's unexpected confession.

"Close your mouth boy, before a bee fly in, sting you on the tongue." J.R. suddenly became consciously aware of his opened mouth then quickly closed it.

"You play with fire, you get burned! Daniel stated, guiltlessly. "And that's all I have to say about that. Now getting back to the question you asked me about your wife." Daniel stared J.R. squarely in the eye.

"She don't want you boy." He said "She don't sleep that much. You gon need to romance that girl."

"Romance?" J.R. looked perplexed.

"You know anything about romancing a woman J.R.?"

"Well, uh, I uh . . . ." J.R. stuttered.

"You uh—what? Daniel questioned. How many women you been with before uh…?"

"Ella Mae?" J.R. teased.

"I thought her name was Effie Mae. Well, anyway—you didn't answer my question.

"Well, you see Cousin Daniel . . . ." J.R. became uneasy.

"Oh boy." Daniel interrupted.

"Now, Cousin you know, I am a preacher. And I believe in living by the good book." He said, religiously standing his ground.

"Calm down J.R., I understand what you saying." Daniel said. "I didn't say but two words. *Oh* and *Boy*. I wasn't trying to embarrass you or make you feel like less of a man." He stated, apologetically. "You know J.R., it's ain't too many men that can make that claim or even would if they could. That's brave of you boy. And I truly respect you for that. You give preachers a good name. I'm proud of you J.R. And I mean that—Reverend." J.R. lessened his defensiveness. His face displayed a look of praiseworthy morality.

"I'll help you out alright. But . . . ." Daniel grinned.

"But what?"

Daniel replied, "You gon need to keep Geraldine busy while, me and Effie Mae . . ."

"Cousin Daniel!"

Daniel began laughing. "I was just playing with you. But if you need any help . . . ."

"I'm serious Cousin Daniel."

"I understand what you saying. It's gon take some doing with that girl. But, if you listen to me J.R. you'll have Ella—uh, your wife, pregnant quicker than a cat can lick his—well, never mind." He took two quick puffs from the pipe, and exchanged a look of guaranteed success with his mentee. "Trust me." He concluded.

Effie Mae waited at the dining room table for her dinner companions to join her. She saw only J.R. in the kitchen preparing a dinner of bread dressing, onion gravy, smothered pork chops, cabbage and biscuits.

"Where's Bonnie and Clyde at tonight?" She asked.

"Who?"

"Ms. Geraldine and Mr. Daniel?" J.R. laughed then looked at her, captivated by her sense of humor.

"Are you cooking tonight J.R.?"

"Yeah." He removed a pan of biscuits from the oven.

"I didn't know you could cook."

"Yeah, you couldn't live in my Momma's house without learning how to cook."

"Your Momma?" She sounds like Ms. Millie Reed."

"You cook Effie Mae?"

"I'll put it this way, it ain't nothing in there you cooking that I can't cook. And probably better!" She laughed. J.R. looked at her and smiled as he tried to remember the step by step instructions Daniel gave him on how to romance her.

"You look beautiful tonight Effie Mae." He said as he placed a pan of smothered pork chops onto the table. Effie Mae gazed at him in response to his uncharacteristic compliment.

"Thank you J.R." She blushed.

"Uh, would you mind if I turned off the lights and lit a few candles?"

"Then how are we gon see our food to eat?"

"I'll make sure we have enough light."

"That's up to you."

J.R. lit four candles then turned off the lights. He stared at Effie Mae from the other side of the table.

"Uh, you like music?" He asked.

"I love music!"

J. R. hurried from the dining room and into the living room. He rushed over to the record player and placed Nat King Cole's—"When I Fall in Love", onto the turn table, then scurried back into the dining room.

"You want to dance Effie Mae?"

"I love dancing!"

Effie Mae quickly rose from her chair and strolled over to him. He nervously embraced her in his arms. She wrapped her arms around his neck as they danced cheek to cheek.

"What's that you have on, J. R.? It smells good."

"Cousin Daniel let me use some of his cologne."

"Well, you smell really good." Her nose touched his neck as she sniffed. Distracted by Effie Mae's unexpected action, J.R. struggled to remember what his next rehearsed move should be.

"Uh— Effie Mae?"

"What J.R.?"

"Can we skip dinner?"

"What?"

"Well, I was kind of hoping that with the candles, dinner, music and all—that, you would." He paused

"Would what J.R.?"

"You know." He cleared his throat.

"Okay."

"What?" He said, surprised by her response.

"I said okay."

J.R. stood completely still. He removed Effie Mae's arms from around his neck then took a hold of her right hand. They slowly walked in the direction of their bedroom. J.R. stopped just outside the door and passionately kissed her. He swept her up in his arm and carried her into the room, lightly kicking the door shut behind him.

It's been one month since J.R. and Daniel set out on their mission to impregnate Effie Mae. Horrendously nauseated, she leapt out of bed and hurried from her bedroom and into the bathroom. She vomited much of the food she ingested last night, into the toilet. She knew without a doubt that her symptoms were morning sickness. She had witnessed it firsthand from the young, unmarried females, who, unlike her, had become pregnant. Effie Mae felt defeated. Despite her many intimate encounters, she had never become—with child. She hurried from the bathroom and reentered her bedroom.

"He tricked me!" She said to herself as she paced back and forth. "He didn't ask me if I wanted to have a baby. He's just trying to slow Effie Mae Reed down!" She walked over to the door and slammed it. She opened it and slammed it again. Effie Mae opened the door for a third time and paused. "Well, Rev. J. R. Smith you'd better get ready to be Momma and Daddy, because Effie Mae Reed ain't taking care no babies! Now how you like that . . . J.R.?" Effie Mae again slammed the door.

Effie Mae picked at the fried chicken, cabbage, cornbread and candied yams on her plate. She thought about how she would share the news of her pregnancy with J.R. And if she should make the announcement during dinner or wait until they were in the privacy of their bedroom.

She glanced across the table at Ms. Geraldine then looked at Daniel seated left of J.R. at the end of the table. She took a deep breath and prepared herself for whatever verbal altercation that might follow her news.

"I'm pregnant."

"Well I'll be damn!" Daniel shouted. "Congratulations J.R., Effie Mae! It's about time." Daniel exchanged a quick wink of the eye with J.R. "I was wondering what y'all was waiting on." He pretended to be surprised by Effie Mae's carefully plotted pregnancy. J.R. smiled then leaned over to his right and kissed his now pregnant wife, on the cheek.

"You sure that baby's yours?" Ms. Geraldine said underneath her breath. She glared at Effie Mae with a look of distrust on her face. Effie Mae ignored her words.

"You say something Geraldine?" J.R. inquired.

"Naw, J.R. . . . Geraldine ain't said nothing." Daniel quickly stated. "She's just running her mouth like she always do. Nope! Don't pay her any attention. She always got something to say, but don't be saying nothing, just talking!" Daniel signaled her with his eyes, instructing her to hush. She ignored his non-verbal cues as she prepared for a second time to cast doubt upon the paternity of Effie Mae's unborn fetus.

"I heard your wife's been seen all over town with that no good Huck." She spooned up a helping of candied yams and dumped them onto her plate.

"Who? Huck?" J.R. asked, innocently.

"That's right! Henry Lee White. But folks around town call him Huck. And he's nothing but a no good hustler." She looked Effie Mae directly in the eyes. "And apparently—he's a real good friend of your wife's." Daniel shook his head, trying to quiet her. Again, she ignored him. "I also heard that she's been spending a lot of time downtown at that jazz club. Down there shaking her behind, just like she's not a married woman."

"Jazz club?" J.R. glanced over at Effie Mae.

"How are things going over at the church, J.R.?" Daniel asked, abruptly trying to change the topic of discussion. Ms. Geraldine continued.

"Instead of being down there at that jazz club, doing who knows what, with who knows who, she ought to have her butt here at the house taking care of her husband."

"Aw, Geraldine, hush!" Daniel snapped. "You ain't doing nothing but spreading that mess from the streets!"

"No I'm not either." She said. "But, I guess if you really want to know . . ." She gazed at Effie Mae. "Why don't you ask your wife, if you don't believe me?"

All eyes locked onto Effie Mae. Suddenly feeling as if she were under attack, Effie Mae slowly rose from the table and prepared to counter Ms. Geraldine's verbal assault.

"Now you hold on just one damn minute Ms. Geraldine!" Daniel swiftly shifted his eyes to Effie Mae, surprised by her aggressive words. "The only man you ever seen me lying with is my husband. As far as Huck, yeah, he's my friend and that's all he is. And I'll be damn if I let a broom riding witch like you say, I have!" Effie Mae glared at her with immense anger. Without warning, she charged towards Ms. Geraldine, holding her fork tightly in her hand.

"Effie Mae!" J.R. shouted. He jumped to his feet and grasped a hold of her arm, pulling her back towards him. Daniel watched in horror, unable to move. Ms. Geraldine quickly scooted her chair away from the table and prepared to escape. J.R. held onto Effie Mae as she fumed with rage.

"It seems to me, if you spend less time sticking your nose in other folks business, Mr. Daniel wouldn't be out there making babies with another woman. Babies your old behind couldn't seem to give him." Effie Mae stopped when she realized the words she'd just spoken. She looked at Daniel. He closed his eyes and lowered his head in response to her outing him, then looked up and stared at J.R., certain that he'd shared the information with her. J.R. shook his head and humped his shoulders indicating that he was not aware of her knowledge of his indiscretion. Daniel gazed at Effie Mae then looked into the face of his dishonored wife and marveled over what his next words would be. Ms. Geraldine looked at J.R. as he gently guided Effie Mae back to her seat. His eyes apologized to her for her biting words. The room remained eerily silent. Ms. Geraldine arose gradually from the dining room table, walked towards her bedroom then entered inside and closed the door. The wailing sounds of her sobbing seemingly echoed throughout the house.

After ten minutes of listening to Ms. Geraldine's continuous weeping, Daniel got up from the table. He walked away, joining his wife in their bedroom. J. R. and Effie Mae maintained their silence as Daniel repeatedly confessed his love for his wife and apologized for the error of his ways.

Effie Mae and J.R. resumed eating the lukewarm dinner as if the entire event had never taken place. J.R. silently chuckled as he thought about what had just happened, being oddly humored by the entire chaotic incident. Thirty minutes would pass before Daniel's pleas ended and the house again filled with silence.

Effie Mae lay in bed alone in the darkness of her bedroom. She rubbed her belly as she surprisingly began bonding with the infant growing inside of her. J.R. and Daniel convened on the back porch. Daniel cleaned his pipe as he prepared to smoke.

"Do you love Effie Mae, J.R.?" Daniel asked. J.R. thought momentarily about his question.

"I do, Cousin Daniel. I don't know when it happened, but yeah, I do." He looked surprised by his own response.

"Well, I'm telling you for your own good, folks ain't gon take kind to that mouth of hers. It's not gon sit well with the church folks around here, having a preacher with a wife that speaks with a devil's tongue like Effie Mae done here tonight." He peered into J.R.'s eyes. "You better talk to her boy. Get her in line before it's too late." Daniel stuffed the pipe with tobacco. "Otherwise folks might be looking to throw both you and her, right out the front doors of the church. And J.R., I sure would hate to see that happen to a decent young man like you."

J.R. listened as he watched Daniel strike a match and ignite the pipe hanging from his mouth. He suddenly envisioned the incident that occurred during dinner and silently chuckled, strangely amused. Then spoke up in Effie Mae's defense.

"Now I know Effie Mae can sometimes have trouble holding her tongue, and she do have her ways." He stated. "I'm not saying that it's right, but that's just who she is. I haven't known her very long, but what I do know, is that she's a good person." Daniel looked at him through doubting eyes. "But, in due time she'll come around. And you'll see what I'm talking about. Besides, once she gives birth to this first baby, there's gon be plenty more to follow." J.R. smiled.

Daniel puffed on the pipe, unconvinced by his cousin's unproven words. He looked at him with cynical eyes, wanting to believe his untested hypothesis.

"Okay." Daniel nodded, but with skepticism. "But, I'll tell you how you have to tame them pretty women." He paused. "Keep their heads empty and their bellies full!" He laughed. J.R. looked at him in disbelief and total disagreement of his antiquated philosophy.

"Cousin Daniel, now . . . . ." Daniel cut him off.

"What? You do!" He took two puffs from his pipe then nodded.

"Effie Mae, can you go get the mail?" Ms. Geraldine asked as she rinsed off a bowl of neck bones over at the sink in preparation for dinner. "My JC Penny's catalog should be here by now." Effie Mae opened the door to exit.

"Girl, if you don't go put on a coat! It must be thirty degrees out there." Ms. Geraldine said as she tossed the meat into a pot of boiling water. "You must be trying to freeze you and that baby to death." She chuckled. "You only have a few more months left and your belly's not that big. You're lucky. I've seen women seven months pregnant who looked like they'd swallowed two bowling balls." She laughed.

"It seems like I been pregnant forever. Now I know how Annie Mae felt."

"I've seen watermelons bigger than that little bulge you have."

"Well, it feels like it weighs a ton." Effie Mae left the kitchen and went into her bedroom. She opened the closet and took out a winter coat. She slipped it on as she walked towards the door and out onto the screened-in front porch. Effie Mae leaned slightly over to gather up the mail, the mailman routinely pushed through the mail slot. When she stood to return inside she noticed Huck, standing on the corner a block away watching her. Mesmerized by his presence, she released the mail, dropping it onto the floor. Effie Mae hurried from the porch and headed in his direction. She smiled as she placed her hand underneath her abdomen and hastily walked. Huck smiled as she approached.

"Huck!" She wrapped her arms around him. He hugged her then stepped away and looked at her.

"Girl, look at you." He placed his hand onto her pregnant belly. "Are you being watched? Huck asked, suddenly realizing that they were out in the open. "Where's your husband?" He glanced at the house "Maybe we should step around this corner." He put his arm around her as they walked out of view.

"I guess now you know why I ain't been down to Blue's."

"I'd heard. I didn't know how true it was, though." He rubbed her belly again. "Come on. Let's get out of this cold." Huck opened the car door and helped her in. Then walked around to the other side and got in. Effie Mae silently stared at him with a large smile on her face. She took a hold of his hand and held it to her cheek.

"What's that for? I told you about that girl."

"No. It's not like that. I'm just so glad to see you Huck. I've missed you."

"You know they miss you down at Blue's? Especially, Blue." He chuckled.

"Well, you can tell them that as soon as I have this baby, Effie Mae's gon be coming back!"

"No you won't." Huck stated. "Once you have that baby, girl your life's gon change."

"But that's not gon stop me from coming to Blue's." She said, smiling. Huck gazed into her eyes.

"You know. I believe you." He said as her words ruminated. "That's it." Huck looked at her as if looking into her soul.

"That's what?"

"I knew it was something different about you."

"Different? What?"

"When I met you Effie Mae, I knew it was something about you that drew me to you." He rubbed her hair. "You and me—we're not like everybody else. We're different." He said. "People like us, we don't fit into this world, like society say we should." Effie Mae listened, intrigued by his words. "Whose idea was it for you to get married? I know it wasn't yours. Naw, you don't seem like the type to want to get married while you're so young." Effie Mae's eyes answered his question. "You weren't pregnant. So why get married? Something was different about you." He gazed into Effie

Mae's eyes as if reading her very thoughts. "Look at you girl. Glowing like the stars. But, it's something in you that's not gon let you continue in that fantasy life."

"Fantasy life?"

"Yeah, it's all fantasy. Because people like me and you, we require more than being married—having kids." Effie Mae thought about the content of his words. "You and I are soul mates Effie Mae. You know that?" He took a hold of her hand. "Getting married, I never gave it a second thought before. But, seeing you here all pregnant and glowing . . . if I did get married, it would be to you." He kissed her hand.

"How you gon marry me? I'm already somebody's wife." She held out her hand and displayed her wedding ring.

"That ring, don't mean nothing. After a while, you'll get tired of that life. It's not you."

Effie Mae turned and looked out the back window. "I guess I'd better get back in the house before Ms. Geraldine gets worried." Huck leaned over and took a hold of her chin then kissed her gently on the lips.

"Slide over here." Effie Mae slid over next to him. He took her in his arms and passionately kissed her. She kissed him back. He stopped then looked her into her eyes. "You understand what I'm talking about now? What do you think your husband would say if he knew you just kissed me like that?"

"What? It was just a kiss."

"This time; One day Effie Mae, a man is gon kiss you, and it won't be just a kiss." He again applied a gentle kiss to her lips. "Go. Get back in the house, before I forget that you pregnant."

"What? I thought you said it wasn't like that between us?" She smiled.

"You know the funny thing about life Effie Mae, it's forever changing. Get on girl." Effie Mae slid back over. She opened the door and prepared to get out. Huck caught her by the arm.

"I'll be around if you need me. You just go ahead and keep trying to fit into your life." He paused. "Bye, Effie Mae." Huck watched as she got out of the car and hurried back to the house.

Chapter Eleven

Effie Mae lay in bed positioned on her back, her knees bent as she prepared to give birth to her fifth child.

"Push Effie Mae, push!" Ms. Geraldine coached as she assisted Ms. Ida, the midwife with the delivery.

"I'm pushing as hard as I can!" Effie Mae shouted; her face drenched with beads of sweat.

"This child is almost here. All I need is just one more push." Ms. Ida stated, clutching the emerged head of the infant in her hands.

"Ahhhhhh!" Effie Mae let out a screech as another excruciating contraction bolted through her pelvis. Compelled by the uncontrollable urge that forced her exhausted body to push, she gave a final thrust and expelled a moderate sized newborn into the world.

"It's a girl Effie Mae! It's a beautiful baby girl!" Ms. Ida stated, customarily informing Effie Mae of the infant's gender.

"And she looks just like you." Ms. Geraldine said. This being the fifth time in the last six years she'd been given the opportunity to witness this miracle of life, all the previous infants, also girls. Ms. Ida placed the healthy crying baby girl into Effie Mae's awaiting arms, minutes after separating the two by way of the umbilical cord.

"Can't you and J.R. make anything else besides these girls?" Ms. Geraldine teased as she used a clean white towel to wipe the fluid from infant's head and body. "You can come on in now J.R." She called out into the living room where he and Daniel patiently waited, as they'd done four times prior when Effie Mae gave birth.

"How you feeling Effie Mae." J.R. asked as he entered into the bedroom to the welcome his new baby daughter. He smiled as he gazed at the beautiful baby girl. "What you want to name her?"

"Sarah." I'm gon name my baby girl, Sarah."

"There you go, naming another one of your girls after a singer!" Ms. Geraldine chuckled.

"Let's see, you have Lena, Billie, Mahalia and now Sarah. The only one that's not named after a singer is Millie Ann. And maybe she should've been." She laughed.

"You making fun of my Momma's name again Ms. Geraldine?" Effie Mae teased.

Ms. Geraldine laughed then left from the room to join Daniel. She looked around the living room then headed towards the back porch, guided by the smell of his pipe. Effie Mae and J.R. admired their newborn daughter as she fell asleep. J.R. placed the sleeping infant in her crib, situated next to their bed.

"I'm gon go sit out here with Daniel and Geraldine and let you get some rest. I'll be back to check on you."

"Okay J.R." He kissed her gently on the lips then exited the room.

Effie Mae decided to enter the birth of Sarah into her diary. She reached under the mattress and pulled out the old red book. She adjusted a few pillows behind her back then began writing. She wrote of her multiple births, her improved relationship with J.R., and Ms. Geraldine. She also entered her unusual relationship with Huck.

Effie Mae, Ms. Geraldine and the children are downtown. Loading her many offspring onto the bus, assisted by Ms. Geraldine, the two women ventured downtown in the early morning, allowing J.R. and Daniel time to prepare for the surprise birthday party they'd planned for Millie Ann—her sixth.

"Oooh, Effie Mae, I don't' know about you, but I'm tired." Ms. Geraldine said as she sat on a bench at the bus stop, holding three year old Billie in her lap. "We've been down here for three hours now. If J.R. and Daniel haven't gotten things together by now, it's not going to be a surprise. Because when this next bus comes . . . I have every intention of getting on it." Effie Mae gave no reply as her eyes seemingly stared into nothingness, as she held two month old Sarah in her arms. "Effie Mae." Ms. Geraldine looked at her with concern when noticing the unfocused gaze in her eyes. "Effie Mae!" Ms. Geraldine reached over and touched her arm. Effie Mae looked swiftly to her, startled. "Are you alright?" Ms. Geraldine asked.

"Yeah, I'm feeling a little tired, Ms. Geraldine."

"I think maybe J.R. and Daniel should've planned something that didn't require us leaving the house. It's too soon for you to be traipsing around out here anyway."

"I'll be alright Ms. Geraldine." She said, exhausted. "It's not every day that Millie Ann's gon turn, six years old." Effie Mae smiled.

"Well, if this bus isn't here soon . . . " Ms. Geraldine paused when three year old Billie slid down off her lap, and four year old Lena broke away from Millie Ann's hold, attempting to run away. Sarah began to cry.

"Get back over here Lena." Ms. Geraldine called out as Effie Mae rocked two month old Sarah in her arms. "Billie, come here to Momma." Effie Mae said as her frustrations grew. Realizing that Effie Mae had become overwhelmed, Ms. Geraldine intervened. She took a hold of the hand of two year old Mahalia's then assisted in organizing the other children.

"Millie Ann, you hold onto Lena's hand, and Lena—you hold onto Billie's hand."

"Thank you Ms. Geraldine. Sometimes, having all these babies make me wish I could start my life over." Effie Mae stated, agitated by Sarah's continued crying. Ms. Geraldine looked in awe, shocked by her words.

"You don't mean that Effie Mae. You're just frustrated right now." She said. "You and J.R. have all these beautiful babies you wouldn't know what to do without them."

"Yeah, you right Ms. Geraldine."

Effie Mae looked up momentarily from Sarah and saw Huck standing across the streets watching her, smiling.

"Uh, Ms. Geraldine, can you take my babies home for me. I'm—feeling like I need some time to myself."

"Are you sure, Effie Mae? You want me to send J.R. back down here to get you?" She asked, worried.

"No—I'll be fine." Effie Mae glanced at Huck. "You think you gon be able to handle Sarah and Mahalia by yourself?" She asked Ms. Geraldine, discretely shifting her eyes again to Huck.

"Don't worry about me, I'll manage just fine." Ms. Geraldine said, trying to figure out how she would secure the infant and toddler.

"You need help Geraldine?" asked, Ms. Rose; a neighbor of Ms. Geraldine's, also waiting for the bus.

"How are you today, Ms. Rose." Ms. Geraldine asked. "I sure do. If you could get Mahalia, I can carry Sarah." She picked Mahalia up and handed her to Ms. Rose, then retrieved Sarah from Effie Mae's arms." Are you sure you gon be alright Effie Mae?"

"Yeah, I'm sure Ms. Geraldine." Effie Mae glimpsed at Huck. "I'll be home shortly. Uh, don't say anything to J.R. about this. If he asks just tell him I . . . ." Ms. Geraldine cut her off.

"Effie Mae, don't ask me to start lying to J.R. I'll just tell him that you needed some time to yourself after being down here . . . all morning, with these children. J.R.'s a good man, and he loves you. He'll understand." Ms. Geraldine hugged her with her free arm. "And don't worry about these babies, we'll look after them." The bus pulled up and stopped. "I'll see you at home." Ms. Geraldine climbed onto the bus with the children. Ms. Rose followed.

Effie Mae watched as it pulled off then turned her attention to Huck, waiting across the street. She hurried over to him as if being drawn by a magnet.

"I see you still trying to live that fantasy!" He laughed to himself. "Come here girl." Effie Mae entered into his open arms. She suddenly felt secure as he lovingly embraced her. She cautiously looked around, worried that they might be seen.

"Oh! You scared somebody gon see us?" He released her. "If you want to keep playing that game its fine with me, Effie Mae." He briefly stared at her. "Let's get in the car." They walked over to his car, parked on the corner. Huck opened and closed the door for her then hurried around to the other side and got in.

"Girl, are all those kids yours?" He asked, surprised.

"Yeah, they mine." She stated, still somewhat stressed.

"I see you still trying to fit into a life that's suffocating you." He gazed at her then smiled. "You know I've missed you. But, I know right now you doing what you think, you need to do."

"I told you when I saw you last year Huck, I've changed." He interrupted.

"Is that what you telling yourself Effie Mae? If you think this housewife, and mother thing is for you—Girl, you fooling yourself!" He took a hold of her arm and tried to pull her close to him. Effie Mae resisted. Huck looked at her in astonishment.

"What's that suppose to mean Effie Mae? I guess next, you'll be telling me that you love your husband? Huh . . . is that what you gon tell me?" He pulled her again. This time she showed no resistance. Huck took her in his arms and romantically kissed her then looked in her eyes and smiled.

"Now that's the Effie Mae I know." Effie Mae's confusion increased as she thought about her chaotic life with J.R. She wrapped her arms around Huck's neck and vigorously kissed him. He gently pushed her away.

"Hold on girl." He stared at her. "What's all that about?"

"It ain't about nothing. It was just a kiss. You know we don't have that kind of relationship—remember?" She giggled.

"Come with me Effie Mae. Leave your husband and come be with me."

"I can't do that Huck! I have my babies to take care of."

"Yeah, I saw. Where your babies at now, Effie Mae? And why are you sitting here in the car with me?" He asked, annoyed. Effie Mae remained silent. "I told you once before—you and me, we soul mates, girl. When I look at you, I see me. Both of us struggling with who we are, and asking ourselves how we fit into this world." Effie Mae attentively listened. "But when we together, it's like that incomplete circle becomes complete." He kissed her. "Come with me Effie Mae." He gazed into her eyes. "If you want to keep playing housewife . . . ." He paused. "I'll marry you, because I know you're not happy." Effie Mae pulled away. "I'm happy."

"What you happy about Effie Mae?"

"My babies, my life—it's okay.

"Okay? And what about your husband?"

"J.R. loves me."

"Do you love him?"

"I need to get home before J.R. gets worried." She nervously stated then slid towards the door, taking a hold of the handle. Huck caught her by the arm and pulled her back towards him, then romantically kissed her.

"I won't come to you again Effie Mae." He said, after their kiss ended. "When you realize the life you living is not real, you'll come to me."

Effie Mae briefly looked at him then slid back over to the door. Huck watched as she opened it and hurriedly climbed out. She ran across the streets and boarded the upcoming bus. Her eyes locked onto Huck's face as she looked through the bus window and into his car. He shook his head in disappointment as the bus drove away. Effie Mae sat quietly as she thought about their conversation and reflected on Huck's penetrating words.

Chapter Twelve

Millie, Annie Mae, Pete and their children were all asleep. Suddenly, the sound of pounding on the solid wood door echoed throughout the house. Millie awakened first. Her head now exhibited salt and pepper strands of hair. She climbed out of bed in response to the persistent banging, hoping to end the loud noise before it awakened the children.

Pete and Annie Mae were also awakened by the mysterious thumping of an unexpected visitor. Moving quietly through the house, careful not to disturb the sleeping children, the three arrived in the living room at the same exact moment. The trio stood in wonder as their unseen guest persisted.

Pete stepped in front of Millie and Annie Mae, guarding them from the individual determined to make their presence known.

"Who is it?" Pete yelled through the door.

"It's me . . . Johnny—Johnny Banks."

"It's three o'clock in the morning. What you want this early in the day, Johnny?"

"I got some news Pete—some bad news!" He replied.

In anticipation of the news, Pete cracked the door and cautiously peered out. After he determined the situation to be safe, he stepped aside and allowed Johnny, a small build, somewhat frail, dark skinned male, wearing horn rimmed glasses, with thick lenses, to enter. A close friend of Pete's as well as to the entire Parker family, Johnny stepped just inside of the living room. He looked at Pete in fear as he prepared to share the horrific news.

"I . . . I need to be speaking to you Pete, uh, it's about your daddy."

"What about my daddy, Johnny?"

"He's dead, Pete!" Johnny blurted.

"What—what you talking about Johnny?" Pete maintained his calm demeanor.

"Mr. Ned, he's dead, Pete! Mr. Jed Russell, he done shot your daddy. Shot him right in the head!"

"You sure about what you saying, Johnny?"

"Yep . . . As sure as I am that if you play with fire, sooner or later you gon get burned!"

"What cause Jed Russell got to want to shoot my daddy?"

"By you asking me that, I reckon you ain't known about your daddy lying up with Mr. Jed Russell's wife.

"My daddy did what?"

"He's been lying with Mr. Jed Russell's wife, Ms. Josephine; And Mr. Jed done found out about it. He headed straight way for your daddy when he heard they were up at the Cozi-T. Mr. Jed caught them . . . right there in the act, Pete! They were laid up in the bed, naked as two jaybirds! And let me tell you, Pete—they wasn't playing Checkers!"

"Lord, have mercy." Millie said as she and Annie Mae looked one to the other in horror.

"That's been when Mr. Jed—he done gon plain crazy! Cocked his shot gun, and took to shooting both of them. First, Ms. Josephine then he turned the gun to Mr. Ned. Shot him right in the head—blew half of it clean off!" A distressed look formed on Johnny's face.

"Where you getting all this from Johnny?" Pete asked in anger.

"I was there when it happen Pete!" Johnny stated, loudly. "I was on my way back home from the fishing creek up yonder near the Cozi-T. I'd been there all day and messed around and drank too much of that old moonshine, and . . . ." Pete interrupted.

"Messed around? That ain't nothing new for you Johnny. You sure it ain't that moonshine that's got you talking?"

"Naw Pete. I heard a man shouting like he's crazy. I turned my truck around to go see what was going on. That's when I seen Mr. Jed Russell standing in the doorway of one of the rooms at the Cozi-T. He's yelling so loud, I thought he'd busted his foot or something. Then before I could see what was going on—that man just up and started shooting!"

Millie and Annie Mae embraced each other, unnerved by Johnny's words. Both women looked at Pete with fret then turned their focused again to Johnny.

"Scared that he might shoot me, I got out of my truck quick! I pushed it behind some trees and hid there, 'til he left." Johnny stopped and stared at Pete in silence. Pete looked at Millie and Annie Mae in disbelief then again turned his attention to a slightly, catatonic Johnny.

"Johnny! Johnny!" Pete called out, breaking Johnny's unrelenting stare.

"Huh?"

"You alright Johnny?

"Yeah." Johnny continued his recollection of the event. "So, I walked over to see what had happened. That's when I seen Ms. Josephine. And she had a hole in her the size of a watermelon!" Johnny became faint. He fell forward. Pete caught him, helping him to again regain his balance.

"You alright Johnny? Breathe . . . breathe." Pete instructed.

Johnny took a few deep breaths. He looked incoherently at his awaiting listeners as he regained his bearings. Pete again shifted his eyes to Millie and Annie Mae. The two women looked on, being somewhat humored by Johnny's peculiar behavior. They fought back their laughter due to the seriousness of the matter. Appearing as if he'd just seen a ghost, Johnny proceeded.

"Even though I was scared, I peeped my head in the room a little further and that's when I seen Mr. Ned and he ain't had but half a head, Pete! Jed Russell—had done shot half of your daddy's head . . . clean off!" Johnny began shaking. He again lost his balance. Pete again caught him.

"You need to sit down Johnny?" He asked, concerned about his unsteadiness.

"I—I—I'm, alright Pete." He said, nervously. Pete shifted his eyes to Annie Mae and Millie. Both being only minutes away from erupting into laughter at Johnny's comical behavior. They maintained straight faces. Pete again turned his attention to a wobbly Johnny as he continued speaking. "That's when I took off running so fast I could've outrun a cheetah, Pete." Johnny half-heartedly joked as he neared the end of his eye witness account. "I ain't stopped running 'til I reached that door right there!" Johnny pointed his trembling finger at the front door. Pete stood motionless, lost for words.

"You gon be alright son?" Millie stepped forward and placed her hand on his shoulder.

"I'm gon be just fine Ms. Millie. Right now I'm thinking about, Momma. My Daddy ain't ever acted like he was a married man, running around with anything wearing a skirt. But bringing shame on Momma like this, it just ain't right." Annie Mae walked over and laid her head against his chest. Pete kissed her on the forehead. He knew that his Momma wouldn't take the news well, despite the circumstances under which Ned had died. Pete put his contempt for his Daddy's behavior aside, and decided to drive over to the Parker's family farm to comfort his Momma. "I need to get to the house before the sheriff arrives with the news. Let me get dressed, and I'll be right out Johnny." Annie Mae took a hold of his hand and walked with him back to their bedroom.

Pete raced down the rocky dirt road in his red and white 1963 Ford F100 truck. His plan being to break the news of his father's death to his Momma in the least upsetting way. He decreased his speed when seeing flashing red lights in the distance as he neared the house. Pete pounded his fist on the steering wheel as he drove past the sheriff's patrol cars parked in the driveway. He pulled along the right side of the cars, then stopped and parked in the front yard. Pete glanced over at Johnny. He suddenly felt apprehensive about entering into the home.

"You gon be alright, Pete?" Johnny asked, sensing Pete's increasing anxiety. Pete nodded then opened his door and stepped down from his truck. Johnny exited from the passenger's side. The two men slowly walked in the direction of the house. They slowed when arriving at the porch stairs. Pete took a deep breath then stepped up onto the porch. He clasped the doorknob in his hand then turned it. He and Johnny entered into the house. They walked through the living room and past the circle of Sheriffs who'd arrived only moments before, with the devastating news. Pete stopped when he saw Jimmy attempting to restrain his hysterical Momma as she cried out in anguish.

"Nooooooooo!" Fannie Mae screamed out as she tried to free herself from Jimmy's strong hold, determined to go to the Cozi-T Motel in search of her husband. "Let me go Jimmy, so I can go and see about Ned."

"Come on now Momma . . ." She cut him off.

"Come on—now what?" She yelled.

"Momma you know . . .

"All I know is that my husband's out there somewhere, and these Sheriffs won't let me go and . . ." She again tried to break free from Jimmy's firm grasp.

"Ma'am . . ." An Officer said, interrupting her. "Ma'am do you need us to call a doctor?"

"Yeah—tell them to go to the Cozi-T Motel, my husband's been hurt." She stated, in denial of the truth.

"Come on and lay down Momma." Jimmy pleaded as tears streamed down his face.

"Lay down for what? I'm alright!"

"Naw. Momma . . . you ain't alright."

Pete cried as he watched Jimmy's wife, Rosetta, watching helplessly. Her face saturated with tears as Jimmy both wept and restrained his combative mother.

Fannie Mae's eyes suddenly noticed the tearful face of her baby boy, Pete. She broke free from Jimmy and rushed over to him then fell into his arms. She dwindled down to the floor and cried at his feet.

"He's gone Pete—he's gone." Fannie Mae said, weeping.

"I know Momma." Pete lowered himself to his knees. Tears streamed down his face as he placed his arms around his worn out Momma then closed his eyes. His hurt being not for the loss of his father, but an empathetic response to the pain he knew burned deep within his Momma's very soul.

Standing guard over Fannie Mae, Jimmy suddenly noticed Johnny standing stationary by the front door. He walked over to him.

"How Pete find out about daddy, Johnny?"He curiously asked.

"It was me— I told him Jimmy."

"You? How you knew?"

"I was there Jimmy . . . saw it all."

"You telling me, Johnny, you know who killed my daddy?"

"Yep, I sure do, Jimmy." Johnny stared into Jimmy's eyes. "Mr. Jed Russell shot your daddy, Jimmy."

"Mr. Jed? Jimmy shook his head. "I told daddy to stop messing with that man's wife." He said, infuriated, then turned and walked away. He rejoined Pete and his Momma as they sobbed endlessly.

The Parker family's farmhouse filled with neighbors and friends, coming to pay their respects, and to—

speculate on the details of Ned's demise out of the earshot of Fannie Mae and her two sons.

Chapter Thirteen

Huck knelt on one knee as he engaged in a game of craps in the backroom of the Envoy Bar & Grill, accompanied by Buckeye and Gus. The establishment functioned mainly as a grill, despite having a license to sale alcohol. This was due in part to the fact that Benny, the owner, nicknamed Boney-nee, for his extremely skinny legs, that matched perfectly with his frail frame, had an addiction to alcohol

Unable to replenish his inventory as fast as he consumed it, he had earned a reputation for replacing genuine liquor in exchange for his uncle's bootlegged corn whiskey. This greatly affected his business in that only a small portion of his regulars had the stomach to ingest the exceptionally strong liquid.

"Snake eyes!" Huck shouted, after Buckeye tossed a pair of dice onto the floor. Friends for over twenty-five years, Huck had given him the unusual nickname based on his extremely large eyes. Huck snatched up the dice, accumulating dust on the side of his hand as he slid it across the un-swept floor. "I need a seven, but I'll take an eleven!" He shouted as he vigorously shook the dice, seconds later releasing them from his clutched fist. The white dotted cubes toppled onto the floor's designated area then tumbled to a halt displaying a *five* on one die. The second die revealed a *two* for a winning score of *seven*. "That's what I'm talking about!" Huck shouted, excited by his ability to skillfully manipulate the dice. "Pay me my money!" He reached down and grasped the twenty dollars he'd just won.

"Hey Huck! Whatever happened to that pretty young girl you had trailing you around town—back here about six years ago?" Buckeye asked as he lifted himself up from the floor. Huck walked over to the lone round table, centered in the middle of the room surrounded by four wooden chairs, and sat down. Gus and Buckeye joined him. "Ooowee! She sure was a pretty!" Buckeye stated as his excitement escalated.

"Hey Boney-nee!" Huck called into the bar area of the establishment. "Bring us something back here to swallow?"

"Yeah! And bring us the real stuff, not that bootlegged poison you get from your Ol' jack-legged uncle!" Buckeye yelled.

Boney-nee rushed into the room carrying a brown bottle of scotch. He positioned three shot glasses on the table, one in front of each man then filled them to the rim. Gus abruptly snatched his up, and guzzled down its content then set the glass back onto the table. He looked at Boney-nee, his eyes requested a refill. Huck and Buckeye marveled at their friend's misuse of the authentic beverage.

"You paying for that Gus?" Huck asked as he watched Boney-nee refill the glass. Gus licked his lips in anticipation of the drink. "You giving away free drinks now, Boney-nee?" Huck asked.

"I thought you were paying for . . . ." Huck interrupted.

"Did you hear me say that Boney-nee?" Huck looked directly at Gus.

"Uh, no Sir, Mr. Huck." Boney-nee reached over and picked up the glass. He tossed back his head then gulped down the entire shot himself. Huck looked up at him.

"Man you need to work on that!" Buckeye shouted. Huck turned to Gus then to Boney-nee. He nodded, permitting him to refill Gus' empty glass. Boney-nee poured the shot then turned to exit. Huck cleared his throat signaling him to leave the bottle. Boney-nee positioned it on the table then hesitated. He suddenly seized the brown bottle and raised it to his mouth. He titled back his head and ingested about two ounces of its contents, then calmly placed it back onto the table and prepared to leave the room. The three men stared at him with unbelief. "What's wrong with you man?" Buckeye shouted as he rose from his chair. Huck glanced at him and shook his head, requesting that he again be seated.

"Now Boney-nee, I know you got a love affair with that firewater, but if you ever do that again to a bottle I'm paying for—your stomach better be able to digest glass." Boney-nee stared at him, uncertain of what his fate would be. "Now go get me another bottle." Huck said in anger.

Boney-nee snatched up the scotch and hurried from the room. He returned with another unopened bottle. He opened it and poured Huck another drink, leaving the bottle on the table. Huck watched as Boney-nee scurried from the room and closed the door. "Now, what was that you were saying Buckeye?" Huck asked as he hurled scotch into his mouth from the shot glass, then poured both he and Buckeye a refill.

"I was asking about the pretty girl you had on your arm a while back."

"Which one?" You know Ol' Huck keeps plenty of pretty women with him." He laughed.

"That one with them cat eyes! Use to be down at Blue's with you." Gus said as he rolled his empty shot glass in his hand. His eyes locked onto the bottle. Huck pretended as if he needed a moment to think. He refilled his glass then capped off Buckeye's.

"Yeah! I know who you're talking about, uh . . . Effie Mae, my little country queen."

"Yeah, that's the one!" Buckeye said as he scoffed down his third refill. "I know some men, would pay good money to have a pretty girl like that. If I were you man, I'd go and find that young money maker. Stop hustling these dice and start making you some real money." He gazed at Huck.

"I heard that girl was married to a preacher, Huck." Gus stated, tapping his glass on the table. "He pastoring at that church just up the block, around the corner." He added.

"Is that right?" Huck's mind reflected on Buckeye's words as he refilled his own glass for the fifth time.

"I also heard that she got about nine or ten children!" Gus said.

"Is it good for woman to be having that many babies?" Buckeye asked. His eyes enlarged as he contemplated Gus' report.

"Huck?" Gus said. His eyes glued onto the brown bottle.

"What is it Gus?" Huck asked, fidgeting with the bottle as he thought about his recent conversation with Effie Mae.

"You think I can get another shot of that scotch?"

"Oh. Yeah. Here—take it." Huck slid the bottle across the table to him. Gus seized it then turned it over, preparing to pour its contents into his glass. A single drop came out. The bottle was empty. Gus licked his lips and wiped his hand across his face. He looked at the bottle for thirty seconds then picked it up again. He tossed back his head, held the bottle over his opened mouth and waited for a drop to drip onto his tongue. Huck and Buckeye shook their heads as they watched their alcoholic cohort.

"Word is Huck—she just gave birth to another baby just last night." Gus said, peering inside of the overturned empty bottle. Huck stared at him then chuckled at his inaccurate report.

"Now that's a lot of wear and tear on a woman's body." Buckeye stated, shifting his large eyes to Gus, who nodded in agreement. "I ain't seen too many women keep their good looks and fine figure after having that many babies!" Buckeye said. "If I were you old friend, before I start counting the green, man I'd make sure your sheep ain't turned into a Billy goat."

Huck maintained his silence. He smiled as he envisioned Effie Mae and the kiss they'd recently shared. "You just might find that your gold mine has turned into gold dust—just blowing in the wind." Buckeye stated.

Chapter Fourteen

J.R. entered into the bedroom where Effie Mae lay in bed taking a nap. He smiled as he watched his sleeping wife hidden under the covers then gently shook her shoulder.

"Effie Mae." He pulled the covers off her head. She pulled them back. "Effie Mae. Wake up. I got some bad news from back home." He stated, softly. Effie Mae uncovered her head and slowly sat up in response to his words. Her eyes, consumed with fear.

"Is it Momma or Annie Mae?"

"No. Ms. Millie and Annie Mae are doing just fine." Effie Mae's thoughts drifted to both Anthony and Jimmy. She knew that she would never receive word of Anthony status. She also knew that Sissy would do anything to keep her past from J.R. And since Jimmy was a significant player in her escapades, word of his present state would likely not be conveyed. "It's Ned Parker." He stated. Effie Mae remained silent. She chose to say nothing about the tumultuous relationship she and Ned Parker shared. She believed that her life prior to marrying J.R. was simply none of his business.

"Cousin Daniel said that he was shot and killed this morning."

"What?" Effie Mae never really liked her younger sister's father-in-law. Yet, she found news of his demise, disturbing. "I guess Fannie Mae finally got tired of him chasing behind every woman in Yazoo County." She said underneath her breath.

"What?" J.R. said. "Did you say something?"

"Now, who would want to shoot Ned Parker?" Effie Mae thought to herself, anybody that knew him.

"Cousin Daniel said it was a man name Jed Russell—said he blew half his head off!" Effie Mae frowned.

"Why would Jed Russell want to shoot Ned Parker?"

"Cousin Daniel said he found him in bed with his wife buck naked."

Effie Mae's mouth flung open in shock of her husband's use of the word *buck naked*. J.R. quickly corrected himself in response to her reaction. "Well, uh . . . neither of them had any clothes on." He rephrased, embarrassed by his prior word usage. "Sissy said Jed Russell caught them up at the Cozi-T Motel. Shot and killed both of them." Effie Mae discreetly smiled as she thought of the multiple times she and Anthony rendezvoused at the Cozi-T.

"Well I'll be damn!" She said as the information digested. "Ol' Ned Parker finally got caught!" Effie Mae burst into laughter. J.R. looked at her, baffled by her odd response. His only reply being,

"Effie Mae Smith, watch your mouth woman. Remember, you the wife of a preacher." He teased. Effie Mae continued laughing as her clueless husband looked at her with peculiarity, unaware of the colorful past she shared with Ned Parker, Jimmy Parker and their numerous indiscretions. Effie Mae ended her laughter when she realized this would be the first time in six years she'd be returning home to Yazoo City.

"I'm gon need to go home to be with Annie Mae and Pete. Ned Parker was my baby sister's father-in-law." Effie Mae sympathized with Pete's loss. J.R. looked surprised when hearing that his sister-in-law, who he'd met only briefly, was the daughter-in-law to the deceased. "How am I gon . . . ." Before she could complete her sentence, J.R. placed a train ticket in her hand.

"I've got your ticket right here. Train's gon be leaving here today at three o'clock this evening."

"I'm also gon need some new clothes." She paused. "You got that too?" She teased. J.R. walked over to the closet and opened the door. He reached inside and took out a sleek black pinstriped skirt, a black satin long sleeved blouse, both still hung on the hanger. He laid them on the bed. Effie Mae looked in amazement at her husband's surprising behavior. He retrieved a bag from the top shelf in the closet, and handed it to her. She opened it and looked inside. She smiled as she removed a patent leather red belt.

"You think those clothes gon be okay for you to wear, to go see Ms. Millie and Annie Mae?" His boyish smile tugged at her heart.

"You said Ned Parker was shot and killed this morning. When did you have time to buy new clothes?" He gazed into her eyes.

"I looked at my beautiful wife one day, and all them beautiful babies she had done gave me, and I . . . ." His eyes moistened.

"I know you didn't pick those out?" Effie Mae said, interrupting as she fought backed her own tears.

"Uh . . . No; Geraldine insisted I let her do it." J.R. wiped the tears from his eyes then cleared his throat.

"If Ms. Geraldine ain't got nothing else, she's got an eye for clothes." Effie Mae thought to herself as she remembered her adventure inside Ms. Geraldine's closet many years ago.

"You better hurry, if you expect to get to that train station in time." J.R. felt a sense of triumph.

"I'm gon take Sarah with me so Momma and Annie Mae can see her."

J.R. nodded without uttering another word. He gazed at his attractive wife as if for the first time, he actually saw her true beauty . . . inside and out.

Chapter Fifteen

The engine led procession of railway cars arrived in Union Station. Millie and Annie Mae awaited Effie Mae's departure.

"Momma! Annie Mae!" She called out as she exited the train and saw their awaiting faces in the distance. Millie's heart filled with delight when she heard the familiar voice she'd not heard in many years. Her wandering eyes brightened when the face of her eldest daughter emerged, her infant daughter cradled in her arms. She reached out and took a hold of Effie Mae, the second her hands were able to touch her. It appeared as if the *mother-daughter* feud, that existed before Effie Mae's departure had subsided. Annie Mae reached inside the huddle formed by her Momma and big sister and removed Sarah from Effie Mae's arms.

"That's my Sarah." Effie Mae said as she continued her embrace with Millie.

Effie Mae's eyes met with Pete's as she entered into the house that she'd always known as home. He slowly rose from the squared pink couch, held by the short wooden legs underneath. He smiled as he walked over and hugged her.

"How you doing Ol' crazy girl?" He asked. "I'm glad to see you finally made it back this way. Your sister's been driving me crazy." He laughed. "I think she thought you had done fell off the face of the earth or something." They ended their embrace.

"Living all the way in New York City, I feel like I did." She chuckled. "How you doing Pete?" Effie Mae asked, sympathetically.

"I'm good. Momma ain't doing so well though, but she's holding."

"How's Jimmy doing?" Pete glanced at Millie before answering the question.

"Uh, Jimmy . . . he's having a pretty tough time. You know he was Daddy's favorite."

"Although I never really liked Mr. Ned, I'm sorry he's dead."

"Effie Mae!" Millie called out.

"What Momma? You know that man didn't like me, him or Ms. Fannie Mae!"

"It's not that they didn't like you Effie Mae, they just didn't want you marrying Jimmy." Pete stated.

"Pete!" Annie Mae yelled.

"What? They didn't!" He laughed.

"It don't matter now anyway. Effie Mae Reed is already married." She smirked.

"Hey, how's J.R.—everything alright?" Pete asked.

"My husband is doing fine." She smiled.

"Look at you." Annie Mae said. "Momma did you hear Effie Mae?"

"Yeah, I heard her." Millie watched with ambiguity. She wanted to believe that Effie Mae had finally settled down. But, in her gut she knew a pending disaster was inevitable. Millie's thoughts were redirected by the sound of a crying infant.

"There goes Little Momma." Pete said. "It sounds like she's hungry too." He hurried from the room.

"Little Momma?" Annie Mae you got a baby?" Effie Mae asked, surprised.

"Yeah, you know I had to keep having these babies, until I finally gave Pete his daughter and Ms. Fannie Mae her granddaughter." She shook her head. "I'm done now! You hear that Pete?" Annie Mae yelled down the hallway that connected two additional bedrooms and a completed bathroom to the Reed's family home.

"Pete sounds like J.R." Effie Mae said. "Sarah's the fifth baby I done gave that man, but he still wants that boy." She chuckled. "He ain't gon let me be done until Ms. Ida's pull that boy out of me!" She joked.

"Effie Mae, you have five kids?" Annie Mae asked, astonished.

Their attention suddenly diverted to the kitchen when the screened back door slammed. One-by-one, four young boys of various ages entered into the house. They looked up at the white and red cookie tin on top of the refrigerator. A blue-eyed, white haired Santa Claus displayed on the side of the container.

Pete returned to the living room. His newborn daughter cradled in his arms; his one and a half year old son, trailing him.

"I already changed her. She's ready to eat now." He handed his infant daughter to Annie Mae. "Look who else woke up." Effie Mae looked at the toddler rubbing his eyes. She smiled.

"And who is this?" She asked.

"That Daddy's boy—is Baby Andy." Annie Mae said.

"Andrew Alexander . . . is his real name." Pete added, sounding like the proud Poppa. He then noticed his other sons standing in front of the refrigerator. Their eyes now locked onto Effie Mae. The tallest of the three boys asked . . ."

"Daddy, who is that?" Pete dashed from the living room and into the kitchen. He reached up on top of the refrigerator and grabbed the tin and opened it. He disbursed three homemade oatmeal cookies to each of his sons.

"Make sure you bring Andy a cookie too Pete. You know if he sees his brothers eating cookies, he's gon want one too." Pete took out an extra cookie then shooed his sons out the back door.

"Uh—uh Pete, bring my kids back in here so they can meet their Auntie."

"Y'all come on back in . . . and watch those crumbs." Pete said. The boys reentered. "You know your Grandma Millie don't like it when y'all start dropping crumbs all over the place." Pete led the boys into the living room then handed Baby Andy a cookie. He picked him up and sat him on his lap as he lowered himself onto the pink couch. Annie Mae began her maternal introductions.

"Little Momma here, is Effie Mae." Effie Mae smiled at the beautiful baby girl.

"Annie Mae! You named your baby after me?"

"I told you that girl loved you Effie Mae!" Pete said.

"I hope she turns out better than I did." Millie glanced at Effie Mae then turned her attention back to Sarah.

"This is Pete Jr." Annie Mae pointed to the boy greatly resembling Pete. "Looks like Ms. Fannie Mae and Pete were right, when they said I was having a boy." Pete nodded. "And this is Frank, Momma named him after Daddy. He ducked his head behind Annie Mae's leg and tried to hide his face. Annie Mae noticed Lil' Ned dropping his cookies. "Pete! Look at Lil' Ned. That boy dropping crumbs everywhere!"

"Annie Mae, Ned?" Effie Mae questioned.

"Now, you know if I name one of these boys after our Daddy, I was gon have to name one after Pete's daddy." She shook her head then noticed Lil' Ned trying to hide the crumbs under his feet. "Pete, this boy's making a mess!"

"Don't worry about it Annie Mae. I'm gon clean it up."

"Momma, I see that child's still lazy. She's working poor Pete to death." Millie gave no reply. Annie Mae and Pete glanced at each other in response to Millie's silence. They hoped Effie Mae's visit would be a peaceful one.

"That's Jimmy right there." Pete pointed to his son trying to stuff all three cookies in his mouth. "Pretty boy—just like his uncle." He laughed. Effie Mae looked at her baby sister in admiration.

"My little sister is all grown up. I'm happy for you Annie Mae." She hugged her adored only sibling.

"Annie Mae, have you seen Anthony?"

Millie briskly walked over and handed Sarah to Effie Mae, then left the room. She entered into her bedroom and slammed the door. Pete and Annie Mae shifted their eyes one to the other, believing that the impending disaster had just reared its head.

Effie Mae relaxed on the couch Millie kept on the front porch for visitors, peacefully enjoying the country scenery she'd not seen in years. She thought about the first time Anthony pulled into the driveway and introduced himself. Effie Mae smiled. Her mind drifted to the look on Anthony's face when he watched her and J.R. exit the church as husband and wife.

Her attention drew to the white convertible cruising down the road. Leaning slightly forward, she tried to catch a glimpse of the driver who she thought bore a similar resemblance to Anthony. Effie Mae dismissed the thought. She told herself that he'd probably married and perhaps even moved away, long ago. She again relaxed.

Effie Mae's peace would be short lived, when a figure suddenly appeared on the side of the porch next to her. She abruptly turned and looked into the face of Anthony. He now wore a shirt and tie.

Effie Mae hurried from the porch and ran into his awaiting arms.

"Anthony!" She wrapped her arms around him and hugged tightly.

"Hey Effie Mae." He took her into his arms then gently kissed her on the lips. Effie Mae kissed back.

"I can't believe you here Anthony."

"I can't believe that you're here, Effie Mae. I think about you all the time. I never thought I'd ever see you again." He kissed her again as they remained embraced on the side of the house.

"I have a surprise for you Effie Mae."

"A surprise? What kind of surprise, Anthony?"

"Come ride with me, I'll show you."

"If you trying to take me to the Cozi-T — I'm still married to J.R., Anthony.

"That's not it. Come ride with me Effie Mae."

"Okay, but I can't be gone for too long. My baby is in the house with Momma."

Anthony smiled. "Your baby? Boy or girl?

"Girl, her name is Sarah."

"I hoped that one day, we would have babies." Effie Mae smiled as she looked into his eyes through his thick rimmed glasses. "Come on." He took a hold of her hand. They snuck down onto the road where Anthony's parked car awaited. He opened the door for Effie Mae then walked to the other side car and got in. They drove away. "Is Sarah your only child?" His eyes alternated from her face and again onto the road.

"I got five babies Anthony. Sarah is my youngest."

"Five! Then my surprise will work out just fine."

"Where you taking me Anthony?"

"You'll see. We're almost there." He smiled. After fifteen minutes, Anthony pulled into the driveway of a two story home and turned off the motor. "Well, this is it!"

"What is it?"

"My home – our home." He said, smiling. Effie Mae's mouth flung open in response to his unexpected words. "Let's go in." He got out and hurried to her door then opened it. She remained inside.

"Anthony! My life is in New York now."

"I bought this house for you. I love you Effie Mae."

"Anthony. I can't . . ." He took a hold of her arm and assisted her out of the car. Holding her hand, Anthony guided her up the stairs and onto the front porch. "Is this where you live Anthony?" She asked, looking around.

"Yes. Come in." He opened the front door and the two entered. "Well, what do you think so far?"

"I like it. It's a nice house, but . . . ." He cut her off.

"I knew you'd like it. I bought it two years ago after I finished college and started working. I'm an Accountant! Marry me Effie Mae."

"Anthony! I already have a husband."

"I asked you first. And you said yes."

"I know, but . . . ." Anthony embraced her in his arms and kissed her. "Let me finish showing you around the house."

"Okay, but . . . ." He kissed her again then took a hold of her hand and continued their journey through the house which ended in the upstairs master bedroom. Anthony stared at Effie Mae and smiled as he sat down onto the bed. She looked around in amazement at the beautifully decorated room.

"Did you do all this Anthony?"

"Yes. Do you like it Effie Mae?"

"It's beautiful. But . . . ." He interrupted.

"Sit down so we can talk."

"I don't know Anthony. Maybe you should take me back."

"Effie Mae." He cut her off. "Sit down." She continued standing. "Before you married J.R., we spent almost every day together. I guess you didn't love me, but you knew I loved you." He gazed at her through pleading eyes. "Can we just talk? I hope that we're still friends." He smiled widened.

"Okay. Talk . . . and that's all!" Effie Mae sat next to him on the bed.

"Tell me about your life Effie Mae."

"What you want to know Anthony?"

"Are you happy?"

"I am. I . . . ." Anthony cut her off.

"Do you miss me Effie Mae? Do you miss us?" He put his arm around her.

"It's been six years Anthony. I thought maybe you got married or something." She said, becoming uneasy.

"You still like to have a good time Effie Mae? Anthony asked, looking into her eyes. "I do." He seductively smiled. You want to have a good time, together? Effie Mae stared at him, unable to speak. Anthony gently lowered her body down onto the bed and began passionately kissing her. Effie Mae surrendered.

Effie Mae uncovered her head and looked around the dark room. She panicked when she realized that hours had passed and it was now night. She thought about how she would explain her absence to Millie.

"Anthony! She shook his shoulder. "Anthony, wake up! I have to get home. Anthony!" He rolled over still half asleep.

"Did you say something Effie Mae?"

"Yeah, take me home! I don't know what I'm gon tell my Momma."

"Stay the night with me Effie Mae."

"I can't do that!" She looked into his smiling face. "Stop smiling and take me home."

"Stay the night with me. I promise I'll take you home early in the morning."

"What am I gon tell my Momma?" She yelled.

"I'll think of something." He and Effie Mae paused then burst into laughter as they remembered their first night at the Cozi-T Motel.

"Now what do you think you can say that my Momma's gon want to hear?" They laughed.

"You said early in the morning, right?"

"Before, the sun comes up." Effie Mae again surrendered.

"Effie Mae! Wake up girl so I can take you home." Anthony said from the opposite side of the bed. Effie Mae turned over and saw his bare back.

"Anthony! What happened to your back?" She asked, alerted to the red scar on his left upper shoulder.

"What? What do you see?" He asked, alarmed.

"It's a red scar on there!"

"Oh. That. It's my birthmark."

"It don't look like any birthmark I've ever seen. And, how come I never seen it before?"

"I don't know. It was there." He slid his t-shirt down over it as he began dressing. "It's unique to my family. My father has one just like it. And my grandfather and so forth."

"Pull your shirt back up." She said. Anthony reached behind and pulled the t-shirt up. Effie Mae gazed at the unusual mark. "It looks like you fell and scrapped it or something." She reached over and rubbed it.

Anthony pulled into the driveway to drop Effie Mae off. She opened the door and prepared to get out. He caught her by the arm.

"Is this it, Effie Mae?" He asked. "It was nice, us having a good time together again." Effie Mae thought about the numerous times he'd dropped her off after they'd spent the night together. This time she thought about the fact that she had a husband. She wondered if her being with Anthony would affect her life. She'd always had special feelings for Anthony, but she had J.R. in New York awaiting her return.

"I got to go Anthony."

"Promise me you'll think about us."

"How can I think about us Anthony? I have a husband!"

"But you shared my bed with me. If you were committed to your husband, I wouldn't be dropping you off this morning." Effie Mae listened to his rational words. She turned around and quickly kissed him.

"Bye, Anthony." She got out of the car and walked onto the front porch. She turned and looked back at him then smiled before entering into the house.

"Effie Mae!" Annie Mae said when seeing her walked through the door. "Where have you been? I know you weren't with Jimmy because he's married." She said in a low tone, as she sat in the living room, feeding Sarah.

"Where's Momma?" Effie Mae whispered.

"In her room, and right now she's so mad at you. Effie Mae did you forget that you're a married woman?" You stayed out all night with somebody! Who?" Annie Mae asked, frustrated.

"Anthony."

"Anthony?" Last I looked Anthony wasn't your husband. Effie Mae what were you thinking?" Annie Mae sat Sarah's bottle on the coffee table then placed her onto her chest and began burping her. "How can you go back home and lay with your husband knowing you been with another man? What if J.R. finds out?

"How he gon find out Annie Mae? You gon tell him?"

"No. But anything can . . . ." Effie Mae cut her off.

"Me and Anthony just had a good time together and that was it." She smiled.

"I hope for your sake, that's all it was."

"It was. Don't worry." Effie Mae reminisced on her evening with Anthony.

"Here! Take your baby." Annie Mae handed her Sarah.

Effie Mae lay asleep on the couch. Millie entered into the room with Sarah in her arms and stood over her.

"Effie Mae!" Millie called out. Effie Mae pulled the cover from over her head. She looked into the glaring eyes of Millie.

"Morning Momma." She said, hoping that Millie would let her indiscretion go unchallenged.

"Are you and J.R. still married?"

"Momma, what goes on between me and my husband is our business. And besides, I'm grown." Millie handed her Sarah as she sat up.

"Maybe I should call him then. Tell him that his wife just walked through the door this morning, after being in another man's bed all night."

"Is that what you want to do Momma?" She asked, loudly.

"Even with a good husband like J.R., you're still acting like …."

"What Momma—a female dog in heat?"

"You ain't changed not one bit!" Millie looked at her in disgust.

"I can see, ain't nothing changed with you either Momma! You been sitting back all this time, waiting on me to mess up? Okay, Momma. I messed up! But even if I hadn't, ain't nothing I do gon ever be good enough for Millie Reed, now is it?" Effie Mae yelled.

Annie Mae hurried from her bedroom and into the living room, awakened by their angry voices.

"My children and Pete are still sleeping! So, if you want to argue with Momma, Effie Mae, you gon need to do it someplace else!" She stated, speaking just above a whisper.

"What you do Annie Mae, tell Momma?"

"Who do you think was sitting up all night with your baby? When you walked through that door this morning, Momma had just gone to her room to get some sleep!" Annie Mae shook her head in disappointment. "And this ain't about Momma. It's about you. And how you couldn't come back here, married or not, without messing with Anthony!"

"Anthony?" Millie looked at Effie Mae in disbelief.

"Yeah Momma, that's right! Anthony." She said. "And, it looks like he ain't changed either." She smirked.

"Effie Mae!" Annie Mae yelled. "Don't come down here disrespecting Momma like that! I should call J.R. right now and tell him how you left his baby here at the house, so you could go climb in the bed with Anthony."

"Go ahead Annie Mae! Call him! He won't believe you. My husband loves me." Effie Mae paused. She thought about the words she'd just spoken. She said nothing further.

"Let's just get through this funeral." Millie said, then walked away and returned to her room.

Chapter Sixteen

A host of family members, friends, and a parade of numerous spectators hoping to catch a glimpse of the half-headed corpse, filled St. Ebenezer Missionary Baptist Church from front to back. Fannie Mae sat on the foremost pew shrouded in all black, from her patent leather shoes, to the veiled black hat obscuring her wet face. Her sobbing echoed through the sanctuary, sounding much like the howling of a wolf. She stared upon the closed casket garnished with a multitude of colorful wreaths then suddenly cried out.
"Ned!!!!!"
Jimmy seated to her left, placed his arm around his Momma and attempted to console her. To his left sat Rosetta, his wife of four years. Pete, Annie Mae and their children sat left of Rosetta. At the very end of the pew sat Millie. Effie Mae took her historical seat on the very back pew.
Suddenly, an unfamiliar woman entered into the church followed by four minor daughters of various ages. The eyes of the congregation and attending spectators, watched as she and her children walked up

to Ned's hidden remains. She stood gazing at the closed box then shriek.

"Ned! Ned! Ned!"

"Daddy!" The children cried out, weeping. Pete looked at his weeping Momma and shook his head, disgraced by his Daddy's endless dishonor. Fannie Mae stopped blubbering when she witnessed the fiasco. She leaped up from her seat and moved swiftly in the direction of the woman.

"Get away from my husband!" She yelled. Jimmy hurried after her. He grabbed her arm, firmly restraining her.

"Leave me alone woman! Let me grieve for my man." The woman shouted.

"Your man?" A female voice yelled out. A second woman stood to her feet then walked in the direction of the casket. Her two sons followed.

"Come on Ned Jr. and Parker!"

The multitude of families created by Ned Parker, paraded throughout the church, all congregated in front of the casket. Jimmy rested his humiliated, weeping Momma's head onto his chest as he escorted her back to her seat. He froze when he suddenly noticed Effie Mae seated in the rear of the church. They momentarily gazed into each other's eyes then blushed. Sissy Hill observed their intimate exchange. Rosetta turned and looked in the direction of her husband's stare, when she too took note of his sudden preoccupation. She watched as he and Effie Mae shared an affectionate smile. Rosetta glared at Effie Mae with rage then turned her attention to her enchanted husband. Jimmy's gaze broke, when he noticed Rosetta's unrelenting stare. Millie also witnessed the intimate interaction.

As the funeral neared its end, the Parker family followed the pallbearers down the center aisle of the church and through the awaiting opened doors at the entrance. Rosetta held onto Jimmy's arm as they prepared to exit. Effie Mae and Jimmy, being unable to resist their lingering chemistry, looked one to the other, smiling. Rosetta watched.

She reluctantly released her hold on Jimmy, when he assisted Fannie Mae into the funeral home's 1965 black Cadillac Fleetwood Limousine, customarily provided to the family of the deceased. Also seated inside were Pete, Annie Mae and their children. Rosetta climbed into the front seat with the driver. She glared into the church's opened doors and watched as Effie Mae talked with Sissy. She gave Effie Mae a final stare before the Funeral Director closed her door. Jimmy also glanced inside the church, catching a quick glimpse of Effie Mae before the driver pulled off.

Millie and Rev. Hill stood at the church doors and watched as family and friends disbursed.

"Now Rev. Hill, you know that was the worse mess . . . ." Millie quieted as the mother of Ned Jr. and Parker exited the church with the two boys. Rev. Hill watched as the multitude of women, claiming Ned as the father of their illegitimate children, departed from the church.

"Sad—truly sad." Rev. Hill shook his head in pity.

"Rev. Hill, have you heard any news on what the Sheriff plan on doing with Jed Russell?" Millie asked.

"Now Ms. Millie, you know I don't like saying things unless I know them to be true." He leaned in towards her and whispered. "But Deacon Bledsoe told me, that he ain't even been arrested." He looked around to make sure there were no other listening ears in the immediate vicinity.

"Well, hush your mouth!" Millie said.

"Said, there weren't any witnesses to the crime." Again, he looked around.

"Rev. Hill, Johnny Banks stood right there in my living room, and told us he seen the whole entire thing!" Millie spoke just above a whisper.

"Did you see Johnny here at the funeral Ms. Millie?" Rev. Hill raised an eyebrow.

"Come to think of Rev. Hill, I sure didn't." A concern look formed on her face.

"Heard, that he was hiding out somewhere in Jackson . . . ." Millie interrupted.

"Now how long, do he think, he gon be able hide out—and right there in Jackson, Mississippi?

"Not Jackson Mississippi, Ms. Millie. Florida . . . Jacksonville, Florida!" Millie's mouth flung open. "Johnny's family got him out of here so fast, looks like he vanished in thin air." He nodded, confirming his mysterious words. Millie looked in wonder.

"Well, tell me this Rev. Hill. I saw that young gal sitting next to Jimmy, that his wife?"

"Now Ms. Millie, you know I don't like no parts of getting into other folks affairs."

"Shame on you Rev. Hill, now you know I wouldn't ask you to meddle in other folks business."

"Is there a reason why you asking Ms. Millie?" He looked around.

"Rev. Hill, I saw that gal, give my Effie Mae a look that sent chills right up my spine!"

"Truth is, I married her and Jimmy just about four years ago. But you know Ms. Millie, funny thing is, neither one of them seemed to be happy about marrying." Rev. Hill huddled close to Millie.

"Well, hush your mouth." She replied. "I ain't seen no children either. Do they got any?"

"Now you know I wouldn't tell this to anybody else except you Ms. Millie." Rev. Hill convinced himself that he wasn't gossiping. "After they'd been married just about a year, her Momma came to me, asked me if I could pray for her daughter."

"You don't say—about what Rev. Hill?"

"She wanted me to pray over her womb." Rev. Hill shifted his eyes towards the church doors then again to Millie.

"Well, hush your mouth." Millie's curiosity heightened.

"Seems she been having female difficulties since she was 'bout twelve years old." He and Millie drew closer.

"Is that right? So what finally happened?"

"Well, let me put it this way Ms. Millie …." He glanced inside the church. "I'm still praying. Some things just ain't in God's will." Rev. Hill and Millie were momentarily, deeply engrossed in thought.

"Momma!" Effie called out, startling them both. You and Rev. Hill ain't out here gossiping are you?"

"Uh, how are you Effie Mae?" Rev. Hill asked. "Uh, it's good to see you again. Uh, how's that husband of yours? Uh, is everything going okay?" He rambled.

"J.R. is doing fine. And everything's okay." She answered. "Come on Momma. If we gon get out to the cemetery, we need to be leaving here now. You know we want to be there in time enough to see them drop that old hateful man in the ground and cover him up with dirt!"

187 | *Effie Mae*

"Effie Mae!" Millie called out, embarrassed by her insensitivity regarding her true feelings for the deceased. "That was your sister's father-in-law. I guess that just about made Ned Parker, family." Millie choked on the words.

"Momma, if you want to claim Ned Parker as kin, that's you. But, you know you didn't like that man anymore than I did . . . ."

"Ahem." Millie cleared her throat, cutting her outspoken daughter off when she observed Sissy exiting through the church doors, baby Sarah cuddled in her arms.

"Sister-in-law, you and J.R.'s gon have to give me this beautiful baby girl." She teased then kissed the infant gently on the forehead. "Y'all have four more at home!"

"You gon have to asked Ms. Millie Reed about that." Effie Mae joked.

"Sissy, now you know your baby brother ain't gon let his wife leave that sweet baby, down here in Mississippi." Millie stated. "So you may as well give her all the love you can while she here." Sissy laughed then walked over to their 1966 black Cadillac Brougham. She climbed inside, taking her usual seat on the passenger's side.

"I guess we gon be seeing you out at the cemetery Rev. Hill." Millie said.

"Alright, Ms. Millie." He concluded their secret discussion. "Effie Mae, you be sure to tell J.R. I asked about him."

"I will, Rev. Hill." Effie Mae strolled over to the car and climbed into the backseat, joining Sissy then rolled down the window. "Come on Momma!" Millie hurried to the car and got in just as one of the church deacons climbed into the driver's seat then pulled off, headed to the cemetery.

    The speculations regarding Ned Parker's violent demise followed people from the cemetery to the Parker family's farmhouse. The attendees gathered in the rear of the home to partake in the customary foods prepared to feed people coming to share their condolences for the bereaved family. The gossiping halted, when Fannie Mae passed out on the back porch as she prepared to enter into the home. Pete broke her fall then carried her inside. He took her into her bedroom, putting her into bed. He knew that the day's events had been far too much for her to bear.
    Outside, Jimmy eyes followed Effie Mae around as she searched for a vacant seat amongst the many chairs located throughout the yard. He watched and waited for the opportunity to make his move as if he'd forgotten that between the two, there were spouses. Effie Mae blushed when noticing his unrelenting gawk.
    Seated at a table with Rev. Hill and Sissy, Millie took note of their foolish exchange. She chastised Effie Mae with her eyes and hoped this time she would remember that she was another man's wife. Rev. Hill and Sissy also noticed the inappropriate transactions.
    "My brother loves that girl so much. Millie it would break his heart if he saw what her and Jimmy were doing." Sissy stated as she held Sarah in her arms. "And look at this precious baby girl they've made." Sissy shook her head with disapproval.
    "Let me go talk to my daughter." Millie said as she stood.

"Ms. Millie if there's anything you need me to do, you know I'm right here."

"Thank you, Rev. Hill." Millie watched as the playfulness between Effie Mae and Jimmy continued. "As much as I loved seeing Effie Mae and my grandbaby, I almost hate that she came home." Millie walked away and headed in Effie Mae's direction. "What's wrong with you child?" Millie asked as she approached her flirtatious daughter.

"What you doing Momma, watching me?"

"It looks like somebody ought to."

"I guess Rev. Hill and Ms. Sissy watching me too?"

"You know they is! That's why I can't understand why you acting like this."

"Acting like what, Momma? I ain't said one word to Jimmy, and he ain't said one word to me. Besides, Jimmy's got a wife now. And I'm sure she ain't gon let me get within ten feet of him."

"And you got a husband! But that ain't stop you from lying up all night with Anthony, now did it?" Effie Mae rolled her eyes.

"I'm grown Momma."

"Then act like it!"

"Don't worry Momma I'm gon be leaving first thing in the morning. So, you don't have to worry about me waking up in Jimmy's bed. Plus his wife, don't look like she'd just get out and let me get in. But, if she did." Millie cut her off.

"Listen at you!" Millie glared at her. Effie Mae shifted her eyes to Jimmy and flirted. He blushed. She gazed at Millie then stood and walked away. Millie stared at her as she strolled across the yard and headed in the direction of the house. Jimmy made his move. He positioned himself in her direct path then stopped. She blushed. Before a word could be spoken between the two, Rosetta moved swiftly in their direction.

"Effie Mae Reed!" She yelled from behind as she prepared to confront Effie Mae and lay claim to Jimmy. Effie Mae turned in response to the unfamiliar voice. She saw Rosetta quickly approaching. Millie took note of the impending altercation.

"Are you speaking to me?" Effie Mae asked.

"Yeah, I'm speaking to you! I'm Jimmy's wife, Rosetta." She stated as though proposing a challenge. "I been watching you—watching my Jimmy. Folks around here told me that you and my husband have a past. Well I'm coming to you woman to woman to tell you to stay your high yellow behind away from my man! Or you just might find yourself missing half of your head, like Mr. Ned!"

When hearing the words *half a head*, all eyes centered on Jimmy Parker's wife and Millie Reed's eldest daughter. Included amid those eyes were Millie's, Rev. Hill's and Sissy's.

"Well, Ms. Rosetta I believe I was just about ten years old when my Auntie Peaches told me that when a woman can't hold on to what she think is hers . . . maybe it's because she ain't have it in the first place." She quoted. "And as far as my behind being yellow, I guess you can get that information from your husband, he done seen it enough times." Jimmy laughed.

Effie Mae turned and looked at him when hearing his laughter. "What? Well you have." She smiled. Rosetta looked around at the crowd of people, all laughing at Effie Mae's *biting* words.

"I don't know who that heifer thinks she's talking too!" She popped off her red artificial nails and kicked off her red shoes as she prepared to launch a physical counter attack.

She curled her fingers into the palms of her hand and formed a fist. Then raised her right arm high in the air and approached Effie Mae from behind. Seconds before she could connect to the back of Effie Mae's head, Jimmy stepped in front of her and intercepted the intended impact. He seized Rosetta by the arms and restrained her. Screaming voices were heard throughout the crowd of on-lookers. Rev. Hill leapt from his seat when he heard screams and saw Effie Mae standing front and center of the commotion. Effie Mae looked around and gazed into the disturbed eyes of Millie. Sissy looked in shame as she observed the dispute. Rev. Hill shifted his eyes to Millie then to Sissy. He hurried in the direction of the altercation as he brought the assembly of people to order.

"Brothers and sisters let us not forget the reason why we're here." He stated. "Let's keep in mind that Sister Fannie Mae Parker just lost her husband. So if everybody would please go back to what you were doing, we can keep this from becoming a fiasco."

Rev. Hill glared at Jimmy as he continued to restrain his wife. His eyes reprimanded him for his behavior, given the circumstances under which his father had recently passed.

Jimmy whispered in Rosetta's ear as a parent scolding a naughty child, as she maintained her eye-to-eye gaze with Effie Mae. When, certain that she no longer posed a threat to the woman at the center of his heart, *Effie Mae Reed,* Jimmy released his hold.

Rosetta strolled around the area of her thrown items, picking up what she could find of the red nails, and red shoes. She moved at a snail's pace as she headed in the direction of the house. She stepped onto the back porch then looked back and exchanged a cold, piercing stare at Effie Mae. She rolled her eyes then disappeared through the back door. As the crowd of onlookers came to order, their gossiping resumed, this time it included, Effie Mae Reed.

Effie Mae walked around to the side of the house and readjusted her composure. Jimmy followed. He moved swiftly in front of her and stopped, placing himself within kissing distance.

"Hey Effie Mae. Uh, I guess you know, that was my wife." He smiled.

"Looks like you done married to a crazy woman!"

"She just jealous is all." Jimmy explained. "How you been doing?" He asked, captivated by her very presence.

"I'm doing fine." Effie Mae blushed.

"So, tell me Effie Mae, what you doing all the way up there in New York City?"

"Taking care of my five babies." She tried to resist his magnetism. She stepped backwards. He moved forward.

"You know them babies should've been mine." He said, flirtatiously. Effie Mae again blushed. "Pete said he told you, I was in love with you. That ain't changed."

"Is that right?" She smiled.

"You know it's right." Jimmy moved closer.

"You must be trying to get me killed?"

"What you mean?"

"Rosetta? Your wife?"

Jimmy laughed to himself.

"Girl, you done gone soft since you left Mississippi. What happened to the Effie Mae that used to burn like fire? She must still be in New York." He chuckled.

"Well, when you see her, tell her Jimmy asked about her." He teased.

"I'm a married woman with babies now, Jimmy."

"I don't know if I should be happy for you or jealous."

"Jealous! About what?"

"You."

"Me? What about me?"

"You being married to another man and giving him my babies."

"Your babies?" She blushed. Jimmy leaned in and kissed her on the lips. Effie Mae kissed him back. He took a hold of her hand and guided her towards the front of the house. He motioned her to climb inside of his Black, 1963 Chevrolet C10 Pickup truck parked on the front lawn. Effie Mae opened the door and climbed in then ducked down on the seat. She laughed as Jimmy reached his hand inside the open window and put the truck in neutral. He pushed it onto the road and jumped inside then started it up. He put his arm around Effie Mae and kissed her. The two then drove away.

Millie watched in silence as Effie Mae stood in the living room and packed her and Sarah's belongings as she prepared to return to New York City. She thought of Effie Mae and Jimmy's extended absence from the gathering at the Parker's family farm. Millie knew that once again her married daughter had given herself to yet another man. She wondered if she would ever desire a need for self-respect. Effie Mae turned and noticed Millie's stare.

"What Momma?"

"I'm not gon ask, because I don't really want to know the answer." Millie held Sarah in her arms." I hope you and Jimmy remembered that both of y'all is married?"

"Yeah, Momma . . . we did. But I figured since Effie Mae Reed had already messed up, what difference would it make?" She glanced at Millie. "I'm gon let Jimmy worry about Rosetta."

Annie Mae hurried into the living room from the kitchen after she heard Effie Mae's confession. Pete followed.

"I know I didn't just hear you tell Momma that you messed with Jimmy?" She asked. Pete reluctantly snickered.

"I was talking to Momma, Annie Mae." Effie Mae gazed at Millie then sat her suitcase down onto the floor." Momma, can you look out and see if Rev. Hill and Ms. Sissy are out there yet?"

"Jimmy's married, Effie Mae!"Annie Mae shouted.

"Well, he sure ain't act like it yesterday." She smirked. Millie ignored her shameless words as she walked over to the opened front door and looked out. Pete chuckled.

"Effie Mae what's wrong with you?" Annie Mae yelled.

"I wish I knew."She said. "But you better hang on to Pete. I just might change my rule about being with brothers." Effie Mae looked at Pete then shifted her eyes to her young sister. Annie Mae turned quickly to Pete. He threw his hands up proclaiming his innocence.

"Momma! You better get her out of here!" Annie Mae shouted then rushed towards Effie Mae. Pete grabbed her from the back, around the waist and held her.

"Let her go Pete!" Effie Mae said." I'd hate to hurt your wife, but, she come over here that's just what I'm gon do."

"This, don't make sense—y'all sisters!" Pete yelled. "Effie Mae's grown and so is Jimmy. They know what they done, wasn't right. But that's for them to answer for. Not you Annie Mae and not Ms. Millie!"

"Here comes Rev. Hill and Sissy, now." Millie said looking out.

"Now, I'm gon carry Effie Mae's bag out to the car. And this here mess that just happened . . . it's over!" Pete gazed at Effie Mae. "It's a good thing that Pete Jr. and them, wasn't in here. I wouldn't want them to see their Momma and Auntie carrying on like that!" He stared at Annie Mae." I mean it Annie Mae!" Pete released Annie Mae. He walked over and picked up Effie Mae's luggage. He stopped when approaching the door. He glanced at each of the women in the room then focused his attention onto Annie Mae. "I mean what I say, Annie Mae." She gave no reply. She watched in silence as he exited through the front door.

Effie Mae shifted her eyes to Annie Mae then walked over to Millie to take Sarah. Annie Mae momentarily stared at her big sister, then turned abruptly away and left the room. She hurried down the hallway and entered into her bedroom, slamming the door behind her. Millie placed Sarah into Effie Mae's arms.

"Effie Mae, I want you to go home to your husband and think about what you done.

"Momma, like Pete said . . . ." Millie cut her off.

"Listen to me child." Effie Mae quieted. "I want you to ask yourself if what you done…" Millie looked briefly away as she thought about Effie Mae's infidelity, then turned again and faced her. "Is it worth losing a husband that loves you and a life that plenty of women would feel blessed to have? J.R. is a good man, and I know in my heart, that he would've never done to you, what you done to him and Jimmy done to his wife."

"Now see, you don't know that Momma." Millie glared into her eyes.

"Effie Mae, do you truly believe that J.R. would lie in another woman's bed?" Effie Mae remained silent. "I want you to think about that. Because inside your head, I know, you do know, right from wrong." Millie leaned forward and kissed Sarah on the forehead then hugged Effie Mae. "Life's got a funny way of catching up to you." Millie turned and walked away. "Bye Effie Mae, Smith."

Chapter Seventeen

Effie Mae awakened with queasiness in her stomach. She sat up in bed then looked over at Sarah's empty crib. She rationalized that Ms. Geraldine had probably taken the infant from the room while she lay sleeping. She noticed J.R.'s absence from their bed and assumed that, it being a Saturday morning, he'd probably gone out onto the back porch to converse with Daniel.

Effie Mae heard the voices of her children, laughing as they watched cartoons in the living room. Her nausea increased from the aroma flowing from the kitchen as Ms. Geraldine customarily prepared her large breakfast every Saturday morning. Effie Mae swiftly climbed out of bed and exited the bedroom, then hurried in the direction of the bathroom.

"Morning Effie Mae." Ms. Geraldine said when she saw her scurrying through the dining room. "If you're looking for Sarah, J.R. just took her outback with him and Daniel."

"Uh-huh." Effie Mae replied as she felt the puke oozing upward through her throat and into her mouth.

"Are you feeling alright Effie Mae?" Ms. Geraldine watched in wonder as Effie Mae entered into the bathroom and closed the door. Placing her hand on her abdomen, Effie Mae vomited into the sink. After five previous births, she knew for certain that she was again pregnant. Her mind wandered back to the intimate evenings she'd shared with both Anthony and Jimmy while home in Yazoo City. She realized that the child she now carried may have been fathered by anyone of the three men she'd shared herself with, within the last month. She placed her hand over her mouth and tried to quiet the sound of her recurring heaves. She wondered if Ms. Geraldine had heard her.

"Effie Mae? Are you alright in there? She asked.

"Yeah Ms. Geraldine, I'm fine." Effie Mae turned on the water in the sink then splashed some over her face. She took a deep breath and turned it off. She looked in the mirror and thought about her dilemma then opened the door and came out. She tried to hurry back into her bedroom, but stopped when hearing Ms. Geraldine's voice.

"Did I hear you in the bathroom throwing up? Effie Mae, are you pregnant again?"

Ms. Geraldine gazed at her. "I can always tell when you're pregnant. It's almost like you have a glow about you." She looked at Effie Mae as if looking for a *glow*. "You and J.R. are around here breeding like rabbits!" She laughed. J.R. entered into the house with Sarah in his hands, held away from his body.

"You just in time Momma—to change your daughter's diaper. This girl is wet!" He said handing her off to Effie Mae.

"My daughter? Why is it when she's wet, she becomes my daughter?" Effie Mae teased.

"Well, when this next baby gets here, all of us are going to be changing diapers. Y'all already have two in diapers now!" Ms. Geraldine said, laughing.

"Next baby? Effie Mae, you pregnant?" J.R. asked.

"Yes, she is." Ms. Geraldine interrupted. "I heard her in there in the bathroom just a few minutes ago— sounded like she was throwing up to me." She gazed at Effie Mae. "And she has that glow again. And I know what that means!" She paused. "That she's pregnant." Ms. Geraldine laughed.

"Glow?" J.R. looked at Effie Mae in search of *the glow*. "Geraldine, it looks like you got a gift." He said, as he continued to stare at his wife.

"I don't know about all that J.R.; I just know your wife— and when she's pregnant." She chuckled.

"Thank you baby." He said then kissed Effie Mae gently on the lips. "We gon have us a boy this time, Geraldine!" He stated with confidence then kissed Effie Mae again.

"J.R., maybe you and Effie Mae need to stop all that kissing?" She raised an eyebrow. "That's why you have all these babies now." J.R. looked at Effie Mae and smiled then applied another loving kiss to her lips.

"I think it takes more than a kiss, Geraldine." He teased. Effie Mae nudged him in the side with her elbow.

"You know my babies in there watching television." J.R. kissed her again then hurried out onto the back porch to share the news with Daniel.

"I guess you won't be eating breakfast this morning, Effie Mae? Ms. Geraldine said, doubtful.

"Why Ms. Geraldine? I got to eat!"

"You're not getting ready to throw all my hard work back up." She laughed. Effie Mae smiled. "Now, you go on ahead and lie back down, and let me cook something, I don't mind you throwing up." Ms. Geraldine chuckled. "I'll be in there in a few to get Sarah . . ." She paused. "After, you've changed that wet diaper." She raised an eyebrow.

"Okay, Ms. Geraldine. I can't wait to see what you gon cook that's gon stay in my stomach."

"You let me worry about that. You just get that baby dry."

Effie Mae playfully kissed baby Sarah on the cheek.

"Come on Momma's baby. Momma's gon get you nice and dry." She again kissed Sarah's cheek as she left the kitchen and returned to her bedroom, closing the door behind her.

Effie Mae laid Sarah inside her crib. Suddenly feeling light headed, she sat on the bed. Admiring her beautiful baby girl, she thought about how disappointed Millie would be if she learned of her pregnancy, and that the child she now carried, may or may not be her husband's.

Effie Mae also thought about how hurt J.R. would be if he knew the child growing in her womb, might possibly belong to another man. Her thoughts were suddenly interrupted by the cheerful sounds of her children in the dining room as they prepared to eat. Effie Mae smiled then again looked over at Sarah lying asleep in her crib. She stared at her wedding ring and thought about Millie's prophetic words. She now feared that her decision to be intimate with Anthony and Jimmy could change her life forever. Her thoughts were cut short when the door opened and Ms. Geraldine entered.

"Effie Mae, have you changed Sarah, yet?" She walked over to the crib and picked the infant up. "Effie Mae this girl is still wet!"

"I ain't feeling good, Ms. Geraldine."

"Well you go ahead and lie down and get some rest. I'll look after Sarah, and the rest of these children."

"Thank you Ms. Geraldine."

Ms. Geraldine grabbed the diaper bag from off the dresser. She momentarily gazed at Effie Mae as she lay resting. She briefly wondered what it might have been like, to have had children of her own.

"Let me know if you need anything." Ms. Geraldine said as she exited the room with Sarah.

Effie Mae awakened after only thirty minutes of sleep. She slid down onto the floor and removed the old red diary from underneath the mattress and began to write. She wrote in great detail of her intimate moments spent with Anthony and Jimmy. She talked about her pregnancy, and her uncertainty of which of the three men, fathered the child that grew inside of her. She quickly dropped the diary when hearing the sound of the door being opened. Before she could pick it back up, J.R. entered into the room. He noticed the red diary lying next to her.

"Effie Mae you still writing in that old red book? I thought once you started having these children, you had stopped that." He chuckled. Afraid that she may be asked to reveal her ugly secrets written on the pages of the old diary, she diverted his attention.

"I have a confession to make." She said, softly. J.R. looked at her with curious eyes. He wondered what secret his wife could possibly be keeping. He hoped her confession would be her love for him.

She looked at him in silence. Her heart pounded and her mouth dried, and for a fleeting moment, she actually thought of revealing her indiscretions. She couldn't do it.

"I, uh—didn't change Sarah. Ms. Geraldine done it for me."

"Looks like you doing all the birthing and Geraldine's doing all the mothering." J.R. teased, feeling slightly disappointed by not hearing the words... "I love you."

"It's just that, I wasn't feeling well . . ."

"That's alright baby. I still love you." He noticed the troubled look in her eyes. "Is something bothering you Effie Mae?"

"I was just thinking—what I would do if I lost all of this."

"All of this? J.R. looked around the room. "All this, belongs to Cousin Daniel and Geraldine." He teased.

"No. I mean . . . my life, you, our babies . . ."

"Well you don't ever have to worry about that. I'm here to stay." He sat down on the floor beside her, and positioned her head onto his chest then put his arm around her. "I love you Effie Mae." He lovingly stated.

...

Drenched with sweat, Effie Mae screamed out in agonizing pain as she prepared to bring another infant into the world. Ms. Geraldine stood close by, as she again assisted the Midwife.

"Just one more push Effie Mae." Ms. Ida said. "Your new son or daughter is about to make its arrival."

"J.R., are you going to come in and see this miracle of life?" Ms. Geraldine yelled into the living room.

"No! I'm gon let you women folk handle that." J.R. stated as he and Daniel waited for the announcement of the birth of the infant. Even better, would be the news that Effie Mae had given birth to their first son.

"Ahhhhhhhh!!" Effie Mae gave a final yell and pushed then thrust out a healthy baby boy.

"It's a boy Effie Mae!" Ms. Geraldine shouted as Ms. Ida cut the umbilical cord. "Did you hear that J.R.?" Ms. Geraldine hollered out.

"Well, I'll be damn! It looks like Effie Mae finally gave you that son y'all been waiting on . . . forever!" Daniel said with excitement. "I guess we all know what y'all gon name him, now don't we? Now this calls for a smoke." J.R. looked at his cousin with peculiarity, in that he viewed smoking as being an unnecessary affliction.

"Come on J.R. and put some tobacco in one of these pipes! Have a smoke with your cousin." He extended one of the many pipes he kept in a glass jar sitting on the living room table.

"Ain't no need in all that Cousin Daniel. And you know I don't smoke."

"What's the matter boy? You think you gon burn in hell for smoking a pipe?" Daniel chuckled.

"It's not that Cousin Daniel. Have you ever seen me smoke anything before?"

"I guess the key words there, would be—have I ever seen you? And the answer is, no, I have not. But I ain't ever seen you preach either." He took a long drag from his pipe. "Does that mean you're not a preacher?" He took another puff from the pipe then looked at J.R. questionably. J.R. chuckled.

"Daniel! You'd better not be smoking in my house— I know that much!" Ms. Geraldine yelled out. Daniel waved his hand dismissing her words then took two additional puffs. He turned to J.R. and defiantly removed the pipe from his mouth.

"Those two puffs were for you J.R." The two men laughed as Daniel got up and went out onto the back porch.

"Well aren't you going to come in here and welcome your new son . . . J.R. the second, into this world?" Ms. Geraldine asked, as she cleaned the large infant off and prepared to present him to his Daddy. J.R. entered into the bedroom, excited to see his *boy* cradle in his Momma's arms. Effie Mae lay resting after her exhausting ordeal. J.R. leaned over and kissed her on the lips.

"Did I hear right Effie Mae? We made us a son?"

"See for yourself." She exposed the naked infant from underneath his blanket. J.R. looked in disbelief at the handsome baby boy, becoming consumed with fatherly pride.

"I'll be damn! I done made me a son!" He shouted. Effie Mae and Ms. Geraldine looked one to the other, shocked by his use of the word, *damn*.

"Now, I know you're excited about this boy J.R., but . . ." Ms. Geraldine stated.

"I'm sorry Geraldine, Ms. Ida; Effie Mae." He said, apologetically.

"J.R., you better watch your mouth. Remember, your wife's married to a preacher." Effie Mae teased. She momentarily paused. "There's something I been wanting to ask you for a long time now, J.R." Effie Mae said.

"What's that?" He asked, curious of her impending question.

"Just what do that J and R stand for in your name?" J.R. laughed, humored by her out of character innocence.

"They really don't stand for anything. After Momma birthed eighteen youngins, I reckon with me being number eighteen; her and Daddy ran clean out of names. So they just named me with two letters in the alphabet." He stated in a matter of fact tone.

"Well, I ain't about to name my only boy with two letters." Effie Mae said.

"Understandable. Anything you name him Effie Mae is fine with me. It's just one thing that I ask.

"One thing—what's that, J.R.?"

"Don't name my boy after any of your old boyfriends." Effie Mae shifted her eyes to her newborn son, internally convicted by her sudden guilt. "I don't care how cute their names were." He chuckled. "I'm just teasing with you." They harmoniously laughed.

"I don't mind using those letters, but I'm gon put a name to them."

"That's fine." J.R. agreed.

Effie Mae considered the possibility that her newborn son could have been fathered by her husband, Anthony or Jimmy. She thought of how Anthony and Jimmy had no children of their own, and rationalized how proud either man would be to have a son named after him, if indeed, he were their son. She convinced herself that if by chance he were J.R.'s, the J and R would still be appropriate.

"Let's see . . . For the J—I'm gon name him . . . ."

"Take your time." J.R. teased.

"Jimmy."

"Okay, Jimmy's fine. As a matter of fact, my oldest brother's name is Jimmy." He smiled and nodded.

"And for the R—I'm gon name him Rae." J.R. nodded in agreement. "I want to add another name too."

"Another name?" An odd look formed on his face.

"Anthony."

"Anthony?" He thought for a moment. "Yeah, I like that. It's got a nice ring to it." He thought for a moment. "So, our baby boy's name gon be . . . Jimmy Anthony Rae Smith." He said.

"That's Ray with an "e" not a "y." Effie Mae added.

"Jimmy Anthony Rae with an "e" not a "y," Smith." J.R. inhaled then exhaled. "That's a whole lot of name for one boy." He said then gazed at Effie Mae with adoration. "But, if that's what my wife wants to name our boy, then that's just what we gon do." He smiled. "But now, I'm still gon call my boy Lil' J.R." He proudly stated.

Effie Mae convince herself that she had done the right thing by choosing to leave J.R. in the dark, about her history with Jimmy and Anthony, and how she'd just named their newborn son after the two men. She thought nothing more of it, as she continued to admire her first born son.

Chapter Eighteen

Ms. Geraldine and Effie Mae relaxed on the back porch, enjoying the warm weather, complimented by a calming, cool breeze. They talked as the children played in the slightly worn grass and J.R. entertained one and a half year old Lil' J.R.

"Effie Mae, I'm sure glad you finally gave J.R. a son. But, sometimes I think he forgets that he even have those girls." Ms. Geraldine stated, jokingly. "The man even spends more time around the house, now!" She chuckled.

"Yeah, he loves his boy." Effie Mae stated. "He won't hardly let me to do anything for my baby!" Effie Mae's mind raced, as she thought of how the son J.R. so dearly loved, may not be his own.

"You can give a man all the daughters in the world. But can't nothing take the place of that son." Ms. Geraldine drifted deep into thought. "But you know Effie Mae, I would've been glad to have either one." She looked briefly at Effie Mae. "But, I guess it wasn't in the good Lord's plan." Ms. Geraldine exhibited vulnerability for the first time as tears fixed inside of her tired eyes. Effie Mae listened sympathetically. "I guess Daniel figured just because I couldn't give him any children, there was no reason why he shouldn't have any."

Effie Mae's eyes widened with surprise, not only from Ms. Geraldine's prior knowledge, but her acceptance of Daniel fathering children outside of their marriage. At that moment, she remembered her hurtful words many years ago.

"Ms. Geraldine, I didn't mean to say what I said . . . ." Ms. Geraldine interrupted her.

"Effie Mae—you didn't tell me anything I didn't already know." She looked away. "Feeling sorry for myself . . . not being able to give my husband children . . . . . ." She stared into nothingness then shifted her eyes back to Effie Mae. "A man has a right to have children. Carry on his seed." She paused. "Even, if it is with another woman." Puzzled by Ms. Geraldine's self-defeating words, Effie Mae maintained her silence as the two women continued watching the children play.

...

J.R and Lil' J.R. played hide-and-seek inside the house throughout the various rooms of the home. Peeking through his fingers as he covered his eyes, J.R. noted Lil' J.R. hurry into the living room and over to the coffee table. He grabbed one of Daniel's pipes from the jar and quickly shoved it in his mouth. J.R. dropped his hands and rushed into the living room.

"What's that you got in your mouth son?" J.R. chuckled then removed the pipe from the toddler's mouth. "Looks like I'm gon have to talk to Cousin Daniel about leaving these things sitting around here where you can get a hold of them." J.R. removed the jar of pipes from the table. He took them into the kitchen and sat them on the counter, then he and Lil' J.R. continued their game of hide-n-seek. "Go run and hide Lil' J.R., so Daddy can find you." The toddler took off running and giggling. He ran from the living room, through the kitchen and in the direction of the dining room. J.R. uncovered his eyes. "Where are you Lil' J.R.? Where's Daddy's boy." J.R. left the living room then headed towards the kitchen. "I'm gon count to ten. Then Daddy's coming to get you. One, two, three, four, five . . . ." J.R. continued counting as his son ran through the hallway and into his parent's bedroom. The door closed silently behind him. ". . . Eight, nine, ten! Ready or not here I come!" J.R. went in his search of his young son.

...

"Slow down now! You're running too fast, Billie!" Ms. Geraldine cautioned then continued her discussion with Effie Mae. "You and J.R. having all these children, in some way, it was like the good Lord gave me the babies my womb was unable to bear." She shifted her eyes to Effie Mae and smiled. "I want to thank you Effie Mae, for letting me be a part of their lives. I know we haven't always gotten along. . . ." Effie Mae interrupted.

"I'm the one who should be apologizing, Ms. Geraldine. I was so busy being mad at J.R. because he took me away from my Momma and baby sister . . . ."

"I know you and J.R. want your own home. And I know that it's because of me carrying on, every time he says something about buying you a house that he keeps putting it off." She light-heartedly chuckled. "Then before you know it, another year's gon by and another baby is here." Effie Mae laughed. Ms. Geraldine took a hold of her hand and gently squeezed it. "Thank you Effie Mae." The two exchanged an endearing smile.

"Ms. Geraldine you probably been more of a Momma to my babies than me. Cooking their food, cleaning their little behinds . . . ."

"Uh huh! And don't forget about all those dirty diapers I changed!" Ms. Geraldine teased.

"Now, you getting them ready for school in the morning, when you have to get ready for work yourself."

"Effie Mae, me taking care of those children means just as much to me as it does to them." She again squeezed Effie Mae's hand. "I know I haven't said it before, but those children give me a reason to get up in the morning." She hugged Effie Mae. "Thank you."

...

J.R. continued his search for Lil' J.R. He looked in the bathroom. "I'm gon find you Lil' J.R." He walked through the dining room then noticed the closed bedroom door. Remembering that it usually remained open during the day, he crept over and quietly turned the knob then entered. He observed Lil' J.R. sitting on the floor flipping through the pages of Effie Mae's old red diary. "Lil' J.R., boy you in here playing with your Momma's old red book? It's a good thing you can't read. Effie Mae would have a fit if she caught anybody looking in that old thing." He removed the diary from Lil' J.R.'s hands. His curiosity suddenly peaked.

J.R. always wondered what Effie Mae had been writing in the red book over the years. Despite his interest, he'd never looked inside. He thumbed through the first few pages which merely reflected the words of a ten year old girl. J.R. positioned himself on the bed then sat Lil' J.R. next to him.

"Now you stay right there Lil' J.R., don't move now. Daddy's just gon take a minute to peek inside, and see what your Momma's been writing in this book of hers." He flipped to the back of the diary then paged forward until seeing the beginning of her last entry.

The sound of J.R.'s rapidly beating heart, throbbed in his ears as he read the details of his wife's adulterous affairs with Anthony and Jimmy. His eyes filled with tears and his mouth quickly dried as he continued reading of his wife's detailed betrayal and the possibility that the son he so dearly loved could have been fathered by either man. J.R. lowered himself down onto the floor, cradling in a fetal position. The words of Effie Mae's adultery repeated themselves over and over in his head, as he lay motionless on the bedroom floor and inaudibly wept.

...

"Sounds like J.R. and Lil' J.R. must have played themselves to sleep." Ms. Geraldine said when she no longer heard their playful sounds for several minutes.

"Let me go see about my baby." Effie Mae stood and prepared to enter into the back door. "He probably wet as a *cat caught in the rain*. I know J.R. ain't thought once about changing that boy's diaper."

"You and J.R. need to think about potty training that big boy." Ms. Geraldine said with seriousness. "It's not too early!"

Effie Mae laughed at her suggestion then entered into the house. She walked through the kitchen then stopped when she arrived at the closed bedroom door.

"I guess Ms. Geraldine was right." Effie Mae quietly pushed opened the door then froze when discovering J.R. lying on the floor, curled up next to the bed, quietly sobbing. The old red diary still clutched in his hand.

Lil' J.R. climbed off the bed and walked over to her. He raised his arms, reaching for her to pick him up. Her life seemed to be moving in slow motion as she realized that at that moment, her two worst secrets had been exposed.

"I'm sorry J.R. I didn't mean to hurt you." She said, trying to explain away her deception. He slowly rose from the floor. He threw the red diary onto the bed then brushed past her without acknowledging her presence. He walked in the direction of the dining room. "J.R., please—wait! Let me explain! Please!" He ignored her words as she continued to follow him through the house. Effie Mae grabbed a hold of his arm and tried to stop him. "I love you." She stated in desperation.

J.R. abruptly stopped. He turned and stared into her deceptive eyes. Infuriated by her shallow words, he yanked his arm from her griping fingers then walked away. Effie Mae selfishly tried to shift the blame to him. "Leave! I don't care! Gone, go head on . . . walk out on your family! You never loved me anyway." She yelled. "Preacher!" She said emphasizing his title.

J. R. stopped. He turned and glared angrily into her eyes, but said nothing. He took a final look at the son he once believed to be his own, then continued walking towards the front door. He again stopped. He momentarily gazed at the only woman he'd ever loved. His ferocious stare frightened her. Without saying one word, J.R. turned away. He opened the door and slowly exited, slamming it shut behind him. Ms. Geraldine hurried into the house in response to the loud noise.

"Effie Mae! What was that? I thought I heard the door slam." She asked. "Is everything alright?" She noticed Lil' J.R. sitting on the floor flipping through the pages of the old red diary. "Where's J.R.? Did he leave? Effie Mae what's going on?" Ms. Geraldine remained puzzled by Effie Mae's troubling silence.

Without speaking one word, Effie Mae returned to the bedroom and removed the diary from Lil' J.R.'s hands. She picked him up and carried him over to Ms. Geraldine, placing the toddler into her arms, Effie Mae reentered the bedroom. She slammed the door, locking it behind her.

Ms. Geraldine watched in astonishment, uncertain of what had just happened. Her attention diverted when she heard the laughter of the children still playing outback. Carrying Lil' J.R. in her arms, she reluctantly returned back outside to continue supervising J.R. and Effie Mae's children.

Chapter Nineteen

Ms. Geraldine stood at the kitchen counter writing a small grocery list. Effie Mae sat at the dining room table and waited, periodically adding food items to the list, she determined would be needed.

"Effie Mae, it's been a year since J.R. left. And you still haven't told anybody why."

"Make sure you put milk on that list Ms. Geraldine. These kids drink milk so fast—they must think we own a cow."

"As much as he loved those children, it's got to be something awful bad to make a man just walk away and never look back." Ms. Geraldine glanced over the list then quickly jotted down milk before handing it over. Effie Mae browsed at the narrow slip of paper.

"I don't see eggs on here either." She disregarded Ms. Geraldine's inquiring words.

"I just can't believe that J.R. would walk away from Lil' J.R. Now that's what really doesn't make any sense to me."

"Does it matter why he left Ms. Geraldine?"

"What matters is that these children haven't seen their Daddy in a long time and nobody seems to know why."

"Tell that to him." Effie Mae folded the grocery list and put it in her purse then walked out the front door.

...

Effie Mae carried two brown paper bags filled with groceries, one in each arm as she returned home from the market. Only a few blocks away from the house, she saw Ms. Geraldine in the distance, standing in the middle of the sidewalk, waving her arms frantically. Her fear mounted. Effie Mae increased her speed, alarmed by Ms. Geraldine's odd behavior. As she drew nearer, she noticed the flowing tears that streamed down Ms. Geraldine's face. The grocery bags involuntarily slipped from her arms, milk and eggs splattered onto the concrete pavement.

Effie Mae's feet moved faster and faster down the sidewalk. Her heart pounded loudly and her breaths deepened. She abruptly slowed a few feet away from Ms. Geraldine.

"They're gone! They're gone!! They're gone, Effie Mae!" She cried out.

"Who? Who's gone, Ms. Geraldine?" Effie Mae's stomach filled with knots.

"The children! All of them! They're gone." She said, sobbing. "J.R. came back and took them — all of them. He said he was never going to bring them back!" Ms. Geraldine dropped to her knees and continued weeping. Her words gradually penetrated into Effie Mae's psyche.

"Noooooo!!!!!" Effie Mae screamed. She melted down onto the sidewalk then laid flat on her back.

"Noooooo!!!!" Tears streamed down her face, trickling onto the concrete sidewalk.

Chapter Twenty

Effie Mae sat alone at the table directly in front of the stage at Blue's Jazz Club. Already intoxicated, she poured herself another shot of scotch from the bottle, watered down per Blue's instruction to the bartender. Blue kept watching her as he performed on stage and ran interference when men in search of an intoxicated female to take home for the night, approached her. After he finished his set, Blue retreated from the stage and joined her at the table.

"You doing alright Effie Mae?"

"I'm doing just fine Blue." She slurred, pouring the last remaining drop of scotch into her glass then tossing it into her mouth. Blue watched with compassion.

"You let me know when you're ready to go home. I don't want any of these hounds in here to take you home with them." Effie Mae picked his hand up from the table, and kissed it.

"Do you love me Blue?" She asked. He gazed at her before answering. He wanted to tell her how he felt, but knew he couldn't.

"I wish I didn't." He said underneath his breath.

"Because if you do . . . don't! I ain't worth loving. I never have been. I'm just gon hurt you." Effie Mae picked up the empty bottle." I need me another bottle of this stuff. What is this stuff anyway, Blue?"

"Scotch."

"Yeah . . . Scotch! Will you buy me another bottle of scotch, Blue?"

"Effie Mae, I think you probably already had enough." He took the empty bottle from her hand and subtly placed it underneath the table.

"I bet its lot's of men in here who would love to buy Effie Mae Reed a bottle of scotch!" She yelled as she looked around the club.

"I bet it is, too." Blue said. "But, you don't want to do that. I'll get you another bottle." Blue gained eye contact with the bartender. He nodded, signaling him to bring a bottle of the watered down liquor. The bartender brought the brown bottle over and set it on the table. Effie Mae smiled at Blue.

"Thank you Blue." She placed her hand on the back of his neck and pulled him towards her mouth then kissed him on the lips. Blue took her in his arms and passionately kissed her back then stopped. He felt uneasy, given her drunken state. She picked up the bottle and filled her glass.

"Did you know I use to have a good husband, Blue? That man knew he loved him some Effie Mae!"

"Yeah Effie Mae, I remember you telling me that several months ago when you first started coming in here."

"We had six children." Effie Mae began crying. "Now he can't stand the sight of me. What's wrong with me Blue?" He laid her head onto his chest and comforted her. "Momma always said that I was sick in the head. Looks like she was right, Blue."

"No, Effie Mae. Your Momma was wrong." He kissed her on the forehead. "I've got another set to play then I can take you home."

"I don't want to go home Blue! Ain't nothing there for me! No J.R., not my babies, nobody, but Mr. Daniel and Ms. Geraldine." Effie Mae looked up at him. "Can I go home with you tonight, Blue?" He wiped away her tears with his hand.

"We can talk about it when I'm done playing. You wait right here. Don't go anywhere, okay?"

"If you don't want to take me home, I bet its lot's of men in here that would love to take Effie Mae Reed home with them!" She slurred.

Blue looked around the club. "Okay Effie Mae. If you wait right here until I'm finished, I promise I'll take you home with me again tonight, okay?"

Effie Mae smiled. "I bet I know what we gon do when we get there." She placed her hand behind his head and lowered it towards her mouth then again kissed him. He took her in his arms and romantically kissed her then stopped. She looked into his eyes and smiled. Blue inhaled and slowly exhaled.

"We'll see when we get there. Now I have to get back up on stage. Remember, don't leave here with anybody, okay?" He hurried onto the stage and picked up his saxophone and prepared to play his last set.

"I'm gon be right here waiting for you Blue." She stated, smiling.

Gus walked into the jazz club in search of Effie Mae, having seen her earlier when she'd entered into the establishment. He looked around and spotted her sitting near the stage then approached her. He looked up at

Blue and smirked, then leaned over Effie Mae's shoulder.

"Hey, Effie Mae." She looked up at him."

"You know me?"

"Yeah, I know you." He stroked his goatee with his thumb and index finger.

"How do you know me?"

"I'm a friend of Huck's. Can I sit down here with you?"

"Huck!" She smiled, fondly. "Yeah, sit down, I need some company." He sat in the chair to her right. Blue kept his eye on him as he played.

"That's my man Blue up there playing that horn." Effie Mae said, smiling at Blue. "He's gon take me home with him after he done playing." Gus looked up at Blue. He remembered Huck's warning that Effie Mae was hands off.

"Is that right? Uh, did you need a ride home Effie Mae? Because I can." She cut him off.

"I'm not ready to go home!" She slurred.

"Well, look here . . . ." He looked up at Blue then again at Effie Mae. "Has, uh Blue, taken you home with him before?'

"Lots of times." She smiled.

"Is that right?" He slid his chair close to hers. Blue watched. His anger grew in intensity. The volume of his saxophone grew louder.

"But I always fall asleep. This time I'm gon stay woke."

"Well, you just let me know when you ready to leave because I can—uh, give you a ride." He put his arm around Effie Mae and kissed her on the neck.

"You ready to go Effie Mae?" Blue asked in anger, startling Gus as he stood over him.

"She said she wanted me to take her home, so back off jack!" Gus leaped to his feet.

"Alright Gus, you go ahead and take her home. But before you can start the engine on your car, Huck's gon be on you like white on rice." Gus gazed at Blue.

"You can bet I'm gon be doing a little talking to Huck myself." He turned to Effie Mae. "Goodnight Ms. Effie Mae, maybe another time." He leaned down and kissed her on the cheek then stared momentarily at Blue. He winked at Effie Mae then turned and walked away, exiting the club.

...

At the Envoy Bar & Grill, Huck engaged in a game of poker with Buckeye, Gus and two other gentlemen. He remained silent as he anticipated his next strategic move.

"Give me two." He said to the dealer. Huck picked up the two cards then discarded two.

"Hey Huck, man I heard Effie Mae was in a real bad way." Gus stated as he proceeded to convey his side of the story. "I saw her down at Blue's the other night. Man, she was so drunk! And get this Huck . . . I heard that Blue's been taking her home with him every night!" Huck looked up from his poker hand and directly at Gus. Buckeye intervened.

"That funny Gus because I spoke with Blue this morning and he said you were just in there last night trying to take Effie Mae home with you." Gus glanced at Huck.

"I—I, know that—Blue's a lie, and the truth ain't in him, if he said that!" Gus became nervous. "You tell him to tell that lie to my face."

"For sure—one of y'all lying." Huck said, staring at Gus. "And why am I just now hearing about Effie Mae?" Huck's eyes returned to his poker hand. "Effie Mae is hands off. You know that Gus."

"Yeah, I know that Huck! But, Blue—see . . . . he don't know that!" He rambled. "Now don't it make more sense that he would be the one . . ."

"Gus." Huck interrupted.

"You called me Huck?"

"You the only Gus sitting at this table ain't you?" Gus took a quick drink from the glass of beer in front of him.

"Yep."

"Now, I'm gon say this one time—and one time only. Are you listening?"

"Yeah . . . . I'm listening Huck."

"And that goes for the rest of you. Effie Mae is strictly hands off! Now, is it anybody sitting here at this table, who don't understand that?" Huck looked at each man.

"Naw Huck." The men said in unison.

"Buckeye." Huck threw more chips onto the pile.

"Yeah Huck?"

"I want you down at that Jazz Club every night, until I tell you not to. Is that clear?"

"Yeah."

"Word on the streets is that her husband, the preacher, left her and took all the kids." Gus said then gulped down another swallow of the beer.

"You sure you heard that right, Gus?" Buckeye asked as he upped the ante, adding to the generous pile of black and red chips stacked on the table. "I know how you can get things all turned around."

Huck gave no reply. He remained silent as he anticipated his next move, this one regarding Effie Mae.

"I'm just as sure about that as I am about them buckeyes in your head!" Gus stated. Huck laughed, quietly.

"You better watch your mouth Gus. I know you don't want me telling everybody about you and Ol' long titty Lila! Now do you?" Buckeye teased.

"Long titty Lila! Man, I told you that wasn't me you saw creeping out of that woman's house last Saturday night after her kids had went to bed!"

"Watch out Gus!" Buckeye shouted. Gus nervously jumped.

"Man what's wrong with you?"

"You better watch where you stepping! Man, I heard that those titties were so long, she once tripped over them herself." Buckeye burst into laughter.

"I told you man, that wasn't me! That was somebody that looked like me. Man I ain't been nowhere near that Ol' long titty . . ." Huck cut him off.

"You know where about Effie Mae staying Gus?" His eyes quickly moved from the cards and directly onto Gus.

"All I know is that she staying with some kinfolks. You remember Daniel—got those two kids by Ol' lying, Sadie Ann?" Gus said.

"Yeah man, I heard she got four other men believing those kids are theirs." Buckeye said then shook his head in pity.

"What you gon do Huck?" Gus asked in anticipation of Huck's next move.

"I'm gon pay Ms. Effie Mae a visit . . ." Huck laid his cards on the table and displayed a royal flush. ". . . And real soon."

Chapter Twenty-One

Effie Mae got out of bed and walked through the open bedroom door. She entered into the dining room then went into the bathroom. She relieved herself, flushed the toilet and turned the water on in the sink. She washed her hands, splashed water over her face and looked at herself in the mirror. She picked up the bottle of mouth wash, opened it then drank from the container. She spit the gold colored substance into the sink then returned the cap to the bottle. She grabbed the large white towel that hung on the towel rack and dried her face. She again looked in the mirror then walked away.

Effie Mae entered into the kitchen in search of something to eat. She glanced out the window and saw Huck in the distance. He stood a block away and looked towards the house. She darted from the kitchen and into her bedroom. She grabbed a jacket from the closet, hurrying through the house and out the front door wearing the clothes she'd slept in. Her eyes locked onto Huck as she ran down the streets, rushing into his open arms. Effie Mae cried. Huck held her.

"It's alright girl. Huck's gon take care of you."

"I messed up Huck!"

"Naw, Effie Mae—you didn't mess up. You were just in a life that you shouldn't have been in, in the first place." Effie Mae continued crying. "Come on and get in the car. I can't have you all out here in the streets, crying like that." Huck put his arm around her then walked her to his car parked on the streets. He opened the door and helped her inside. Then walked to the other side and got in. "Come on over here, girl." Effie Mae slid over. "Stop crying." He wiped her tears with his hand. "What's going on with you and Blue?" She looked into his angry eyes, surprised by his question.

"Blue, is my friend." Effie Mae became frightened.

"Uh-uh. You got one friend . . . and that's me." He glared at her. "You messing with Blue, Effie Mae?" She turned and attempted to exit the car. Huck grabbed her by the arm. "Where you think you going?" He hit her in the face with his opened hand.

"Ahhhhhh!" Effie Mae screamed.

"Stop screaming."

"Ahhhhhh!"

"You want me to hit you again? If not, you better stop screaming right now!" She stopped. "Now answer my question." Effie Mae looked at him in fear.

"He wouldn't touch me."

"He wouldn't touch you? Is that what you telling me?" He wrapped her hair around his right hand and pulled it.

"You're hurting me Huck." Effie Mae grimaced with pain.

"Tell me right now, why I shouldn't hit you in the mouth?" He pulled her hair tighter.

"Ahhhhhhh!" Effie Mae hollered out.

"Didn't I tell you to shut up?"

"Yesss!" I was drunk! I was drunk, Huck!"

"Yeah, I knew it had to be something. You'd have to be drunk to mess with Blue's ugly ass." He laughed. "Ain't that right?" Effie Mae remained silent. Huck pulled her hair tighter. "Ain't that right Effie Mae?"

"Yesss!" She cried out.

"But, you know Effie Mae . . . I don't think even that matters with you. Nope. You know why? You nasty Effie Mae." He looked at her in disgust. "You just nasty." He released her hair. Effie Mae looked at him. "You think I don't know why your husband left you?" She fixed her eyes on him and wondered if he really knew. "Daniel?" Huck tilted his head to the side and looked at her. "That your cousin or your husband's? Because if he's your cousin, girl—you need to think about getting yourself some new relatives." He chuckled. "He's out there putting all your business in them streets! "Two men, Effie Mae?" He frowned. Effie Mae looked away and silently stared through the windshield. "I'm curious though. Did you do them both at the same time?" Huck laughed. "Girl, you are nasty! I don't blame your husband for leaving your nasty ass. I would've left you too." He raised his hand as if preparing to hit her. Effie Mae flinched. "That's what your husband should've done. And I almost married you." He laughed to himself. "Girl, if you had done that to me, I would have hurt you Effie Mae. I would have put your ass in the hospital!" He glared at her. "You know what else Daniel said? That from all that nastiness, that you had a son. And you don't even know which man got you pregnant." He momentarily raised his hand. "I ought to hit you again." He shook his head. "Damn shame. But, I tell you one thing I'm grateful for .

. . . ." Effie Mae looked at him as he gave a sigh of relief. "That I never touched your nasty ass!" She abruptly looked away.

"Let me out Huck!" She shouted.

"Oh, you mad Effie Mae?" He laughed. "Ol' Blue's gon be glad to hear that he dodged that bullet." Effie Mae turned to him in response to his words. "Oh, yeah. I'm gon tell Blue." He nodded. "I like Blue. I'm just looking out for him, in case you come at him again." Effie Mae turned away and stared through the windshield.

"Let me out Huck."

"You know what you sound like Effie Mae?' He grasped a hold of her hair and lightly pulled. "You sound like an unpaid whore."

"You hurting me Huck." He released her hair and laughed.

"Girl, if you gon be giving it away like that, you need to be getting paid for it. And I know just the place where you can do that."

"Let me out Huck."

"Oh, you can go. But I'll be back on Friday. I got some work for you." He laughed. "Now get your nasty ass out of my car." Effie Mae slid over, opened the door and began to get out. Huck reached over and squeezed her butt. "You know Effie Mae . . ." He smiled. "One day I just might change my mind about us. You and me—we still have a connection." He laughed to himself. "Kiss me." Effie Mae gazed at him, afraid that he might hit her again. "I ain't gon hit you." Effie Mae slid cautiously over towards him. Huck took a hold of her chin, looked into her eyes then kissed her gently on the lips. "Get on." He watched as she got out of the car and hurried away. He realized that the connection between him and Effie Mae had grown into something that now encompassed his heart.

...

Ms. Geraldine entered through the front door, as she returned home from work. She noticed Effie Mae making her way through the dining room headed towards the kitchen carrying two suitcases.

"Are you going somewhere Effie Mae?" She asked concerned about her state of mind.

"I'm going out here to find my babies!" She shouted, intoxicated.

"Why don't you go back to your room and lay down?" Ms. Geraldine reached towards her to remove the suitcases from her hands. She smelled liquor radiating from her breath.

"Effie Mae, I don't think drinking all that liquor's going to help you with anything." She took a hold of the luggage and guided Effie Mae back into her bedroom. "You go ahead and lie down, get some rest. I'll have Daniel see if he can get a hold of some of their people in Mississippi, to see if any of them have heard from J.R."

"You think he took my babies back home to Mississippi, Ms. Geraldine?" Effie Mae asked as she fell onto the bed.

"I guess that could be possible." Ms. Geraldine stated unaware that her answer could set Effie Mae on the pathway back to Yazoo City. She helped her under the sheets, pulling the plaid blue blanket over her, hoping that she would remain sleep throughout the night.

She closed the curtains to darken the room, then walked out and quietly shut the door.

...

Ms. Geraldine and Daniel convened at the dining room table eating a dinner of meatloaf, collard greens, fried okra, and hot water cornbread.

"Daniel, have you been able to find J.R. and those children yet?" She asked, picking at the scarce amount of food on her plate with her fork.

"J.R. ain't lost." He stated matter-of-factly then wolfed down, half a slice of meatloaf. He washed it down with a swallow of ice tea.

"What do you mean he's not lost? Daniel, do you know where J.R. and those children are?"

"Yep." Daniel mixed his greens, okra and cornbread together using his right hand then began eating with his fingers. Geraldine watched in amazement as he shoved the green pasty looking mixture into his mouth.

"Why am I just now hearing about this, Daniel?"

"You just now asked, Geraldine." He said with full mouth.

"So where is he?"

"I can't tell you that!" He swallowed.

"Well, can you please tell me why he left here in the first place?

"Yep." Daniel continued eating.

"Daniel!"

"I'm eating Geraldine! What you want?"

"Can you stop eating for a minute, so you can tell me what's going on?"

Daniel stopped. He wiped his hands with the white towel lying next to his plate then stared at her.

"Now that I've stopped eating my nice hot food . . . Geraldine, you know I don't like eating cold food!" He said, irritated. "Just what is it that you think you need to know?" He gave her his undivided attention. "You get two questions, so what's your first one?"

"Well, first I need to know what happened, that J.R. left here like that."

"Okay. The boy ain't his." Daniel looked down at his half-eaten plate of food then again to Ms. Geraldine.

"What boy? Lil' J.R.?" Her mouth flung open.

"Yes and yes. Now close your mouth." He said. "And that was three questions." Daniel resumed eating, again using his right hand. Ms. Geraldine watched in silence. Daniel again stopped. He wiped his food covered hands with the towel then gazed at her.

"What, Geraldine?"

"If he's not J.R.'s son, then whose son is he?" She asked with suspicion.

"What? Huh? Naw! Geraldine I ain't even gon think about what you thinking!"

"Well you said he wasn't J.R.'s. The only other man she'd been around was you."

Daniel glared at her in dismay.

"Geraldine? Where was Effie Mae at about a month before she told J.R. she was pregnant?"

"I don't know."

"Think Geraldine!"

Ms. Geraldine thought for approximately two minutes before she remembered.

"I know, she went back home to Mississippi. But she wasn't there long enough to get pregnant. Was she?"

"How long you think it takes for a woman to get pregnant, Geraldine?

"Well I just thought . . . ." Daniel cut her off.

"Stop, thinking! J.R. said when she went home to Mississippi she messed with some old boyfriends. Anthony and, uh . . . . Jimmy."

Ms. Geraldine gasped.

"Jimmy? And Anthony? Daniel, is J.R. sure about that?"

"You think he would've left, if he wasn't?"

"Oh, my goodness! And she named Lil' J.R. after both of those men. She just played poor J.R. for a fool!" Ms. Geraldine looked bewildered.

"She did more than that. Effie Mae damn near destroyed that boy!"

"Oooh, Daniel. Why would she do something like that?"

"Why would anybody do anything like that Geraldine? She low down!" Daniel judged as if he'd forgotten about the two children he'd fathered outside of their marriage. Ms. Geraldine raised an eyebrow and looked at him as a hypocrite.

"Well, uh . . ." He stuttered.

"Close your mouth Daniel."

"J.R. said, Sissy told him that before he married her, every man in the county had—had her. But I knew it. I kept telling J.R . . . it was something wrong with that girl. Good looking woman like that, marrying J.R."

"Uh-huh." Ms. Geraldine gaped at him.

"Well, uh . . . ."

"Close your mouth Daniel."

"Anyway, I told him! Don't trust anything Sissy or Rev. Otis T. Hill said about that girl. I told him Geraldine. Boy didn't want to listen—now look!"

"And, Sissy's J.R.'s sister! Daniel, why would she set her baby brother up with a girl like that?" She shook her head. "Shame on Sissy." Daniel looked at her with a silent stare.

"What?" She asked.

"Can I finish eating now?"

"Don't let me stop you." Daniel shook his head then used his fork to quickly toss a piece of meatloaf into his mouth. He stopped chewing. His face displayed a looked of frustration.

"What's wrong?" She asked as if she didn't know the answer.

"Now what you think is wrong, Geraldine?"

"It's cold?"

"You know damn well it's cold! Now it's gon have to be heated." Daniel shoved his plate across the table to her. She picked up the plate of lukewarm food and went into the kitchen.

"Geraldine, don't burn it!" He yelled.

"Uh-huh."

"Now, what's that supposed to mean Geraldine? Oh boy. I guess now I'm in trouble for saying Effie Mae was a good looking woman?"

Ms. Geraldine came out of the kitchen with the plate of food and placed it back onto the table. She slid it over to him. Daniel looked at the food and then to her. He took a swallow of his tea. The ice cubes, now chips, floated in the glass. He took a final look at his defiant wife, and then with his right hand, he mixed the cold food with his fingers and resumed eating. Ms. Geraldine stood over the table and watched.

Chapter Twenty-Two

The next morning, Effie Mae boarded the train after she'd convinced Ms. Ida to drive her to the train station, before Ms. Geraldine and Daniel returned home from work.

In Yazoo City, Millie and Pete waited and watched as the inbound locomotive rolled into the station. The train doors opened and Effie Mae stepped out onto the concrete pavement. Millie and Pete rushed over when they observed her intoxicated state. Effie Mae collapsed in Millie's arms as she approached. Pete picked her up and carried her to his truck parked out front. Shaken, neither, he or Millie said one word during the entire ride home as the aroma of alcohol fragranced the inside of Pete's truck. Effie Mae rested her head on Millie's shoulder, passed out drunk.

...

Millie watched Effie Mae as she lay sleeping in bed. She blamed herself for her daughter's consequential behavior. She clearly understood what Effie Mae had experienced, since she too had been molested by a family member as a child. And like her own mother, who believed soap and water would simply wash away the shame and guilt, Millie looked the other way. She allowed Effie Mae to suffer through the dehumanizing trauma in her own way. She hoped that like her, marriage would dismiss the demons that haunted.

"Effie Mae." Millie whispered as she attempted to awaken her. Effie Mae rolled onto her back and gradually opened her eyes, uncertain of her whereabouts.

"Momma . . . is that you?" She slurred, reaping of alcohol. "When did you get to New York?"

"Child, where's J.R.?" Millie asked greatly disturbed. Effie Mae laughed.

"He left me Momma! And he took my babies—all of them. You were right, Momma!"

"What do you mean he left you? And right about what?"

"You told me Momma!"

"Told you what? What's going on Effie Mae? And why do you smell like you fell inside of a whiskey still?"

"Did you know Momma, that my baby boy might belong to my husband" She paused. "Or Anthony or Jimmy?" Millie gasped as she looked in astonishment. Effie Mae sat up in bed and cried through dry eyes. "I need me something to drink. What you got around here to drink Momma?" She slurred. "Blue always buys me scotch. But I'll take whatever you got." Effie Mae got out of the bed and staggered through the hallway and living room then into the kitchen. She plopped down in a chair at the table.

"Blue? Effie Mae, what've you done, child? And who is Blue? Where your husband at?

"And if I'm good, he's gon take me home and let me stay all night with him." Effie Mae smiled, as she delighted at the thought. Millie looked around in response to her words. She hoped that Annie Mae's children had not heard their drunken Auntie.

"Stop it! Stop talking like that!" Millie yelled." Annie Mae! Come in here. I want you to call Sissy Hill right now! And see if she knows what's going on with my daughter!" Effie Mae held her finger to her lips.

"Shhhhhhh. Don't tell Huck. He'll put me in the hospital if he finds out. So, me and Blue, we just keep it as our secret. Huck's gon put Blue in the hospital too." Millie's mouth flung open as Annie Mae hurried into the kitchen.

"Where's your children Annie Mae? I don't want them to see this mess!"

"Pete took them over to Ms. Fannie Mae's right after he carried my drunken big sister into the house and put her in bed." She looked at Effie Mae in anger. "Momma, do you know that Pete told me that Effie Mae kissed him on the neck, then pulled him down on top of her, and tried to mess with him.

"Your sister's drunk Annie Mae!"

"That doesn't give her the right to try to mess with my husband!"

"Child, you ain't got nothing to worry about! You know Pete ain't gon touch your sister."

"Still Momma!" Millie looked at Annie Mae and shook her head then chuckled. "That ain't funny Momma. Well, when she sobers up, I owe her a butt whooping—kissing on Pete." Annie Mae picked the phone up from off the kitchen counter and called Sissy Hill. "How are you doing Ms. Sissy? Momma wants to speak to you about Effie Mae." Annie Mae looked at the phone." Momma this woman done hung up!"

"Give me that phone!" Millie snatched the phone from Annie Mae's hand then called Sissy back. "This is Millie Reed, and you better not hang up on me! 'Cause if you do, I'm gon bring your brother's drunken wife down there and leave her. Let you and Rev. Hill listen to all that mess coming out of her mouth."

...

Effie Mae awakened in Millie's bed the next morning to the aroma of a homemade southern breakfast. She entered into the kitchen and stood at the large round table surrounded by several wooden chairs of various styles.

"Morning Effie Mae—you rest well, child?" Millie asked as she flipped over a thick round slice of ham in a black skillet.

"Morning, Momma. All I dreamed about was my babies." Effie Mae walked over to the refrigerator and took out a bottle of orange juice and sat it on the table. She went over to the cupboard, and retrieved a glass filling it with juice.

Annie Mae entered into the kitchen carrying three year old Lil' Effie Mae on her hip. She sat down at the table as her children entered one-by-one and were seated. Millie placed a plate of scrambled eggs, buttered grits, ham, sausage gravy and biscuits in front of them each. Annie Mae sat gawking at Effie Mae without saying a word.

"Morning, Annie Mae." Effie Mae said. "Where's Pete?"

"Don't be asking me about my husband. Pete told me how you tried to mess with him yesterday!" Annie Mae loudly stated.

"I was just playing with Pete." Effie Mae chuckled.

"Once a slut always a slut!" Annie Mae shouted.

"Annie Mae! You got children in here!" Millie yelled.

"Let her talk Momma. If I had wanted to be with Pete . . . ." Effie Mae took a sip from the glass of orange juice then turned to Annie Mae. ". . . he would've never made it to your bed last night, little girl." Annie Mae leaped up from her chair still holding her toddler daughter in her arms. Millie seized the iron skillet from the stove.

"Stop it! Stop it!" She shouted. "Or I'm gon take this pan and knock both of you into the next year! Annie Mae, get your children out of here!"

"They ain't done eating yet, Momma."

"They can take it with them! Gone! Get out of here!" Millie shouted. Annie Mae glared at Effie Mae then rolled her eyes. Millie watched as the children took their plates from the table being escorted by Annie Mae from the kitchen through the living room then disappeared down the hallway. Millie again turned her attention to Effie Mae.

"She started it Momma. All I said was . . . morning, Annie Mae." Effie Mae said, maintaining eye contact with her angry Momma. She picked the glass of juice up from the table and took another swallow. "I can't drink this stuff." She frowned. "I need me something stronger than this. You got any scotch Momma?"

"What happened to you, child? Look like since you got married only thing you done, is gotten worse." Millie gazed at her in wonder.

"Well, you said it Momma. You told me that I was sick in the head. You remember that Momma? Now you know how people that's sick in the head, act." Effie Mae shed a single tear. "You satisfied Momma, because it looks like you spoke this one into existence." She walked over to the sink and dropped the glass of orange juice inside, breaking it. "Oh, Momma can I use your phone to call long distance? I need to call New York. Blue told me to call him when I got here." Millie gave no reply. "I guess not." Effie Mae humped her shoulders then exited through the screened back door allowing it to slam shut behind her. Millie watched in anguish as Effie Mae proceeded down the dirt road, still wearing the clothes she'd arrived in—yesterday.

...

Millie instructed Pete to take Annie Mae over to his Momma's house, joining her children. She feared another altercation like the one that morning would again ensue. Alone in the house, she sat at the kitchen table picking turnip greens for dinner. When she rose to retrieve a large pot from the cupboard, she noticed an unfamiliar man standing at the front door. He looked through the screen, attempting to get her attention. Millie walked over to the door, curious of his reason for being there. She looked out and wondered if he were a salesman.

"What you selling? It seems like every time I look up, somebody at that door trying to sell me something."

"Uh, no Ma'am, I'm not selling anything. I'm looking for Effie Mae."

"Effie Mae? Who are you?"

"Uh, my name is Blue." He paused. "I mean, Tyrell." Millie looked at him with peculiarity. "Uh, Effie Mae told me to meet her down here.

"Well, Effie Mae ain't here right now. But, I guess it would be alright for you to wait inside. I can't say when she gon be back though." Millie opened the door and let him in.

"Thank you Ms . . . . ."

"Reed . . . Millie Reed. And I'm Effie Mae's Momma." Millie returned to the kitchen. "Come on in Blue and have a seat, so you can tell me what's going on with my daughter." Millie opened the refrigerator. "Can I get you something to drink? Scotch?" She peered at him. "Effie Mae mentioned you. She said something about you being the one that's been giving her all that scotch." Blue looked like a child about to be scolded.

...

Effie Mae walked down the dirt road headed in the direction of the Parker's family farm. She contemplated as to whether she would tell Jimmy of the possibility that he may have fathered her three year old son. She stopped when she heard the sound of a horn.

"Effie Mae—is that you?" A voice called out. She turned around.

"Hey Jimmy." She smiled.

"Girl, when did you get here . . . and where you on your way to?"

"To see you."

"See me? Well you looking at me." He chuckled.

"This is serious Jimmy. I need to talk to you about something"

"Get in, let's talk." Jimmy reached over and opened the door. Effie Mae climbed inside. He slowly proceeded down the road.

"You remember the last time I was here?" He smiled.

"After I tell you what I'm about to say. You may not be smiling."

"I guess this is serious."

"Three years ago I had a baby boy." His smile slowly faded.

"I'm listening." He gazed at her in silence, lost for words.

"You ain't gon say nothing?"

"Wow. I guess I ain't sure what to say."

"You can ask me who I think my boy's Daddy is."

"Okay . . . who's the Daddy of your boy Effie Mae?" He joked.

"You! My baby boy Jimmy Anthony Rae . . . is your son Jimmy."

"What make you say that? Ain't you got a husband?"

"When I count up the months, it goes back to when we were together. And besides, when I look at Lil' Jimmy, that boy look more like you in the dark, than he ever could J.R. in broad daylight." She laughed.

"Jimmy Anthony Rae? You name your boy Jimmy—after me, Effie Mae?"

"Somehow I knew that boy was yours, so naming him after you was the right thing to do."

"Lil' Jimmy. Wow! Tell me about my boy. Is he like his Daddy?"

Effie Mae stared through the windshield. A tear rolled down her cheek.

"I need something to drink."

"Drink? Like what? Coke? Pepsi?"
"Scotch."
"Scotch? When you start drinking liquor, Effie Mae?"
"Since Blue started buying it for me."
"Blue? Who is Blue?"
"Blue is my special friend." She smiled.
"Do J.R. know about your special friend, Blue?"
"J. R." Effie Mae laughed to herself. "J.R. left me Jimmy."
"What? Left you?"
"Yep. He took all my babies too. I haven't seen them in over a year. When he found out that my son might be yours, he left."
"Who told him . . . Sissy?"
"Right now, how he found out don't matter."
"Yeah it do—if that man plan to come looking for me, like Jed Russell looked for my Daddy!"
"I think J.R.'s already done whatever he was gon do." She paused. "Now, you gon take me to go, get something to drink or what?"
"I can't do that Effie Mae. Drinking scotch ain't gon get your kids back. And it sure ain't gon change what's done happened. So you need to tell Blue to stop buying it for you."
"Let me out!" She yelled.
"What?" Let me take you back to Ms. Millie's."
"I ain't ready to go back to Momma's." She shouted then looked at him and smiled. She scooted over towards him. Her eyes invited him to a kiss. Jimmy put his arm around her and complied. "Let's go to the Cozi-T." She said.
"You sure?" He asked, puzzled.

"Yeah, I'm sure." They kissed again. "But first, I'm gon need something to drink." Jimmy released her.

"You think I'd touch you like that?" He stared at her then shook his head. "I knew I should've married you back when Pete married your sister—listening at Daddy . . ." He laughed half-heartedly. "He just couldn't let it go." Jimmy gazed into Effie Mae's eyes then softly kissed her on the lips. "I know one thing . . . I could've done a better job of taking care of you than J.R." Effie Mae listened. "He left you because of one stray child." He shook his head in disagreement. "You seen all them women and their kids—Daddy's kids, at his funeral. When Momma said, till death do us part, she meant that Effie Mae."

Jimmy laid her head onto his chest then put his arm around her. Effie Mae looked up at him. They kissed. A car pulled up from the rear and blew its horn. Jimmy looked into his rearview mirror and saw Kenny, an old friend.

"Hey, that looks like Kenny. I ain't seen him in . . . you remember Kenny don't you Effie Mae?" Jimmy said, excitedly.

"Yeah, I remember Kenny. He owes Momma a sheet." She laughed. Kenny positioned his car parallel to Jimmy's truck and coasted beside him. He peeked over from the driver's side.

"Hey Jimmy! What you up to man?"

"Hi Kenny!" Effie Mae looked past Jimmy's head and over at Kenny.

"Effie Mae, is that you? Girl I ain't seen you since . . ." Effie Mae cut him off.

"Boy, you owe my Momma a sheet!" He chuckled. Effie Mae noticed the case of beer on Kenny's back seat.

"I'm gon ride with Kenny, Jimmy." Jimmy's eyes shifted to Kenny's back seat, and the beer.

"Come on now Effie Mae. Let me take you home."

"Hey Kenny!" She hollered. "I'm gon ride with you!"

"Let me take you home Effie Mae." Jimmy pleaded.

"You just go home and see about you wife, Rosetta. Don't worry about Effie Mae Reed." She took his arm from around her then stared into his eyes, her own showing no emotion. Jimmy gazed at her then shook his head.

"If you need me for anything Effie Mae, you call me. I don't care what time it is. You hear me?" He stopped the truck.

"Right." Effie Mae dismissed his words. "Bye, Jimmy." She slid over and opened the door then hopped out. Jimmy watched as she got into the car with Kenny. "Take me to get some scotch, Kenny." Effie Mae looked at Jimmy momentarily then Kenny sped off.

...

Millie and Blue sat on the front porch, their dessert bowls filled with Millie's peach cobbler.

"Ms. Reed, thank you for the dinner. Everything was delicious and this peach cobbler." He paused. "The last time I had peach cobbler this good, my grandmother made it."

"Thank you Blue. I'm glad you enjoyed it."

"Can Effie Mae cook like that?" He asked. Millie hesitated before answering. She thought briefly of Effie Mae's personality prior to her radical change.

"Oh, yeah, Effie Mae's an excellent cook" She stated, proudly.

"Just what every man wants, a wife that can cook." Blue chuckled. Millie gave no reply.

She suddenly noticed headlights coming down the dark road heading in the direction of the house.

"Maybe that's Effie Mae coming now." Millie tried to recognize the car. "That car, don't look familiar. But Effie Mae was raised down here, so she could've got a ride from anybody." The car pulled into the driveway and the passenger's door swung open. Effie Mae climbed out and stumbled as she closed it. Kenny backed out of the driveway and sped away.

"Thanks, Kenny." She slurred. Blue hurried from the porch then rushed over to her. He put his arm around her and prepared to escort her onto the porch.

"Hey Blue!" Effie Mae stopped and embraced him then kissed him on the lips. "I'm so glad you came." She smiled then noticed Millie sitting on the porch. "See, Momma. I told you that Blue loves me. Don't you, Blue?" She kissed him again.

"You know I do Baby girl, always." He said. Millie looked at Effie Mae and shook her head in shame.

"Don't bring her in my house. She done caused enough trouble for today!" Blue looked in wonder puzzled by Millie's refusal to allow Effie Mae to enter into her home.

"Where, uh . . ." Millie interrupted him.

"There's a motel down the way called the Cozi-T. Effie Mae can tell you exactly how to get to it. She's been there enough times." Millie stood abruptly to her feet. She entered into the house, slamming the door behind her. Minutes later the door opened. Blue watched as Millie brought Effie Mae's suitcases out onto the porch, then went back in and again slammed the door.

...

At the Cozi-T, Blue lay next to Effie Mae in bed as she lay sleeping.

"Wake up Effie Mae" He pulled the covers from over head.

"I don't want to wake up, for what?" She rolled over onto her back and opened her eyes. She saw Blue sitting up in bed looking at her. She smiled.

"You know your Momma threw us out last night—right?" He chuckled.

"My Momma hates me Blue. I should've warned you."

"Warned me, about what? What did you . . ." He stopped.

"What did I do? Is that what you were gon say Blue?" He remained silent.

"It's something wrong with me Blue. Ever since I was sixteen, I just been different." Effie Mae stared at him.

"What happened when you were sixteen?"

"Hold me Blue." She said, frightened. He lay back down and pulled her into his arms then rested her head onto his chest. He kissed her gently on the lips. "You love me Blue?"

"With all my heart Baby girl— you know that." He kissed her again.

"Promise me that you won't ever leave me Blue, no matter what." He stared at her through curious eyes.

"I'll never leave you Effie Mae." He again kissed her.

"When I was sixteen, my daddy's cousin David, his wife Helen and their boy Willie Lee came here for a visit." Effie Mae stared into nothingness. "It started when David messed with me in his car. He told me if I said anything, he would take me away from Momma. So, I didn't." Her eyes watered. "Because I didn't tell, he told Willie Lee that I could keep a secret. So, Willie Lee came to me in the outhouse." Effie Mae tensed up. "It felt like fire in me Blue. It hurt so bad, I thought I was gon die." Tears streamed down her face as she relived the horror. "Then it was David's turn. He told Momma, he was taking me and Willie Lee for ice cream." She halfheartedly laughed. "He drove way out somewhere then pulled off the road. He made Willie Lee, get out the car and walk away." Effie Mae shook her head. "Then he told me to get in the back seat." She stiffened. "He got in and lay on top of me. But, he didn't hurt me like Willie Lee." She paused. "It was then . . . something changed in me Blue." She looked at him. "It was like my body wasn't mines no more." Effie Mae silently wept then suddenly stopped. "I been with so many men Blue, I don't even remember all of them." She paused. "And it seems that with every man, Effie Mae Reed lost a part of herself." She gazed into his eyes, trying to read his thoughts. "Do you know what it's like to feel nothing on the inside Blue?" She looked away. "It ain't nothing in me, Blue." She closed her eyes and wept. Blue held her. "Why didn't I tell, Blue? Why didn't I tell Momma?"

Chapter Twenty-Three

Effie Mae stood next to the bed in the bedroom she now shared with Blue since their return to New York City. She watched as he got dressed, preparing to go downstairs to the Jazz Club before it opened. She strolled over and wrapped her arms around his neck, kissing him. He subtly pushed her away.

"I, uh—got to go downstairs and get ready to open the club. And, I need to get in a little practice time too." Effie Mae began unbuttoning his shirt. He moved her hands away and re-buttoned it. "Baby girl, I told you, I got to go." Effie Mae stared at him momentarily then walked away. She went over to the closet and opened the door.

"You know Blue you haven't touched me since we got back from Mississippi . . . three weeks ago. Before that, you couldn't keep your hands off me."

"I guess that long ride back from Mississippi, got me kind of tired." He avoided eye contact as he walked towards the door to leave.

"Being tired never stopped you before." Feeling rejected, Effie Mae gazed at him as he prepared to walk out. "Am I nasty to you too, Blue?" Blue turned around. "You know that's what Huck said." She half-heartedly laughed to herself. "By the time, you was with me Blue, the damage had already been done. Does knowing it somehow make me different?" Effie Mae reached inside the closet and took out a suitcase. "I'm gon save you the trouble of putting me out." Blue watched as she walked over to the bed and laid her luggage on top then opened it. He rushed over and took a hold of her hands.

"What you doing?"

"I'm leaving Blue. You ain't no different than any other man."

"I love you Effie Mae." He embraced her.

"Love?" She laughed. "Why is it Blue that every time a man tells me that he loves me, he leaves me?" Effie Mae broke free from his hold and walked over to the dresser. She opened the top drawer and began taking out her clothes and tossing them onto the bed.

Blue gathered them up, putting them back inside the drawer. He wrapped Effie Mae's arms around his neck and kissed her on her lips.

"Put the suitcases back Baby girl. Please . . . don't leave me." He took a hold of her hands and walked her over to the bed then pushed the suitcase off onto the floor. She gazed into his eyes as he lowered her down onto the bed and passionately kissed her. "You want me to touch you Baby girl? I'll touch you." He continued to kiss her. "I love you Effie Mae. I'll touch you." He began unbuttoning his shirt.

...

Gus rushed into the Envoy Bar and Grill. He burst through the doors of the back room where Huck engaged in a game of poker with four other gentlemen.

Down to his last two chips, He looked away from his cards, startled by Gus' entrance.

"Hey Huck!" She's looking for you! She wants you! She's . . ." Huck cut him off.

"Slow down Gus." He laid his cards on the table then covered them with his right hand. "You know, you interrupted me just as I was about to take these gentlemen's money, right?" Whatever you want, it better be worth it." The other players gazed at Huck's hidden cards in wonder.

"She's looking for you Huck." Gus repeated.

"I'm listening, whenever you ready to tell me who *she* is."

"Effie Mae! She's looking for you Huck."

"Why is she looking for me Gus?"

"You want me to find out?"

"Gus. Why is Effie Mae looking for me?" Gus looked puzzled. "Do you know where I am Gus?"

"Yeah."

"So, I'll ask you one more time. Why is Effie Mae looking for me?"

Gus glared at him, confused by his repeated question. He pondered for a minute then smiled.

"You want me to bring her to you?"

"Is that a question I even need to answer, Gus?"

"I'll go and get her right now." Gus turned away and exited the room, leaving the door opened.

"Gus!" Huck called out.

"Yeah, Huck?" He turned and looked into Huck's eyes. Then as if reading his mind, Gus closed the door.

...

Gus returned thirty minutes later. He entered into the bar, Effie Mae followed him.

"Hey Huck!" He called out, his eyes squarely focused on Effie Mae. "It looks like you got a visitor!"

The back door swung open. Huck stood in the entranceway, exquisitely dressed. He looked at Effie Mae and smiled.

"I see you finally got tired of playing house with Blue." Effie Mae looked surprised. "You didn't think I knew about that?" Huck titled his head. "Effie Mae, I make it my business to know everything you do, even your little trip to Mississippi." Her eyes widened. "You and Blue." She remained speechless. Huck smiled. "Come on over here girl and give me a hug." Effie Mae walked into his open arms and hugged him. "When are you gon learn, that what you looking for, you ain't gon find in nobody else but me?" He looked at Gus and winked. Huck ended their embrace. "I heard you were looking for me. What you want Effie Mae?"

"I don't have nobody Huck. Blue, he . . ." Huck cut her off.

"You don't need Blue. What you need him for when you got me?" He motioned to his fellow players, instructing him to leave and allow him and Effie Mae some privacy. Huck closed the door as the gentlemen cleared the room and he and Effie Mae sat down.

"You hurt me girl. When I heard about you and Blue . . ." Effie Mae stood and prepared to flee. "Sit your ass down, Effie Mae." She complied without resistance. "I'm not gon hit you . . . I should." He glared at her. "I told you to stay your ass away from Blue, didn't I? Then I hear about you living with him." He laughed to himself. "Now, look where you at." He hesitated. "Well, if you want something from Huck, you gon have to play by

Huck's rules now." Effie Mae listened quietly. "And if you can't do that . . ." He stared at her. " . . . Blue can have your ass." Huck reached inside his right shirt pocket. He took out a small piece of white paper and handed it to her. "Here, take this." Effie Mae took the paper and awaited an explanation of its purpose. "Now here's what I want you to do." He explained. "When you walk out of the front door, turn right. Go two blocks down and take a left. Turn at that second block. Walk three more blocks and take a right at that first block."

Effie Mae listened, confused by his twist and turn instructions. Huck continued. "It's gon be that big red brick house on the corner—the one on the left hand side of the streets. I want you to go inside and keep straight down that long hallway. Don't turn to the left or to the right—just keep straight." He stated. "It'll be the fourth door to your right. Once you get there, knock twice, wait for about thirty second then knock twice again." Effie Mae nodded her head, still baffled. "The lady answering the door, name's Libby. Now if you can't remember what I just said, that piece of paper I gave you, has all that information written down on it, including Libby's name. Effie Mae looked at the paper. "Now when you speak to her, let her know that Huck sent you. And she'll take it from there. She's good people. And I know she'll take real good care of you." He concluded with a wink of his right eye. "Now this will get you a place to stay."

"I'm grateful to you Huck." She said.

"Kiss me." Effie Mae stood and walked over to him. He sat her down onto his lap, enclosed her in his arms and passionately kissed her. "I'll come and see you." He gently kissed her on the lips again and stared into her eyes. "Get on." Effie Mae smiled then got up. She opened the door and walked through the establishment to the front entrance then exited.

Gus hurried into the room. Through his eavesdropping, he'd heard the entire conversation. He grinned then winked at his old friend's new found fortune.

...

Effie Mae walked aimlessly around the neighborhood. She tried to follow the directions on the written piece of paper, challenged by Huck's verbal instructions. When not finding it, she ended her search and decided to return to the Envoy Bar & Grill. She wandered around another corner and saw the brick house Huck described.

Effie Mae entered into the mysterious house and attempted to remember Huck's detailed instructions. She walked straight down the long hallway and arrived at the fourth door to her right. She knocked twice, paused then knocked two more times.

Effie Mae glanced around the enormous seemingly vacant, building. She tried to visually count the multitude of closed doors as she waited for the mystery woman to reply to her coded knocks. After five minutes with no results, she turned to walk away. The door slowly opened to a crack. A thirtyish, large busted, dark complexioned woman, wearing bright red lipstick, a large semi-curly black wig, and a cherry red negligee, stood on the other side.

"What you want, honey?" She asked, loudly.

"I'm looking for Libby. Are you her?" Effie Mae asked, alarmed by the woman's attire.

"Who wants to know?"

"My name is Effie Mae . . . ."

"Effie who?" She interrupted.

"I was sent here by Huck to see Libby."

"Huck!" She stated. "Honey, why didn't you say that in the first place? Come on in here and get out of that hallway." Libby ushered Effie Mae inside and looked mystifyingly from left to right then closed the door.

"Sure is pretty! Where did Huck find you?" She looked Effie Mae over.

"Oh, Huck and me, we been friends for a long time."

"Friends! Hah!" Libby laughed out loud. "Honey, Henry Lee White ain't got no friends!" She continued her unflattering remarks of Huck. "Honey with Henry Lee White . . . you only as good as what you can do—for him!"

Effie Mae's ears deafened as she looked around the gaudy red and black efficiency apartment. She observed the room's décor of tasteless bright red and black, shiny curtains; red carpet, and red silk sheets covering the enormous mattress canvassed in the wrought iron canopy bed frame. A large, red velvet sofa with two matching Queen Anne chairs, complimented by a marble coffee table and two matching end tables, occupied the right side of the room. To the left, an oversized vanity piled with several bottles of cheap perfume, a two burner stove, a small refrigerator and a complete kitchen set with three chairs and a table. On the walls were several bulky gold framed mirrors and pictures of different shapes and sizes.

"So you're looking to get started in the business, huh?" Startled by Libby's loud voice, Effie Mae's attention diverted from the room's furnishings and back to the lady of the house.

"I ain't ever really worked before. But my Momma always thought I was good at cooking." Effie Mae stated. Libby looked at her with oddity. She shook her head in disapproval, when she realized Huck had again betrayed a so-called friend.

"Cooking?" She said. "I see Huck's up to his old tricks again." She muttered. "Well around here honey services like cooking—ain't what our customers, pay us for." She chuckled. "You ever heard the word *whore* before? Because honey that's what all the ladies living in this building do. We work around the corner at Ms. Norma's Hospitality Parlor." Effie Mae's mouth opened as she looked at Libby in astonishment.

"Well I ain't no whore!" She stated.

"You think you too good to be a whore or something, Ms. Effie Mae?"

"I sure do. My Momma . . . Ms. Millie Annabelle Reed, didn't raise me or my baby sister to be whores!" She stated, judgmentally. "My Momma would take the skin clean off my hide if she even thought, she heard about me being a whore!"

"Where you from honey? I know it can't be from around here!"

Effie Mae said nothing further. She walked over to the door and opened it then departed from the room. Purposely leaving the door wide open, she headed down the long hallway and in the direction of the front door. Libby watched with both hands propped on her hips as Effie Mae exited the building. "You'll be back!" She hollered. "Honey, if you had to go to Henry Lee White for help, you'll definitely be back!"

Effie Mae wondered aimlessly down the maze of streets. She tried to navigate her way back to the Envoy Bar and Grill by reversing Huck's directions. After several minutes of reading multiple streets signs, and turning various corners, she arrived. Effie Mae turned the doorknob and tried to reenter. She discovered that the door was now locked. After frantically twisting and turning it several time, without success, she waited in the hope that someone would ultimately respond, to her repeated knocks. The blue sky suddenly turned pitch black, flashes of lightning and claps of thunder prevailed.

Effie Mae pounded on the door as the rain poured down and instantly saturated her. Bony-nee mysteriously appeared; He looked out, but said nothing. He stood frozen as he gazed through the rain drenched windows. Huck watched in silence from a table to the right of the entrance.

Bony-nee turned to Huck and awaited his instruction. Huck signaled him with a shake of head—no, denying her admittance. Bony-nee took a final look out the window as Effie Mae stood dripping wet. He reversed the sign inside of the door from "open" to "closed."

Effie Mae continued banging as she watched the forest green window shades being pulled down, one-by-one. Her presence ignored.

"Hey Boney-nee." Huck said, deviously.

"Yes, Mr. Huck?"

"I want you to put the word out . . . Henry Lee White is open for business. And look here Bony-nee; make sure you get the word to Blue first . . . it's Effie Mae." Huck laughed to himself.

Effie Mae turned and ran away when she realized her efforts were pointless. She raced through the puddled streets. Her feet repeatedly splashed over the wet concrete pavement. Returning to the red, brick house, for a second time she arrived at the door of Ms. Libby. She reluctantly raised her hand to knock on the partially opened door.

"It's open Effie Mae." Libby called out from inside. Effie Mae pushed opened the door and again entered.

"You ready now honey?" She asked in a huff. "Just let me put on some traveling clothes then we can go around here to Ms. Norma's. I know she'll probably want you working right away." Libby shook her head in pity as she looked at Effie Mae. Her clothes soaked clean through.

...

Effie Mae and Libby entered into the parlor. They immediately caught the attention of Ms. Norma, a White, fiftyish, southern-bell that exhibited flaming red hair, and emerald green eyes. Her flawless good looks were brought to life by several layers of foundation, face powder, mascara, eye shadow, lashes, and ruby red lipstick, all designed to recreate her once youthful beauty.

Ms. Norma stood to the left of the winding staircase, engaged in naughty pillow talk as it related to a customer. The information being shared by one of her blonde hair, blue eyed girls, displayed in a hot pink, laced negligee. Ms. Norma laughed, cleverly.

"He said what? Oh dear. If only walls could talk." She chuckled. Her eyes locked onto Libby and her unfamiliar companion.

"Ms. Norma!" Libby called as she prepared to introduce Effie Mae. In response to her familiar beckoning call, Ms. Norma prepared to end her conversation.

"If you'll excuse me Olivia dear, it looks like we have company." Ms. Norma politely turned to walk away. She stopped and looked back. "And Olivia dear—please be sure to jot that information down. And, uh . . . don't forget to include that gentleman's name." She laughed half-heartedly.

Ms. Norma had worked in the business during her formative years, but now functioned as the Madam of the house. As a challenge to herself, given the girlish figure she'd, over the years, meticulously preserved, she occasionally competed with her much younger contenders to capture the best paying customers. But these days, found it more advantageous than necessity to entertain the clientele.

"Well now, who do we have here, Libby dear? " She asked, eyeing Effie Mae.

"Look like we got another one from Huck." Libby said. "Her name is Effie Mae."

"Effie Mae?" Ms. Norma's face displayed a bizarre look. "What an odd name. Well it's a good thing our customers don't pay our girl's for their names—now isn't it?" She chuckled. "Hmm . . . If I recall, I think my dear Great, Great, Aunt was named Effie Mae. Oh wait! It was Ella Mae. Or was it Ethyl Mae? I guess at this point it really doesn't matter, rest her dear soul." She concluded. "So you're an acquaintance of our dear friend Huck?" She rhetorically asked as she continued her inspection . . . of Effie Mae. "Pretty! Wet, but still pretty."

Effie Mae stood mute as Ms. Norma walked around her. She carefully scrutinized every inch of Effie Mae's well defined anatomy. "Oh, you'll do really well here dear." She stated, completing her appraisal. "Many of our best paying customers like pretty Colored girls. Why, would you believe, some have even done better than some of our Caucasian, blonde hair, blue eyed girls? Now who would've ever thought that was even possible?" Her eyes remained fixated on Effie Mae, as she literally saw dollar signs. "Libby dear, why don't you be a sweetheart and show dear sweet Effie Mae here . . . upstairs to our makeup and wardrobe room." She said. "Tell Dorothy Jean to dry her up. And, uh . . . give this poor dear—the works, please!"

Ms. Norma politely instructed. She watched as the two women began their journey up the stairs. "And of course she'll have to be seen by Doc, so she can be checked for pregnancy and diseases. Thank you Libby dear." She stated, graciously.

The following evening Ms. Norma and the other ladies greeted their many gentleman callers. They presented with little more than their winning smiles, seductive hugs, and tender kisses. The ladies wore negligees of various styles and colors, revealing their feminine attributes as they awaited both regular as well as new customers, arriving. Ladies new to the establishment customarily waited in the downstairs parlor being selected at random by their overly eager clientele.

Effie Mae remained hidden in a corner of the dimly lit parlor, wearing a passion pink laced negligee. She hoped that amongst the many women, she would not be noticed. She gasped when noticing Ms. Norma escorting a customer, quite fond of Colored girls, in her direction.

"Well J.T., isn't she everything I described?" Ms. Norma watched with a million dollar smile on her face as the gentleman took a hold of Effie Mae's hand. "Effie Mae dear, I'd like you to say hello to one of our dearest and most prestigious customers, Mr. J.T. And lucky you, he's selected you to be his entertainer tonight."

"Good evening, Effie Mae." He greeted, virtually salivating. Effie Mae looked at the three hundred pound, red faced, pot bellied gentleman wearing a thick toupee plastered on top of his head. She swallowed the lump in her throat and wished that she could at that moment, simply disappear. "Hell Norma, I'd be willing to pay double for this whore!" He stated as he lifted Effie Mae from her chair. He retrieved a red and white striped hanky, from his left shirt pocket and wiped the drool from the right corner of his mouth.

"Should I take that as your final offer?" Ms. Norma asked in a negotiating tone.

"Well, what are we waiting for Effie Mae? It looks like you and I have a date!" He clasped her arm, nearly dragging her from the parlor and over to the staircase.

"You be good to J.T. now dear." Ms. Norma urged. "Remember, he's one of our best paying customers." She watched as J.T. pulled a very resistant Effie Mae, up the stairs, then two seemingly disappeared as they reached the top.

They entered into one of the many gaudy bedrooms. Effie Mae watched as he loosened his tie and unbuttoned his shirt then dropped then both onto the floor. She looked away when he unbuckled his pants and stepped out of them. J.T. gazed at her as he stood wearing only a white ribbed tank top with wide straps and red polka-dotted boxers.

"Well Effie Mae . . . looks like it's just you and me." He smiled then walked over and cradled her in his arms, lowering her down onto the bed. Effie Mae struggled as she tried to release his overpowering hold. After several minutes of defensive tackle she broke free and tried to escape. His hands continued to paw and grope at the various parts of her female anatomy. Effie Mae kicked him in the groin then ran from the overstated blue bedroom. She hurried down the stairs and directly into the presence of Ms. Norma.

"And just where on earth do you think you're going?" Ms. Norma snapped.

"I think I made a mistake coming here."

"You do—do you? Well perhaps you may have dear . . . ." She stated with a kind and understanding tone. ". . . . but you're here now. And you have a customer upstairs, who requested your company."

"I ain't . . . ." Effie Mae began. Ms. Norma raised her jewelry covered wrist, and painfully slapped Effie Mae's face.

"Now you're gonna take your little butt back up those stairs and in that room. And you're gonna give J.T. exactly what he's paying for!" She demanded. "Because if you don't, I'll throw your little tail out of here so fast, and out of that nice apartment you're staying in—free of charge!" Ms. Norma stared into Effie Mae's face. "Do I make myself clear, dear?" She asked, softening her southern tone. "Now go!" She shouted, pointing her finger, adorned with several large diamond rings, in the direction of the stairs.

Effie Mae turned around and began her journey up the stairs, step by step until she reached the top. She reentered the room where J.T. lay nestled under the blue silk sheets, wearing only the gluttonous smile on his face. Effie Mae climbed in under the covers, closed her eyes, and lay still, as J.T.'s extremely large physique covered her completely.

...

After several months of entertaining gentleman callers at Ms. Norma's, Effie Mae had accumulated a regular flow of customers. Upstairs, she tidied her assigned room and prepared to receive her first scheduled customer for the evening. She sauntered down the staircase, flaunting a cherry red negligee. She wore a red flower attached to the left side of her head, complimented by the bun hair style she wore, as her skin radiated with an aroma designed for seduction.

Entering into the parlor, in search of her unknown customer, she saw Blue seated in one of the oversized, olive green, Queen Ann chairs. She hurried into the room, surprised to see him there.

"Blue?" Effie Mae approached him. He stood and gazed into her eyes, unable to speak. She hugged him. "How you been doing Blue?" He took her into his arms and passionately kissed her.

"I've missed you Baby girl. I came home that night and you were gone." He continued to hold her. "I'm sorry Effie Mae. I didn't mean to treat you like that—I didn't know how to react after you told me about your past."

"Blue, it's alright! I'm just glad to see you. But, right now, I have a customer scheduled and he should be here any minute now." Effie Mae looked at the gaudy watch on her arm. "If you want to talk, you can come back at midnight. I'll be done for the day." Blue stared into her eyes. "Did you hear me Blue?"

"I paid Ms. Norma for my time with you."

"What? You? You my customer, Blue?" Effie Mae pushed him away. "No!"

"Is there a problem Effie Mae, dear?" Ms. Norma asked when seeing her resistance to a paying customer.

"Uh, no, Ms. Norma, it's just that I . . ." Ms. Norma cut her off.

"Know this gentleman? Yes, dear. I'm well aware of that. But a customer's a customer." She smiled. "Time is money." Effie Mae took a hold of Blue's hand and led him up the staircase. Ms. Norma watched as they disappeared at the top, then put on her warm smile and began greeting the parade of men entering into the establishment. Effie Mae escorted Blue into her personal entertainment room and closed the door.

"Why are you here, Blue?" She whispered.

"Why are you here Effie Mae? He put his hands around her waist. "I've missed you." He kissed her on the neck. She pushed him away.

"Just go Blue! I'll give you back your money."

"It's not money I want, Effie Mae. It's you."

"Not here. Not like this. How am I supposed to be with you Blue?"

"Like, you would any other customer."

"That's just it Blue . . . you ain't like any other customer. We have a history. It wouldn't be the same. It would be personal. My response wouldn't be the same. When we work, our job is to get these men so excited that by the time we actually make contact, it's over. They're satisfied we wash up and move on to the next customer." Blue pulled her close then kissed her. "Blue—don't." Effie Mae again pushed him away.

"Come back to me Effie Mae." He took her into his arms.

"What?" She shook her head, no. "I can't do that Blue." Huck would kill both of us. And if he knew I was working here as a whore . . ."

"Then let's leave." Blue interrupted. "I have family in Pennsylvania. We can go there and start over."

"Blue . . . I got six babies out there somewhere. I want my babies back, Blue!"

"I can help you find them. Then they can come with us."

"Did you hear me Blue? Six! I can't ask you to take on that kind of responsibility."

"I want you Effie Mae. And that means I want whatever comes with you."

"Don't make me do this, Blue." He looked into her pleading eyes then released her.

"You left because you said I didn't want to touch you. Well, I'm here Effie Mae." She looked into his begging eyes, being unsure of what to do.

"Just come to my apartment tonight after I get off work. I'll give you what you paid for there, but not here." He smiled. "You once told me that you loved me Blue, and I know you meant it." Effie Mae wrapped her arm around his neck and passionately kissed him then released him. "I'll see you tonight." She smiled. "Here, let me give you my address." Effie Mae grabbed a Kleenex from the box sitting on the dresser and an ink pen. She wrote the information down and stuffed the tissue inside his shirt pocket. "Now don't blow your nose on that and throw it away." She teased. Blue put his hands around her waist. Effie Mae closed her eyes and wrapped her arms around him then allowed him to romantically kiss her.

Chapter Twenty-Four

A 1967 Gold Cadillac Eldorado Convertible pulled in front of Effie Mae's apartment building. The door opened and Huck stepped out, dressed in a pin stripped, navy blue three piece suite, complimented by a red tie and gold Raleigh Fedora on his head. He walked up the stairs and onto the front porch then entered into the building. He proceeded halfway down the hallway, turned to his left then stopped at the first door to his right. He knocked twice then paused. He waited approximately one minute then again knocked twice. The door opened. Effie Mae stood on the other side. She wore a lime green robe, covering her lime green negligee.

"Huck! She said, delighted to see him. He entered into the apartment then looked mysteriously down the hall before closing the door.

"I see you still looking good." He took her into his arms. "Didn't I tell you that Huck would take care of you?"

"I need you to get me out of here Huck." She said quietly. He glanced around the apartment then smiled.

"You know Effie Mae, I could do that, but then I'd be losing money." Effie Mae pulled away and stared at him. "And besides, I hear that you've earned quite a reputation over at Ms. Norma's." He smiled.

"You know about Ms. Norma?"

"Of course I do. You see me and Ms. Norma . . . we got sort of a partnership."

"Partnership?" Effie Mae said, shocked by his words.

"Yeah, I bring her pretty young girls like you, and whatever she makes from the business well—you might say I'm compensated with a percentage." He looked at her then slightly tilted his head. "But, now I'm shocked! It seems you proved Ol' Huck wrong. Girl, all this time, I thought you were all looks." He laughed to himself.

"And I thought you were my friend." She said, disappointed. "But I guess Libby was right when she said, people are only good for what they can do for you."

"Libby said that?" He chuckled. "Libby needs to learn how to keep her mouth shut. I'm gon have to talk to her about that."

"What you want Huck?"

"Like I said, girl . . . you got quite a reputation over at Ms. Norma's. Gus, I hear he's become one of your regulars." He smiled. "It seems you got him thinking about making you wife number five. And well, you see after a while, a man gets tired of just hearing about it. He might want to come find out for himself." He grabbed Effie Mae by the arm and tried to kiss her.

"You touch me and I'm gon scream, Huck!" She shouted. Huck released her and looked around the room then laughed.

"And just what you thinks' gon happen if you do? Even if somebody did come to your rescue—and I doubt they will, what do you think they gon do, Effie Mae?"

"Ms. Norma don't allow us to entertain customers in our apartments."

"Customer?" He stepped back and looked at her. "Is that what you think I am Effie Mae, a customer? He laughed "Well, I've got news for you girl. I ain't your customer. Heifer, I own your ass! That means I can do whatever I want to you. And if I want to touch you . . ." He smiled. "Then that exactly what I'm gon do." He took off his hat and tie then laid them on the sofa.

"Don't nobody own me!" Effie Mae yelled, closing the lime green robe in an effort to shield herself. Huck again, pulled it open and smiled, as he gazed at his *property*.

"Girl, if I had known then, what I know about you now, hell—I would have made you my woman way back when." He took off his suit jacket and vest, and laid them neatly across the gold Queen Anne chair. Effie Mae began backing away. Huck unbuttoned and removed his shirt. He tossed it over a kitchen chair as he continued moving towards her.

"I thought you were supposed to be my friend, Huck." Effie Mae stated, hoping to detour his advances. He chuckled as he walked towards her and unbuckled his belt.

"I am your friend. Didn't I help you get this nice apartment?' He stepped out of his pants. "And after I'm done with you . . . . . ." He smiled. "Girl, I'm still gon be your friend. And if you live up to your reputation, Effie Mae, Girl . . . I'm gon be your friend at least once a week." He pushed her down onto the bed and climbed on top of her.

An hour later, Effie Mae lay in bed under the sheets. She felt betrayed, as Huck prepared to leave. She watched as he walked towards the door carrying his suit jacket and tie over his shoulder. He stopped at the door, his shirt and vest half buttoned then gazed at her and smiled.

"You try to get some rest before you head over to Ms. Norma's. I want you performing at your best." Effie Mae ignored him. "I guess you mad." She looked at him and rolled her eyes. Huck quietly chuckled. "You mad Effie Mae?" He teased. "Maybe your Momma should've kept your country ass in Mississippi." Effie Mae watched him in anger as he slowly opened the door.

"Oh, and uh—Effie Mae, I'll see you next uh . . . . ." He paused. "I'll be back to check on you tomorrow. He cleared his throat. "And keep Blue's ass out of here. If he want it, let him get it like every other paying customer . . . over at the parlor." Huck strolled out, closing the door behind him, but not before taking one last look at Effie Mae. On his way down the hallway, he encountered Libby as she entered into the building. She noticed his disheveled appearance.

"I know you didn't . . . . ."

"What if I did?"

"Ms. Norma don't allow . . . . ." Huck cut her off.

"That's my property. I do with it what I want. And what business is that of yours, anyway Libby?" She glared at him with uneasiness.

"Huck's business . . . is Huck's business. You remember that Libby. And maybe I'll let you keep working over at Ms. Norma's. Don't forget, Huck owns your ass too." Libby watched as he stepped off the porch and got into his Cadillac then sped off.

...

It's Friday, the day that each lady meets with Ms. Norma at the Hospitality Parlor to receive their wages.

"Effie Mae! Ms. Norma wants to see you honey!" Libby said, hollering into the parlor. "It's payday!" She said as she danced around and counted her money. Effie Mae watched as Libby boogied her way up the stairs then disappeared when reaching the top. Walking in the direction of the north end of the massive home, Effie Mae arrived at Ms. Norma's half opened, office door. She stood momentarily on the other side, as the reality of her employment challenged her southern values. She knocked.

"It's open." Ms. Norma's sang out the words.

"You want to see me Ms. Norma?" Effie Mae entered.

"Yes dear, I do. And, uh—would you please be a dear and close the door? I like to keep these meetings as confidential as possible." Effie Mae shut the door then sat in the large, burgundy, leather chair directly in front of Ms. Norma's extravagant, cherry wood desk.

"Well dear, as you well know . . . today is yet another payday." She began. "I'm not sure if you're aware of how certain things work around here . . ." She stated, staring at Effie Mae. "Many of the girls here work through what we customarily identify as middlemen. And although we truly appreciate their assistance in bringing us some of our best girls, they understand that once she's working here at the parlor, they're strictly hands off for at least six days out of the week." She raised an eyebrow." Huck?"

"It ain't my doing, Ms. Norma . . ." Ms. Norma interrupted.

"Now I know that Huck's a very attractive man, and I can see why you might select him as a man of your choosing, to spend your personal time with. But, it's been reported to me that he's spent the night in your apartment, at least eight days in the past two weeks. And that's totally unacceptable!"

"It ain't my doing Ms. Norma . . ." Ms. Norma again cut her off.

"I've already spoken to Huck." She shook her head. "And that wasn't an easy thing to do." She muttered. "He understands that if this continues, I'll simply have to terminate your services here. Do I make myself clear?"

"Move me Ms. Norma. Put me someplace where Huck can't find me."

"What?"

"I need to be someplace where he can't find me."

"If that's what you want, that can be arranged. But if this continues, I'll have to ask you to leave. Is that clear?"

"Yes, Ms. Norma." Effie Mae's head began to spin. Beads of sweat formed on her forehead as she fought to maintain her conscious state. Ignoring Effie Mae's deteriorating state, Ms. Norma continued.

"It's also been reported to me by some of your regulars, that when they've arrived for their scheduled visits—you were nowhere to be found!" She snapped.

"I'm not feeling well Ms. Norma." Effie Mae's words went unheard.

"Are you drinking again, dear?"

"No . . . I, uh . . . ain't had a drink in—uh, five months Ms. Norma.

"Good! Because I simply will not tolerate that type of behavior! Our customers expect our girls to be disease free, drug free and alcohol free. That's what separates us from those girls on the street corners. And that's what, our customers pay us for!" Ms. Norma took note of Effie Mae's half closed eyes.

"Effie Mae . . . are you alright dear?" She asked as Effie Mae appeared, somewhat woozy. "Are you taking the birth control pills that Doc provides to you ladies? The last thing we need is you getting pregnant." Effie Mae conscious state diminished.

"I'm—uh, on pills—Ms. Norma." She garbled.

"Good! Huck warned me that you were unusually fertile." She stated, glancing at Effie Mae's abdomen. "I believe he said you have nine . . ." She hesitated. "Or was it, ten children?" Ms. Norma talked continuously. Effie Mae's ears deafened to her voice as she began to hallucinate about her absent children. As her reality lessened, she heard their voices calling out to her. "Are you keeping all of your appointments with Doc?" Ms. Norma's voice startled Effie Mae, increasing her alertness. The sound of her children's voices ceased. "We can't have you girls spreading diseases, now can we?" She concluded. "That'll be all dear." She said disregarding Effie Mae's fragile mental condition. She handed Effie Mae two hundred dollars, in tens and twenties. "Oh, and Effie Mae, would you be a dear and tell Amanda I'd like to speak with her, please? And, don't forget to close the door on your way out. Thank you dear." Ms. Norma stated, as she continued sorting through the numerous papers spread out on her desk.

Effie Mae rose slowly from the chair then exited the room . . . closing the door behind her.

Effie Mae laid face down on the bed of her entertainment room and wept. She reminisced on the life she had with J.R. then recalled the look on his face when he learned of her betrayal. She began hallucinating. Again she heard the voices of her children. Effie Mae rose from the bed and followed the voices which led her to a second story window. Believing herself to be seeing her children just below, looking up and beckoning her, she opened the window.

"Lil' J.R., is that you baby?"

Effie Mae gazed down and tried to focus on the unclear face of the son she hadn't seen in over a year. No longer able to distinguish reality from fantasy, she climbed up onto the window sill, thinking herself to merely be walking through an open door. The voices of her children echoed, becoming louder and louder. Effie Mae's eagerness to join them escalated.

"Effie Mae!" A voice called out through her closed door, persistently knocking. Effie Mae continued in her trance-like state. The sound of her children's voices growing louder.

"Effie Mae!" The voice on the other side of the door increased in volume as the knocking turned into pounding.

"I'm coming Momma." Effie Mae replied as she digressed into a childlike state. After several minutes of unanswered banging, the uninvited visitor turned the doorknob and opened the door. Ms. Libby entered into the room. She panicked when seeing Effie Mae as she stood unbalanced on the ridge in front of the opened window.

"Effie Mae!" She screamed. Then rushed over and pulled her down seconds before she toppled from the window. "Effie Mae!" Libby yelled, positioning Effie Mae's arm around her neck then assisting her over the couch.

"Libby. I didn't hear you come in." Effie Mae stated, having no remembrance of her near death experience.

"Are you alright Effie Mae?" Libby asked, nervously. Effie Mae laughed at the question. Libby looked at her with oddity. "Honey, Ms. Norma's downstairs arguing with Ol' crazy Huck, again." Effie Mae looked at her with questioning eyes.

"Yeah, it's about you. Can you believe he's down there trying to convince that woman to let him move in with you?"

"What did Ms. Norma say?" Effie Mae asked, panicked.

"Honey . . . What you think she said? No!"

"Ms. Norma said she's gon move me someplace else."

"Hah! That man is hooked on you like a drug! Ms. Norma could move you out of the country and he would still find you!" She stared into Effie Mae's eyes. Girl—you not gon be able to get away from Huck."

"Then I'm gon leave, Libby." Effie Mae stood to her feet.

"And go where?" Libby stated, loudly." And, don't even think about moving back in with Blue. You know, that's the first place Huck's gon look!"

"Then I'm gon live on the streets . . . if I have to."

"Is that what . . . that was all about?" Libby pointed towards the opened window. "Huck?" She glared at Effie Mae. "I can understand wanting to get away from

Huck, but that? Uh-uh!" She again looked over at the window."You gon jump out the window to get away from a man?"

"Jump out the window? Why would I jump out the window, Libby—when I can just as well, walk out any one of these doors?" Libby looked puzzled by Effie Mae's lapse in memory of her near death plunge.

"Look here Effie Mae, I been talking to a cousin of mines that cleans house. She said they always need help over there. So if you interested, honey . . . all you got to do, is say the word and you can start there tomorrow! Ain't no reason for you to be doing anything like, jumping out of a window." Effie Mae remained silent. She felt hopeless. "Honey, did you just hear what I said?"

"Libby, you said it yourself. It won't matter where I go. Huck's gon always find me."

"I tell you what we gon do." She said, realizing that her persistence would be required. "We gon go down there to Ms. Norma's office and make sure, she moves you out of that apartment—today!" She took a hold of Effie Mae's hand, assisting her up from the couch. "Sometimes honey, you just have to light a fire up under Ms. Norma. Because, when it comes to following through on stuff, Ms. Norma ain't always on top of it!" Libby escorted Effie Mae out of the room and down the stairs, stopping when the two women arrived at the slightly ajar door of Ms. Norma's office. Libby knocked.

"What can I do for you dear ladies?" Ms. Norma asked as she shuffled through the mess of papers still lying on top of her desk.

"We need to talk to you Ms. Norma about Effie Mae's situation with Huck! It seems Huck's got himself an itch, and seems to think that only Effie Mae can scratch it."

"Is that so?" Ms. Norma stated in a matter-of-fact, tone. "Well ladies, in this business we always run the risk of things like that happening. But I tell you what were going to do . . . ."

Chapter Twenty-Five

Effie Mae returned home late Saturday night from the Hospitality Parlor. She stood in the hallway of her new apartment building and prepared to unlock the door. There for only three weeks, she'd heard nothing from Huck.

She glanced around her immediate surroundings then stuck her key inside the lock, anxiously pushing open the door and hurried inside. Effie Mae quickly closed and relocked the door. Nervous, she conducted a quick search of the premises. She walked through the kitchen, the bathroom then looked around her bedroom. Feeling somewhat safe, she began preparing for the evening she'd planned for her and Blue.

Effie Mae opened a dresser drawer and retrieved a purple negligee then went into the bathroom. She removed the clothes she'd worn home from the parlor, took a quick sponge bath then slipped into the lingerie. She reentered the bedroom and took inventory of the various bottles of perfume lined up on her vanity table. Effie Mae picked up a small pink, crystal bottle and prepared to apply the sweet smelling spray to her neck.

The phone rang. Quickly sitting the bottle back down, Effie Mae hurried from the bedroom and into the living room. A large smile formed on her face as she picked up the receiver.

"Hello." She answered, blushing.

"Hey Baby girl." Blue said from the other end of the phone.

"Hey Blue."

"You ready for me to come see you?"

"I'm gon be mad if you don't." She teased.

"What about Huck?"

"What about Huck? He don't own me!"

"He thinks he does."

"Don't nobody own me Blue. Besides, Huck don't even know where I am."

"Effie Mae. Huck would find you if you were lost in the dessert."

"Well, he ain't found me yet."

"If you're okay with it, that's all that matters, I'm not gon let Huck keep me from being with my woman." Effie Mae heard the smile in his voice. "I'm about a block away, but I'm not sure which building it is."

"It's the building, right on the corner—on the left side of the streets. I'm on the third floor. Apartment 3C."

"I'll be there in a minute."

"Okay." Effie Mae said with delight. "I'll see you when you get here." She smiled.

"Hey!"

"Huh?"

"I love you Baby girl."

"I know." Effie Mae grinned. "Bye."

"Bye." Blue hung up.

Effie Mae held the phone momentarily in her hand as she thought about, how this could be a new beginning for her and Blue. She hung it up then hurried into the bedroom and freshened her make-up. She picked up the bottle of perfume and applied three sprays to her neck. Seconds after returning the bottle to the table, Effie Mae heard a knock at the door. She hurried from the bedroom and into the living room. Her excitement grew as she eagerly opened the door.

"That was quick!" She stated, seductively. Standing on the other side stood Huck.

"You expecting somebody Effie Mae?" He smiled then pushed open the door. "I know you didn't think you could get away from me?" Effie Mae tried to run past him, and out the door. "Come back here girl!" Huck caught her by the arm and pulled her back inside then shut the door. He smiled as he gazed at the inviting negligee. "Girl, you look better every time I see you." He said as his eyes raked over her seductive presentation. "I know you ain't bringing customers to your apartment? Didn't I hear you say that Ms. Norma don't allow that?" He slightly tilted his head. Effie Mae remained silent. "So, who's coming to see you Effie Mae?" Blue?" She began backing away, afraid that he might hit her. "Yeah, it's Blue. I followed him over here. He didn't see me though." Huck laughed to himself. "Effie Mae, you still messing with Blue?" He raised his hand. Effie Mae flinched. Huck grabbed her by the arm. "Is he paying for that, Effie Mae? Or are you giving my property away?" He hit her in the face with his open hand and knocked her down onto the floor.

"Ahhhhh! She cried out. "Blue's gon call the police if I don't answer the door!" She yelled.

"Blue won't be calling, nobody!"

"Nooooo!!" Effie Mae shouted.

"Shut up! I didn't kill him. I know you'd shut down if I did that. I need you working." He looked down at her lying on the floor. "Get up." Effie Mae lifted herself slowly from the floor. "Naw, Effie Mae—I didn't even hurt him. I just took my money, for what he was trying to get for free . . . that's all. And because of that, I had to charge a little more interest." He quietly laughed then again took note of Effie Mae's enticing appearance. "Since Blue ain't coming, ain't no point in wasting good talent." He smiled. "Get in the bedroom." Effie Mae turned and walked in the direction of the bedroom. Huck began undressing as he followed her.

"Wake up sleeping beauty." Huck pulled the cover from over her head. Effie Mae rolled onto her back and opened her eyes. She saw him standing over her, dressed in a brown pinstriped three piece suite, complimented by a yellow tie and a white Fedora on his head.

"What time is it?"

"Twelve o'clock—noon. Go fix me something to eat." Huck chuckled. Effie Mae rolled her eyes. He continued laughing. "You still mad at me, Effie Mae?" He teased. "Yeah, well, you be mad. You sneak Blue's ass back up in here, I'm gon give you something to be mad about." Effie Mae stared at him. "Only person getting anything free in here—is me." He laughed. "I got some business I need to take care of today, but I'll be back. So don't do nothing stupid." He leaned down and kissed Effie Mae on the lips then gazed at her with questioning eyes. "Girl, I'm gon have to thank Blue! Is that what being with Blue do for you, Effie Mae? I think

I'm jealous." He laughed to himself then left the bedroom, exiting the apartment through the living room.

Effie Mae wrapped herself in the sheet then hurried into the living room. She looked out the window and saw him standing next to his car. Huck looked up at her, smiling. Effie Mae gave him the middle finger. He laughed then got into his Cadillac and drove off.

Effie Mae rushed back into the bedroom and opened the closet door. She pulled out a suitcase in hopes of getting away before Huck could return. One-by-one, she snatched opened the dressers drawers and began tossing her clothes onto the bed. She filled one suitcase then looked inside the closet for additional bags. She discovered the luggage she'd carried with her, when returning from Mississippi. Effie Mae unzipped the bag and curiously looked inside. She found the old red diary tucked away inside. She removed it then held it in her hand. Her mind returned to the day that J.R. learned of her indiscretion. Effie Mae threw the book back inside the suitcase, without looking inside. She swept the many bottles of perfume off the vanity and into the luggage then re-zipped it. Holding both pieces of luggage in her hands, Effie Mae dashed out the front door, her destination – unknown.

Chapter Twenty-Six

Huck drank scotch in the backroom at the Envoy Bar and Grill. Seated at the table with Buckeye, he drank shot after shot, as he wondered of Effie Mae's whereabouts.

"Man I ain't never seen you like this before!" Buckeye tried to slide the bottle of scotch away. Huck stopped him then picked it up and poured himself another drink.

"Buckeye, if you touch this bottle again, you gon get real familiar with the taste of glass." Huck gulped down the entire shot.

"That's what I'm talking about. Man, its ten o'clock in the morning and you already drunk."

"Why you worried about how much and what time I started drinking? You find Effie Mae, yet?"

"Naw . . . And I've looked everywhere, Huck! I got Libby keeping an eye out, too."

"Libby? You keep Libby out of my business." Huck yelled. "Don't you know, she probably helping Effie Mae?' He paused. "She was jealous anyway." Buckeye glared at Huck, troubled by his current status.

"Then you tell me what you want me to do, Huck?"

"The first thing you can do, is get over to Libby's, and see if Effie Mae's over there. And Buckeye, while you doing that—make sure you send Libby a message. If I find out that she's been helping Effie Mae . . . she'd better get lost out there with her."

"Huck, Libby don't know where . . . ." Huck cut him off.

"Do it! And get your best suit out." Buckeye eyes widened.

"Man, I told you that Libby . . . ." Huck interrupted.

"This ain't about Libby. I'm done with that. This about Blue."

"Blue?" Buckeye looked surprised.

"He's been too quiet. He knows something." Huck stared into Buckeye's eyes. "He's got a real thing for Effie Mae. You remember it wasn't that long ago, that they were over there playing house."

"Yeah, I remember, Huck."

"That man's in love, Buckeye." Huck laughed to himself. "And a man in love can do some crazy things." Huck threw back his head and tossed down another shot. "Yeah, I think it's time we paid Ol' Blue a visit." Buckeye nodded in agreement. "Buckeye!"

"Yeah Huck?"

"When's the last time you seen Gus?"

"I haven't." Buckeye pondered.

"Look here Buckeye, when you leave Libby's, I want you to pay Gus a visit too. Give him the same message you giving to Libby."

"Okay Huck."

"Be up at Blue's tonight at eight. And look here Buckeye—make sure you let Blue know I'm coming." Huck chuckled as he tossed back another shot. Buckeye stood up to leave. He walked towards the open door of the back room.

"Buckeye!"

"Yeah Huck?"

"You don't have her do you?"

"Huh?" Buckeye turned hastily around in response to Huck's off-base accusation.

Huck laughed then waved his hand, gesturing him to go. Buckeye exited the room and departed from the establishment.

"Bony-nee! Come in here . . . I need to ask you something."

...

The music blared from inside Blue's Jazz club. Huck stood out front dressed in a deep burgundy pinstripe three piece suit, a white shirt and off-white tie. On his head, he wore a black Stetson hat, complimented by his black and white leather shoes. Buckeye, dressed similar. The two men entered into the club. Huck stood at the entrance until Blue took note of his presence. Blue continued blowing his saxophone as he performed with his band.

Huck and Buckeye walked over to the center of the room, being seated directly in front of the stage. Huck beckoned Blue's number one man Melvin, a gentleman dressed in a tuxedo, over to his table.

"Tell Blue to be at my table in ten." Melvin nodded then walked over to the platform where Blue and the band played. Blue leaned forward, his saxophone still in his mouth. He looked in Huck's direction, indicating that he'd received the message. Blue shook his head, no. Melvin returned to Huck's table.

"He said he ain't coming."

"Here's what I want you to do, Melvin. I want you to go back up there, and you tell Blue that I said, if he don't get his ass over here and see me, that before he can play his next set, I'm gon have my people come in here, and take this place apart. And, the only place he's gon be blowing that horn—is on a street corner."

Melvin returned. Blue leaned down to receive the message then looked directly at Huck. He spoke in the ear of another saxophone player then propped his horn against the wall, and walked off the stage. He approached Huck's table and stood.

"Go ahead and have yourself a sit down, Blue." Huck said. Blue sat in the chair to Huck's left. He looked at Huck then shifted his eyes to Buckeye then again to Huck. The waitress returned with drinks. She placed them on the table and walked away. Buckeye followed her with his eyes from the table and back over to the bar. He smiled. Huck chuckled as he watched him.

"Ain't that your cousin Deborah Ann, Blue?" Huck asked.

"Yeah."

"You related to Melvin too, ain't you."

"That's my cousin."

"You got the whole family working down here don't you, Blue?" Blue gave no reply. "How you been doing Blue?"

"I'm doing fine Huck."

"I'm looking for a woman. I heard you might know where she is."

"What woman is that, Huck?"

"Don't play stupid with me, Blue. It makes me think that you got something to hide."

"I heard you were looking for Effie Mae, but I haven't seen her Huck."

"You sure about that, Blue?" Huck shifted his eyes to Buckeye then back to Blue. "I tell you what I'm gon do, Blue. I'm gon have Buckeye and a few of his associates, run upstairs to your place and search it . . . tear it apart."

"Search it?" Blue asked, nervous.

"Yeah, you got a problem with that, Blue?"

"Uh, no, I don't have a problem with that. But . . ." Blue hesitated.

"But what Blue?"

"I saw Effie Mae one day last week. Man she looked bad. I heard that she was living on the streets."

"Is that right?" Well you do me a favor Blue, the next time you see Effie Mae—you call me. You understand me, Blue?"

"Yeah, Huck. You might also try over at her kinfolk's house. They might know something."

"Kinfolks? Daniel?" Huck said.

"Yeah, you know Daniel, don't you Huck?" Buckeye said, interrupting. "He's the one that have those kids by Sadie Ann." Huck glanced at him then again turned his attention to Blue.

"Thanks Blue. You just keep on playing that horn." Huck shook Blue's hand then held onto it. "Oh, I—uh, wanted to thank you. That night you tried to get something for nothing, I had to step in and take your place." Huck cleared his throat. "You gon have to tell me Blue . . . what you got that I don't? Effie Mae almost sent me to the hospital." He laughed. Blue snatched his hand away then turned and walked away. He returned to the stage, picked up his saxophone and resumed playing. He stared at Huck in anger.

"Yeah, he know something."

"You think so Huck?"

"When he saw her last week, she said something to him." Huck glared at him with curious eyes. "Buckeye, I want you over at Daniel's house, until I tell you not to."

"Okay Huck."

"Now let's get out of here." The two men swallowed their drinks then stood and walked over to the front door, exiting. Blue gazed at the door.

Chapter Twenty-Seven

"Lord, have mercy!" Effie Mae is that you?" Ms. Geraldine looked in horror when she opened the front door and saw a physically drained, unkempt female. She bore little resemblance to the attractive young woman that once sparkled as an 18 karat Diamond, but looked much like a vagabond. "We've been looking all over this city for you! We didn't know what had happened to you." Ms. Geraldine said as she assisted Effie Mae into the house. Her once rippling black hair now resembled tumbleweed. The radiant complexion that greatly contributed to her grandeur had darkened with smudges of dirt, and her bright hazel brown eyes, dim.

"I just need a place to lay my head, Ms. Geraldine." She stated, somewhat deliriously.

"Lay your head! Effie Mae, are you okay?" Ms. Geraldine couldn't make sense of her statement. "Maybe you ought to let me help you to your room so you can lie down." She lifted Effie Mae's arm and prepared to place it around the back of her neck. She suddenly got a whiff of the nose piercing, body odor, radiating from her. "Maybe I better get you to the bathroom first, so we can get you cleaned up." Ms. Geraldine grimace from the smell.

That night Effie Mae lay in bed asleep. Ms. Geraldine and Daniel congregated outside on the back porch as he prepared to smoke.

"You should have seen her Daniel. She looked like something the cats' drug in." Ms. Geraldine scowled.

"Did she say where she been?" Daniel filled his pipe with tobacco.

"And smelled! I had to take her in the bathroom and wash what looked like, a month's worth of dirt off of her."

"You see there, Geraldine. God don't like ugly!" Daniel struck a wood stemmed match on the bottom of his shoe then ignited his pipe with the flame. "She ain't on that stuff is she? Cause if she is, she gon have to get her butt out of here."

"No. She's not using." Daniel took a puff from the pipe then stared his wife squarely in the face.

"Now how do you know that, Geraldine? You don't know where she been or what she been doing."

"Because Daniel, I checked her arms when I washed her up." A guilty look formed on her face.

"Geraldine!"

"What, Daniel? Like you said, we don't know where she's been or what she's been doing."

"Did you ever check with her Momma in Mississippi?" He asked as he lodged the pipe in his mouth.

"I didn't see any point in worrying her poor Momma. And besides if she'd been down there, I'm sure J.R. would've known."

"So how she been taking care of herself?" They looked to each other with suspicious eyes.

"Daniel! Effie Mae's a married woman. I don't think . . ." He cut her off and removed the smoking pipe from his mouth.

"Stop thinking Geraldine. You ain't doing it right! Since when have Effie Mae being married, ever meant anything? That's what started this whole mess in the first place—now ain't it?"

"But still Daniel . . ."

"Geraldine! Geraldine! I don't know what I'm gon do with you, woman!" Daniel shook his head. "Let's just take a look at this. First, before her Momma and Sissy pushed her off on poor J.R., the girl was the town tramp. Secondly, she got a son around here she had by another man . . . .

"Daniel . . . .

"What? I'm just saying Geraldine! A leopard, don't change its spots!"

"Well, all your saying, is giving me a headache. So please don't say anything more. And besides, that's all water under the bridge."

Daniel took two puffs from the pipe. "Can you say, where she been, and what she been doing, Geraldine?"

"Right now, all I care about is that she's back home safe."

"Home?" Daniel yelled. "I know you don't think she staying in here?" The pipe fell from his hand and down onto the concrete porch. "Noooo! We sending Effie Mae's butt, right back down there to Mississippi with her Momma." Daniel stated, adamantly. "She raised her!"

"Daniel, you don't mean that."

"Yes I do, too!"

"Well, we can talk about it in the morning." Ms. Geraldine rose from her chair and prepared to go inside.

"Naw Geraldine, we gon talk about this tonight . . . and right now!"

"Goodnight Daniel." She opened the back door and went inside.

"Come back here Geraldine!" Daniel leaned over to retrieve the fallen pipe. His chair slipped and he landed on his behind. He looked down at the spilled contents of the pipe, the tobacco still burning.

Awakened from the voices of children, Effie Mae climbed out of bed. She looked around the room then walked over to the window and looked out. She felt grateful to be back home with Daniel and Ms. Geraldine.

Buckeye remained parked out front of the home, in his 1967 red Cadillac Coupe Deville, where he'd been Huck's eyes and ears, for the past 48 hours. He'd witnessed Effie Mae's return home, information he'd already reported to Huck.

Virtually asleep for the past two days, except for her sporadic, semi-alert trips to the bathroom, Effie Mae opened her eyes to the sound of her children's voices. She walked over to the closed bedroom door, opened it and inquisitively peeked out. Her eyes brought into focus the faces of the children that were taken from her, almost two years ago. Effie Mae's heart pounded in her chest. And felt as though it were about to leap from her body. She stood immobilized with joy and fear. On one hand, she doubted that her eyes were actually seeing the children she so longed to see. On the other, she thought, what would she say to them if it were true. Effie Mae burst open the bedroom door and hurried into the living room.

"Are those my babies?" She asked as her eyes moistened with tears. Effie Mae reached out and touched the faces of each of her six children as tears rolled down her cheeks. Wanting desperately to see the son she'd not seen since J.R. took him away. She wiped away her tears. Clearing her vision, Effie Mae gazed into his tiny face. Hoping that he would possess features unique to any of the three men, she saw only his hazel brown eyes. Effie Mae took Lil' J.R. into her arms and kissed his cheeks. He looked at her with unfamiliarity then began to cry. He retreated from her hold and scurried over to Ms. Geraldine.

"That's your Momma, Lil' J.R. Don't you remember her?" She asked. The three and a half year old young child shook his head—no then buried it underneath Ms. Geraldine's arm. Effie Mae's eyes asked the question her mouth was too weak to speak. "He brought them back about three months ago. I guess J.R. realized that these children needed to be with their Momma." She hesitated then stared into Effie Mae's eyes. "He also wanted me to tell you that he was sorry. And that he still loves you." Effie Mae ignored Ms. Geraldine's words, as she continued taking pleasure in the return of her children.

...

Effie Mae awakened to a new day, and to the sound of the children she thought she'd lost forever. She climbed out of bed like a child on Christmas morning. She hurried from her room and entered into the living room. She silently watched in amazement as Ms. Geraldine prepared them for school.

"I still can't believe J.R. brought my babies back." Effie Mae said, smiling, joyously. "If he loved me like he said, he would've never, took them in the first place." She stated, minimizing the role she played in igniting the flame that torched her life.

"Now Effie Mae, if you're going to sit there and start pointing fingers, you'd better point the first one at yourself. Remember it was you—not J.R., who was out there committing adultery." Effie Mae lowered her head in response to hearing the truth.

"Ms. Geraldine, what's adultery?" Five year old Sarah asked, repeating what she'd just heard.

"Hush Sarah." Ms. Geraldine said, before returning her attention back to Effie Mae. "You know . . . J. R. told Sissy and Daniel the reason why he left." She hesitated then shifted her eyes to Sarah. "But that's not something we need to discuss right now." Ms. Geraldine looked at Effie Mae. Her eyes indicated that the subject was not to be discussed in front of the children.

"Now, remember Millie Ann, wait for Ms. Alberta to get Lil' J.R. in the house before you leave." Ms. Geraldine stated as she handed the last lunch box to eleven year old Millie Ann. "Now y'all hurry on before you're late for school."

The children scurried out the front door and down the streets. "You hear me Millie Ann? You remember what happened the last time!" Ms. Geraldine yelled out the front door. She casually took noticed of the red Cadillac parked on the streets, but made no mention of it to Effie Mae. "Ms. Alberta, don't have any business watching children, anyway." Ms. Geraldine said closing the door. "Woman so old . . . she probably babysat Moses." She chuckled as she tied a white apron around the plain, black, short sleeved dress she wore. Effie Mae laughed.

"Now, that's old Ms. Geraldine."

"Ms. Alberta must be close to eighty!" She sighed. "But it's so hard to find a woman who's not already working—cleaning house, cooking or doing some type of work outside the home." She thought for a moment. "And she's cheap!" She and Effie Mae laughed. "Ms. Alberta charges me little to nothing for watching that Ol' hard-headed boy of yours."

Effie Mae virtually glowed as she listened to Ms. Geraldine speak on the dilemmas of motherhood. "If you're looking for work Effie Mae, you know Mrs. Winchester can always use extra help at her place. I can talk to her when I get to work today, and see when she'd like you to start." Ms. Geraldine walked over to the window and peeped out of the kitchen curtain. She noticed the red Cadillac still parked out front. "Now that's strange, they must be waiting for somebody." She said to herself then turned and walked away.

"I guess it's about time for me to start working anyway." Effie Mae said." I don't want you and Mr. Daniel to have to keep taking care of my babies."

"Uh-huh." Ms. Geraldine muttered. "Well if you want to get in some practice working, you can start by washing those breakfast dishes your children dirtied up. That sink is full!" She again peered through the kitchen curtains. The car was now gone. Ms. Geraldine thought nothing more of it. "I'll talk to you when I get back home."

"Bye, Ms. Geraldine."

"Bye, Effie Mae." Ms. Geraldine said, then hurried out the front door and headed in the direction of the bus stop.

The following morning, Ms. Geraldine packed lunches and stuffed extra clothes in the diaper bag that accompanied Lil' J.R. to Ms. Albert's house. Effie Mae stood in the living room, dressed in her black maid's uniform, a proud look plastered across her face.

"How come you dressed like Ms. Geraldine, Momma? Lena asked.

"Now you stop meddling Lena." Ms. Geraldine scolded.

"It's okay Ms. Geraldine. I want my babies to know that their Momma's gon be working." Effie Mae smiled as she responded to her young daughter's question. "I'm gon be working with Ms. Geraldine, so I can take care of y'all." She replied. The children looked at her with excited eyes.

"You all hurry on to school now. And make sure Ms. Alberta gets Lil' J.R. in the house before you leave. You hear me Millie Ann?" Ms. Geraldine said.

"Yes Ma'am." Millie Ann replied.

"Bye Momma! Bye Ms. Geraldine!" The children said as they hurried out the front door.

Ms. Geraldine again saw the red Cadillac parked out front as she closed the door behind the children.

"Oh, Effie Mae, when I was bathing Lil' J.R., the other day, I noticed that he had some kind of mark on his shoulder—right at the top, on his left side."

"Mark? What kind of mark, Ms. Geraldine?"

"The only way I can described it, is that it looked like a red scar or something. I asked Millie Ann if he had fallen, but she said that it's always been there." She stated, perplexed. "I guess I just never notice it before."

"Scar? Effie Mae suddenly remembered the scar on Anthony's back, located in the exact area as Ms. Geraldine described. "Uh, I'll look at it when he gets home." She stated, delighted by the fact, that she now knew without doubt, that Lil' J.R. had been fathered by Anthony. She smiled.

Chapter Twenty-Eight

"Well now you must be Effie Mae? Geraldine has spoken very highly of you." Mrs. Mildred Winchester stated through her evenly lined dentures. Middle-aged, with curly blonde hair and an assortment of gaudy jewelry that garnished her chubby wrist and neck, she extended her hand. Effie Mae shook it with distrust. "Now, if you could just give me a little more information regarding your last place of employment that should tie up all the loose ends."

Effie Mae stood paralyzed. She realized that she'd not worked anyplace else besides Ms. Norma's Hospitality Parlor. Her mind raced for the words that would spill through her lips.

"I . . . uh, worked for Ms. Norma." She stated, truthfully.

"Ms. Norma? Hmmm. I don't believe I've ever met Ms. Norma. But for some reason it seems as if I've heard her name in passing." She searched briefly through her memory bank. "I believe it was amongst my Randolph and some of his friends." She again turned her attention back to Effie Mae. "So Effie Mae, what exactly did you do when you worked for Ms. Norma?"

Effie Mae's mind again hunted for a satisfactory answer.

"I worked entertaining her guests." She said, sugar-coating the truth.

"Oh, I see. You were a hostess. Well you'll certainly be doing plenty of that around here. Isn't that right Geraldine?" Ms. Winchester yelled into the kitchen then chuckled. "Well that's good enough for me. Welcome aboard Effie Mae!" She again shook Effie Mae's hand then retreated from the room.

Effie Mae joined Ms. Geraldine at the kitchen table where she'd begun preparing food items for the Winchester's Annual Fundraiser.

"So, how much do you know about cooking, Effie Mae?" Ms. Geraldine asked. "Mrs. Winchester's real picky about how she likes her food prepared." She whispered. "So for today, I'm just going to have you watch. Basically you'll be serving the guest and cleaning up after it's over.

"That's fine." Effie Mae withheld the fact that she was a far greater cook than Ms. Geraldine.

"Now the Winchester's are having their annual fundraiser this afternoon. So, we're going to be really busy setting up, arranging flowers, and a whole lot of other things, to make sure that it's exactly how Mrs. Winchester wants it."

"Just let me know what I need to do Ms. Geraldine, and I'll do it."

"I think I'll have you start by taking all those flowers sitting in there on the dining room table, out into the Winchester's garden. You can start arranging them on the tables." She explained. "Just make sure you put a set of flowers on each table . . . that should be good enough. The main thing is to make sure there's enough food, and that it taste good!" Ms. Geraldine lightly chuckled. "We also need to make sure that the silverware and dinnerware are correct." Ms. Geraldine exhaled then retrieved a long list of chores from the upper right pocket of her dress.

"That looks like a pretty big list, Ms. Geraldine." Effie Mae stated.

"Oh, yes—it is. But don't worry about that, we'll have plenty enough help here today to do everything, on this list."

"Well, I guess I'm gon get started." Effie Mae stated as she headed towards the dining room. Taking a deep breath, she began her duties of transferring the multitude of flowers out into the garden.

Effie Mae worked steadily and arranged the various colored flowers on each of the tables. Remembering the decorative array from her own wedding, she admired her handy work as each table blossomed with colorful arrangements.

Mrs. Winchester watched from the French patio doors in the den. She peaked through the pink custom-made drapes that hung from the sixteen foot window, impressed by Effie Mae's demonstration as a hard and competent worker.

Effie Mae entered into the kitchen twenty minutes later. Ms. Geraldine and several other women arranged hors d'oeuvres on silver serving trays.

"What you need Effie Mae?" Ms. Geraldine asked as she placed a tray of the food inside the enormous commercial refrigerator.

"You need me to help with anything in here, Ms. Geraldine?"

"When you finish putting the flowers on the table, I guess you can start placing the dinnerware and silverware on there too."

"Oh—me, and Mr. James done that already." Effie Mae said.

"Mr. James!" Ms. Geraldine quickly shifted her eyes to Effie Mae. "I see he's gotten started already." She shook her head as she attempted to arrange several food trays inside the refrigerator. "You watch that old Colored man, Effie Mae. He has quick hands, if you know what I mean."

"Ms. Geraldine, compared to the men I've dealt with lately, Mr. James ain't gon be no trouble." Ms. Geraldine abruptly stopped what she was doing. She looked at Effie Mae and thought about Daniel's harsh words, then closed the refrigerator door and walked over to the kitchen counter.

"You ever made hors d'oeuvres before, Effie Mae?"

"Made what?"

"I can only show you once, since we're so busy today. So pay close attention."

"Ms. Geraldine—once is all I need." Effie Mae said with confidence.

Effie Mae learned quickly how to prepare the various exquisite food items, as the watchful eye of Mrs. Winchester took note. She paraded in and out of the massive kitchen, observing Effie Mae's skillfulness.

As the morning quickly became afternoon, the Winchesters, known for hosting many charitable events prepared for their annual fundraiser luncheon, in honor of the New York City Orphanage. Ms. Geraldine, Effie Mae, along with several other women and men, hurried busily about the Winchester's magnificent flower garden, serving their many elite guests.

Amongst the many distinguished personalities in attendance, was none other than Mr. J.T., the mayor of New York City and a regular at Ms. Norma's Hospitality Parlor.

Effie Mae noticed him right away. She slipped inside of the house and hoped to stay out of sight for the remainder of the afternoon. An excessive boaster, Mrs. Winchester stood mid-center of the beautiful gazebo as she'd always done and prepared to speak.

"Welcome, our distinguished guests and friends. Isn't everything simply magnificent?" She boasted. "That's only because here at the Winchester Mansion, we hire only the best workers in the city of New York." Her many guests applauded. "Our girls are hand-picked special, as I'm sure most of you, who've ever attended any of our fabulous events, well know. They're strictly the cream of the crop." She bragged. "And today we've added a new addition to our staff. Not only has she proven to be one of the best, but she's also pretty." She chuckled. "And I'm very pleased to introduce her to you all, right here today." She looked around the garden. "Effie Mae! Where are you dear? Effie Mae, come out— come out wherever you are."

Ms. Geraldine remembered she'd last seen Effie Mae entering into the servant's entrance to the kitchen. She hurried inside to inform her of the great honor, and to personally escort her back out into the garden, for all to see. Ms. Geraldine hurried inside the house.

"Effie Mae! Mrs. Winchester's looking for you." She said, excitedly.

"What she want with me? She, don't even know me." Effie Mae stated, trying to avoid the impending disaster.

"She's told her guests all about you. And now she wants to introduce you to everybody."

"I don't know them people. And I don't want to know them."

"It won't take but a second. Come on Effie Mae!" Ms. Geraldine took her by the arm and guided her out the door.

"Oh, there she is." Mrs. Winchester stated when seeing the two women exiting the house, again entering into the garden. "Come on over here dear." She pulled Effie Mae front and center. "Isn't she simply the prettiest Colored girl you've ever seen? Come on now dear, don't be shy."

Effie Mae smiled. She hoped that Mr. J.T. wouldn't remember her. And, in the event that he did, he wouldn't recall the circumstances under which they'd met. He recognized her almost instantly, minus her negligee. He also remembered their numerous evenings shared at Ms. Norma's Hospitality Parlor. With no thought to how his identifying Effie Mae might damage his own reputation as Mayor, he blurted out in the midst of the Winchester's distinguish guests.

"That girl's a whore! Are you taking in the leftovers from Ms. Norma's whore house now, Mildred?"

Humiliated, Mrs. Winchester's mouth flung open as she looked at Effie Mae in disgust. She quickly turned to Ms. Geraldine in fury.

"Geraldine!" She screamed. "I'm holding you personally responsible for this!" She pointed her finger to Effie Mae. "Now you get that filthy whore off my property this very instant! And I'd better not ever see her here again at the Winchester Mansion!"

Effie Mae darted through the white picket fence surrounding the garden. She ran aimlessly through the streets, crying. After she'd run a total of six blocks, the red Cadillac began following then trailed alongside of her.

"Are you alright Ms. Lady?" Effie Mae ignored his words as she slowed. She looked briefly over at him. "You need a ride? I promise I won't bite you." He teased.

"I don't know you. The last man that picked me up off the streets . . ." He interrupted.

"I'm not that man. I bet I don't even look like him . . . now do I?" He joked. Effie Mae leaned down and again looked inside the car.

"I guess you don't." She quietly chuckled.

"What's your name Ms. Lady? I don't want to keep calling you Ms. Lady—if you have a name." Not certain how wide spread her tarnished reputation had gotten, Effie Mae thought for a moment.

"Geraldine." She replied.

"Pleased to meet you . . . Ms. Geraldine." Effie Mae gave no reply. "Well since you gave me your name, I guess it's only fair that I give you mines. My name is Lawrence." He stated, giving her his legal name.

"Pleased to meet you too, Lawrence." Effie Mae continued walking.

"Now will you please let me give you a ride?" Effie Mae stopped.

"Since I don't exactly know where I am, or where I'm going, I guess it won't hurt nothing." Buckeye stopped the car. He reached over and opened the door from the inside. Effie Mae hesitated then got in.

"If you don't know where you're going, and I don't know where you're trying to go, how about I pull into the service station about six blocks up. And while you're trying to figure out where you need to get to, I'll pay the water bill?"

"Huh?" Effie Mae looked at him, confused by the meaning of his words.

"I gotta pee!" He laughed as he drove several blocks up the streets then turned into the service station. "I'll be right out."

"Then I guess I'm gon be out here waiting."

Buckeye opened his door and got out. He briefly glanced back at her. Effie Mae watched as he walked in the direction of the small blue and white building then went inside, disappearing through the glass doors. He hurried over to the payphone inside and called Huck.

"I got her Huck! She's out there right now, sitting in my car."

"Where you at Buckeye?" Huck asked.

"I'm at the Blue and White Service Station, out here in this rich, White neighborhood. You'll see my car parked; it's right here on the corner."

"Stay there. I'll be there in fifteen."

Effie Mae grew restless as she waited. She wondered what was taking him so long. She looked around repeatedly. She stared at the transparent door, to see if she saw him. After ten minutes had passed, Effie Mae opened the door and prepared to continue her journey on foot. Buckeye rushed out when seeing her. He ran over to the car and hopped in, then started it up.

"Ms. Geraldine, please accept my apology. I thought I had to do the number one, but it turned out—I had to do the number two." He laughed. Effie Mae grimaced.

"Don't be telling me that. That's nasty!"

"I'm sorry Ms. Geraldine. I wasn't trying to make you sick." He pulled his car out and onto the streets then drove in slow motion. "You know what?" He glanced over at her. "You don't look like a Geraldine to me." Effie Mae turned away and stared through the windshield. "So, are you gon tell me?"

"Tell you what?"

"Your real name, because I know it's not Geraldine."

"Don't you worry about what my real name is . . . as a matter of fact, why don't you let me out, right here?" Buckeye looked in his rearview mirror and saw Huck driving up behind him. He pulled over to the curb and stopped. Effie Mae reached for the doorknob. The door swung open before her hand could touch the handle. She looked up, and into the face of Huck.

"Hey, Effie Mae, you remember me?" He smiled. Effie Mae tried to get out of the car. Huck pushed her back inside. "Where you think you going?"

"I have to get home to my babies, Huck." Effie Mae became frightened as she gazed into his angry eyes.

"Your babies, huh?" He chuckled as he took note of the black maid's uniform she wore. "Is that what you're doing now Effie Mae . . . playing Momma and cleaning White folks houses'?" He shook his head. "Girl . . . you wasting your talent." He smiled. "Damn shame! And you costing me money!" His anger heightened. Effie Mae looked at Buckeye, her eyes pleaded for help.

"Get out of the car Effie Mae." Huck ordered. Effie Mae grabbed a hold of the steering wheel.

"I said . . . get out of the car Effie Mae." She again looked to Buckeye for help.

"Please get out of the car Effie Mae. I don't want to see Huck do anything to hurt you."

"Take me home. I want to be there when my babies get home from school." Effie Mae's fear grew. Huck glared at her then reached inside the car and took a hold of her by the arm. He tugged as she continued holding onto the steering wheel.

"Buckeye!" Huck called out. Buckeye forcibly removed Effie Mae's fingers from the steering wheel. Huck quickly dragged her from the car and threw her down onto the ground. "Buckeye; go get behind the wheel of my car." Buckeye hurried from his car and got behind the wheel of Huck's.

"Please Huck—please!" Effie Mae sat on the ground and refused to get up.

"Effie Mae. You got thirty seconds to get your ass up off that ground, before I kick you so hard in your head, Buckeye's gon have to walk two or three blocks to find your eyeballs."

Effie Mae slowly rose to her feet. She looked into Huck's infuriated eyes and realized that her life was in danger.

"Huck, I just got my babies back. Please don't take me away from them." She pleaded as he pulled her by the arm, over to his car.

"Get in the car Effie Mae." She reached for the front door and prepared to get inside.

"Uh-uh! I want you in the back." He opened the back door. "Get in!" Effie Mae got in and sat upright on the seat and awaited her fate.

"Uh-uh. Lay down." Effie Mae didn't budge.

"Huck, please!" She said, her eyes pleaded.

"Girl, if you don't lie down on that back seat. I'll take you right here on this ground. And I won't care who sees it. Now is that what you want, Effie Mae?"

Effie Mae remained upright on the seat. Huck took off his charcoal gray hat and sat it on the roof of the car. He looked in at her then reached inside and forcefully snatched her out, throwing her down onto the ground. He climbed on top of her.

"Okay! Okay!" She cried out. Huck got up, then lifted her to her feet. She climbed into the back seat of the car and laid, down.

"Turn around. I'm coming from the other side." Effie Mae turned. Her head faced the opened passenger side door. Huck closed it then retrieved his hat from the roof. He walked around to the driver's side and opened the back door. He handed the hat across the seat to Buckeye.

"Lay this on the front seat Buckeye." He took off his suit jacket, vest, and tie and also handed them to Buckeye. "Lay these on the front seat too." Standing in the streets, he took off his shoes—one at a time. He loosened the buckle on his pants and stepped out of them. Buckeye reached his hand through the open back door and took the items and laid them neatly on the carpeted floor in front. Huck stood in the streets wearing only his white ribbed tank top, red, silk boxers and black nylon socks. He climbed into the car and on top of Effie Mae.

"Close the door." He said. Buckeye retreated from the car and closed the back door then returned to his place behind the wheel.

"Drive." Huck said. "Turn the music up, and keep your eyes on the road."

...

"Man I've been driving now for the last forty-five minutes! I'm gon have to pull over and get some gas soon."

"Yeah, do what you need to do Buckeye." Huck said, exhausted. "Uh—just pull over and park."

"Park? Man I've been sleeping in the car for the past four days!" He stated, continuing to look forward. Huck man, I just want to go home and stretch out in my bed."

"Well, just take us to your place."

"I thought she said she wanted to get home to her kids?" Buckeye stated.

"Is that what you heard Buckeye? Cause, that's not what I heard."

"Yeah, you remember . . . it's was when you told her to get out of the car."

"Buckeye!"

"Yeah Huck."

"Stop talking. You ruining my concentration."

...

The next morning Buckeye parked on the streets a few houses away from Ms. Geraldine and Daniel's. Huck sat in the front passenger's seat. Effie Mae lay in back. Huck watched as Daniel exited the house for work.

"Is that her husband?" He asked.

"Naw, man, that's Daniel. You remember Daniel don't you, Huck? He's the one that's got those two kids by Sadie Ann.

"That's him? Looks like Daniel's gotten a little old." Huck laughed.

The door again opened. And Effie Mae's children rushed out. Ms. Geraldine stood on the porch and watched as they began their journey to Ms. Alberta's then to school. She went back inside and closed the door.

"Are those your babies, Effie Mae?" Huck took a visual inventory. "Look at Effie Mae's babies, Buckeye. All those girls . . . I can retire on that." He chuckled as he rubbed his chin and contemplated the idea. "How old is your oldest girl, Effie Mae?" Effie Mae refused to answer. Huck crack opened his door. "Maybe I'll go ask her myself."

"Millie Ann's eleven!" She blurted, frightened that he might harm her daughter.

"You hear that, Buckeye? Millie Ann's eleven. And she's cute just like you Effie Mae." He shifted his eyes to Effie Mae in the back seat then closed his door. "What you think Buckeye? You think she's old enough to work at Ms. Norma's?" Buckeye looked at him with disturbed eyes.

"Huck, man you alright? That's a child!"

"Yeah, I'm alright, Buckeye. I'm just picking at Effie Mae."

The front door again opened and Ms. Geraldine walked out onto the porch as she prepared to go to work. She closed and locked the door then walked down the streets and waited for the bus.

"Is that your Momma, Effie Mae?" Huck teased.

"Naw, that's Daniel's wife—Geraldine. You remember . . . ."

"Buckeye!" Huck interrupted.

"Yeah Huck?"

"Did I ask you anything? You speak for Effie Mae now?" Buckeye said nothing further.

"What time do they usually get back home? Huck turned and looked at Buckeye as if waiting for him to respond. "I'm talking to you." He looked in back at Effie Mae. She remained silent. "Maybe you should be speaking for Effie Mae, Buckeye. She don't seem to want to talk to me. But it don't matter. If they get back while I'm still in there, I would love to tell them what Effie Mae's being doing. How she's been selling her . . . ." Effie Mae cut him off.

"Mr. Daniel gets back at around five, and Ms. Geraldine gets home at about four." Huck watched until Ms. Geraldine climbed onto the bus and it drove off.

"Let's go." He opened his door then turned to Effie Mae. "Girl, if you try to run . . . I'll wait right here in the house, with your babies, until you bring your ass back." Huck got out then opened the back door. "Get out." Effie Mae sat up and slid towards the open door to exit. "Girl, you look a mess! Fix your hair and straighten out your clothes. I don't want to make your neighbors nervous." He stood outside the door as Effie Mae rubbed her hands over her face then ran her fingers through her hair. She pulled her dress down towards her knees and attempted to rub the wrinkles, out of the black uniform. "That's enough. Get out." Huck stated.

Effie Mae exited the car. Huck closed the door behind her. He put his arm around her as they walked towards the house. Buckeye followed. The trio went up the three stairs and onto the front porch. Huck gripped Effie Mae by the neck and kissed her on the side of the head. "Girl, if you try anything . . . ." He took a deep breath and blew it out.

Buckeye looked around and inspected the neighborhood for possible onlookers, while Effie Mae unlocked the door and the three entered into the house. Huck looked around and smiled. "Is this where you play Momma, Effie Mae?" Look Buckeye, this is where Effie Mae and her babies live." He laughed. "I guess whoever said that you can't turn a whore into a housewife, never met Effie Mae." He chuckled. "Get in that bathroom and clean yourself up! I can't take you back over to Ms. Norma's looking and smelling like that!" He looked at her in disgust. Effie Mae looked him directly in the eyes, no longer afraid.

"I ain't doing that no more, Huck." He rushed over and grabbed her by the face.

"You going back! And not only that, but you gon to take your ass in there and apologize to Ms. Norma for leaving the way you did! Because if you don't . . . ."

"I ain't going back, Huck." Effie Mae stood her ground. Huck drew back his fist and hit her in the face, knocking her down onto the floor.

"Ahhhhhhh!" Effie Mae cried out as she fell.

"You gon do what I tell you to do! Do you understand me, Effie Mae?" He straddled himself across her body and repeatedly hit her in the face with his fist. Buckeye watched in horror.

"Huck! Stop man! You gon kill her!"

"Uh-uh. I got to show this whore who's in charge." He continued to punch Effie Mae in the head and face as she squirmed. "Buckeye . . . you got your knuckles?"

"Come on Huck man let's go! Don't hit that girl with them knuckles."

"Give them here." Buckeye reached into his pocket and pulled out his brass knuckles then handed them over. Huck slid them onto the fingers of his right hand. He raised his fist and forcefully struck Effie Mae in the front of her head, with the metal weapon. She stopped moving, rendered unconscious. Huck glared at her motionless body.

"Hey Buckeye, man I think I killed her!" He stood up. Buckeye rushed over and looked down at Effie Mae.

"Man, I told you to stop!" He shouted.

"What am I gon do Buckeye?"

"Man, we can't leave her there!"

"So, what you recommend we do Buckeye? Are you gon carry her body outside in broad daylight, and put her in the trunk of the car? Huh? Or do you think maybe we should walk her out and prop her up in the front seat?" He asked, sarcastically.

"Maybe we can wrap her up. It has to be a blanket or rug—something in here, that we can put her in." Buckeye visually searched. "Then we can take her out, and throw her in the Hudson."

"Man, are you crazy?" Huck shouted. "She has children! I can't do her kids like that. They have a right to at least bury their Momma." Buckeye looked at him in awe of his twisted rationale.

"Why don't we just put her in the backyard and let her people find her?" Buckeye stated.

He noticed a green rug in the living room lying under the coffee table. "There's a rug in the living room, Huck."

"Bring it here." Huck stared at Effie Mae as he knelt over her body. Buckeye pulled the rug from under the table. He dragged it through the kitchen and into the dining room. He laid the rug next to Effie Mae's body then he and Huck rolled her onto it—then up in it.

"Open the door Buckeye." Buckeye hurried over to the back door and opened it. He looked around, checking for possible witnesses. "What you see?"

"Man, I don't see nobody."

"Let's get her out there.

Huck and Buckeye lifted the rug, with Effie Mae wrapped inside and carried it out onto the back porch. They transported it into the backyard then lowered it onto the grass. Effie Mae's hand tumbled out. Huck stared it for a minute then picked it up and kissed it. A tear rolled from his right eye. Buckeye watched with concern at his old friend's odd behavior.

"Huck, man, let's go!"

Huck pulled open the rug and exposed Effie Mae's battered face. He gently kissed her on the lips then recovered her and walked away.

"Get the doors." Huck said as he exited through the back gate. Buckeye entered into the back door. He locked both the back and front doors, then walked away as Effie Mae's body lay enclosed in the rug, still dressed in her black uniform.

Chapter Twenty-Nine

"Well I'll be damn! Didn't I tell you Geraldine?" Daniel said, giving Ms. Geraldine his, *I told you so,* speech. "Working in a whorehouse, woman married to a Preacher!"

"Are you going to smoke your pipe Daniel? Or are you going to sit out here condemning your cousin's wife?"

"And that's another thing!" Daniel said. "Next time I speak to Sissy, I'm sure gon tell her about herself." Daniel attempted to fill his pipe. His hands were unsteady from the excitement of *hitting the nail on the head*—about Effie Mae. He dropped bits of tobacco onto the concrete porch. "Girl, wasn't nothing but the devil!"

"Daniel!" Ms. Geraldine stared at him, disturbed by his harsh words.

"She was!" He yelled.

"Keep your voice down, Daniel. You know her children are right there in the house."

"Oh boy." Daniel shook his head in sympathy.

"What?"

"I feel sorry for those kids. Uh-hum—I sure do." He stated. "Momma's a whore. Daddy's a runaway!" He said as he continued, unsuccessfully to fill his pipe.

After several failed attempts, Daniel succeeded. A victorious looked covered his face as he then tried to ignite it. Still excited, he dropped the lit match. He reached behind his ear and retrieved a second match. Striking it on the heel of his boot—it lit. Daniel again dropped it.

"Here . . . take this thing!" He shoved the unlit pipe into Ms. Geraldine hand in frustration.

"The situation's not that bad, Daniel." She looked at the pipe with a sour look displayed on her face. "Calm down."

"I can't!"

"Well you can sit out here and gloat. Or you can calm down and put this pipe in your mouth and smoke it."

"Oh, I see you trying to be funny."

"I'm just saying."

"Well, stop saying!" Daniel snatched the pipe from her then looked at it. "Aww forget it!" He stuffed the pipe into his left shirt pocket spilling tobacco inside." He turned to Ms. Geraldine and stared. "So what's next?"

"What do you mean, what's next?"

"What we gon do about these kids? All those girls; this ain't a whorehouse, Geraldine!" He blurted.

"Daniel!" She looked astonished, alarmed by his statement.

"I mean it Geraldine! Ain't nobody gon turn my house into a whorehouse!"

Ms. Geraldine thought about his words and shook her head.

"Right now Daniel, my main concern is about Effie Mae. Nobody's seen here since she ran away from Mrs. Winchester's."

"What you concerned about Effie Mae for? She made her own bed! And she almost cost you your job!" He stated. "Concerned about Effie Mae—my foot."

"Don't forget Daniel, you have a daughter too."

He turned quickly to her, surprised by the mention of his illegitimate daughter. Daniel stood and prepared to enter into the house then noticed the rug lying in the backyard.

"Ain't that the rug from the living room?" You see what I'm saying, Geraldine.

"Now, I wonder which one of those children brought that rug out here? Just go get it Daniel, and take it back inside the house?" Daniel walked off the porch and over to the rug. He knelt down to pick it up.

"This thing feels kind of heavy."

"Heavy?" It shouldn't be. Why would it be heavy Daniel?" He rolled it over and began opening it. He suddenly looked down into the unconscious, badly beaten face of Effie Mae.

"Geraldine! Geraldine!" He looked horrified.

"What's wrong Daniel?"

"Get those children out of here!"

"What's wrong?" Ms. Geraldine stood to her feet.

"Geraldine! Have somebody from Ms. Alberta's come pick those children up and take them over to her house! Now, Geraldine!" Daniel demanded. She asked no further questions. Ms. Geraldine hurried into the house and made the call.

Effie Mae lay in bed, semi-conscious, after four days of being comatose. The entire top of her head wrapped in white bandages. A line extended from a manual IV inserted into her arm. She gradually opened her badly bruised eyes, surrounded by dark circles. Incoherent, Effie Mae gazed into the worried faces of Daniel and Ms. Geraldine. Also present in the room, was Dr. Brown, one of the few Colored doctors in the city. The trio gawked at the badly disfigured human being, uncertain if she would live or die.

"Ma—Ma." She muttered. Ms. Geraldine trembled as she looked upon the unrecognizable sight lying there.

"Mom—ma?" Effie Mae said, confused. Ms. Geraldine rushed from the room in tears, unable to bear looking upon the disoriented creature. Daniel turned to Dr. Brown, at a loss for words. He took a nervous breath then prepared to speak.

"Uh . . . Effie Mae" His worried eyes shifted to the doctor then again to Effie Mae.

"Mom—ma?" She repeated.

"It's me Effie Mae, Daniel." Somebody beat you half to death! Do you know who did this to you? Who did this, Effie Mae?" He stopped when he noted Dr. Brown subtly shaking his head, forbidding him to speak on the incidence.

"Mom—ma?"

"It's me Effie Mae, Daniel." Effie Mae again closed her eyes and slipped into a medically induced sleep.

"Why don't we let her rest for now? Dr. Brown said. "Even though she's regained consciousness, she'll need to be monitored at all times."

"Okay." Daniel nodded. "We can do that."

Dr. Brown walked over to Effie Mae. He placed two fingers on her wrist and checked her pulse. He held his stethoscope to her chest and listened to her heart as he counted her respirations. He turned to Daniel.

"I already checked her blood pressure, and right now her vital signs are all stable. Be sure to check her temperature regularly." Daniel nodded. "I've given her medication that should keep her sedated for a good while. I've also given her something for pain and infection. It's important that she be turned every two hours." He glanced at Daniel. "She's lucky to be alive. I'll be back tomorrow morning to check on her."

Dr. Brown exited the bedroom and entered into the dining room where Ms. Geraldine waited for the prognosis.

"Who would do something like that, Dr. Brown?" She asked, greatly disturbed.

"Right now, Ms. Geraldine we can't worry about that. Our greatest concern—is whether she'll survive, and if she does, how severe the damages are from the beating. The fact that she's out of the coma is a good sign. But she's not out of danger, yet." He pessimistically stated. "We'll just have to wait now, and see if she has any signs of permanent brain damage."

"Tell me what we need to do Dr. Brown." Ms. Geraldine asked.

"Like I told Daniel—it's important that somebody's with her at all times. She'll also require daily hygiene to keep her skin from breaking down, creating bed sores."

"Daniel and I will do as much as we can to take care of her."

"Daniel?" Dr. Brown asked, puzzled by her statement. Daniel entered into the dining room and picked up a chair. Dr. Brown watched in question as he walked past him, holding the chair, balanced on his shoulder. "Ms. Geraldine, do realize that caring for Effie Mae will mean washing her body from head to toe?" He spoke just above a whisper. "Now, I know a few nurses that won't mind coming over and helping out two or three . . . maybe even four times a week, but after that you'll have to provide any additional care."

"I'm sure I can get some of the ladies from the church to help out." She stated.

"Well be sure you do. Because head injury patient's behavior, can be hard to predict. "I'm not sure if she'll be sound enough to understand what she might say or do."

"I'll be sure to let the ladies know that, Dr. Brown."

"It's not the ladies I'm worried about." He warned. "If her condition should worsen, call an ambulance immediately."

"Thank you, Dr. Brown." Ms. Geraldine escorted him to the front door.

"Remember what I said." He cautioned then exited.

...

Effie Mae sat up in bed comforted by the pile of pillows stacked behind her back, two months after, her life-threatening attack. Daniel and Ms. Geraldine faithfully rotated shifts, aiding in her recovery. Tonight, Ms. Geraldine prepared dinner and helped the children with their homework. Daniel nestled in the high-back, living room chair, next to Effie Mae's bed.

"I guess you stuck with me tonight, Mr. Daniel."Effie Mae teased.

"You know I don't mind. I'm just glad to see you getting better." He hesitated. "Effie Mae you never did say who beat you like that. That tells me it's somebody you know."

Effie Mae looked at him as if she wanted to reveal the identity of her abuser. She maintained her silence. "And, I know it's somebody you scared of. That's why you haven't said anything" Daniel said, pursuing the issue. "The talk on the streets is that it was Huck." Effie Mae stared at him without saying a word. She gave no indication whether he was right or wrong. "Okay. If you don't want to talk about it, I won't force you."

"I want to thank you Mr. Daniel." She said breaking her silence

"I already told you Effie Mae, I don't mind taking care of you.

"That ain't what I'm talking about." She gazed into his eyes, ashamed. "I want to thank you for not asking me about working as a whore."

"Now I know, Huck had something to do with that!" Daniel insisted. "You're not his first."

"You know Mr. Daniel . . ." Effie Mae gazed into his eyes as she prepared to confide in him. "Men have been using my body since I was sixteen. It started with my daddy's cousin David then his son Willie Lee. After that, it seems like everybody wanted a piece of Effie Mae Reed." She laughed half-heartedly. "And I didn't seem to mind letting them have a piece." Daniel listened without judgment, surprised to hear Effie Mae's straightforward words. "I guess if I had loved myself, things might have been different. And Momma always made it so easy for me to hate myself more than I already did." Tears rolled from Effie Mae's eyes. Daniel rose from his chair to comfort her. She held her hands out and blocked him from touching her. "Careful Mr. Daniel, Effie Mae Reed has a history of making any man that touches her, the next man in her bed. You know I'm sick in the head." She joked through tear-filled eyes.

"I'm not gon just sit here and let you cry." Daniel sat on the bed and put his arms around Effie Mae then wiped away her tears. "Talking about you sick in the head—ain't nothing wrong with you Effie Mae." She laid her head onto his chest and briefly closed her eyes. "Effie Mae, I'm sorry." Daniel felt ashamed for his harsh judgment of her. "When I heard about Lil' J.R, I uh . . . thought you had to be one of the most lowdown women, I ever seen. I didn't know all that. I, uh . . ." Effie Mae interrupted him.

"That don't make what I did right, Mr. Daniel." She stated with remorse. "I hurt J.R. bad. Then somebody hurt me, bad." She half-heatedly laughed to herself. "I guess what goes around, really does come back around."

"Daniel! Dinner's ready. Come and get you and Effie Mae a plate." Ms. Geraldine yelled from the kitchen. Daniel and Effie Mae ended their odd embrace.

"When am I gon see my babies again?" Effie Mae asked.

"Geraldine thinks maybe you should wait until some of the swelling and bruises are gone. She thinks it might be too much for the children to deal with." He explained. "You know you look like you been in the ring with Joe Louis?" He laughed. "And you lost!"

Effie Mae took a pillow from behind her back and hit him with it. She laughed briefly then looked at him with seriousness.

"Mr. Daniel, I need to see Blue." Her eyes pleaded. "I know he's probably going crazy, worrying about me."

"Now, Effie Mae, I don't want all that all that mess from the streets, in my home."

"Please, Mr. Daniel, Blue is special in my life." Daniel hesitated then sympathized with her plea.

"If seeing Blue means that much to you, Effie Mae, I guess it'll be alright for him to come by here to see you. But I got to check with Geraldine first. If she okay with it, I'll get in touch with Blue, and let him know. Effie Mae smiled.

"Ouch!" She rubbed her swollen cheek. "Thank you Mr. Daniel."

...

Daniel looked through the widow of Blue's Jazz Club. He saw Blue sitting on stage, adjusting his saxophone between his lips, as he prepared to begin practicing. He knocked on the locked door. Blue looked up in response to the unexpected knock. He saw Daniel peering through the window. Blue's heart rate instantly increased as he wondered if Daniel's visit would bring him news of Effie Mae's demise. He rose from his chair, and apprehensively walked off the stage. Blue's breaths deepened as he approached the door, his eyes never left Daniel's face, as he tried to read the vague look in his eyes. Blue unlocked the door then opened it.

"Hey Blue."

"How you doing Daniel?" Blue hesitated. "Uh—come on in." He maintained eye contact with Daniel as he entered inside. Blue closed and relocked the door, his heart vigorously pounded.

"I know you probably heard about Effie Mae." Blue's eyes widened.

"Uh, yeah—is she, uh . . . "

"Oh! No! But for a while it looked like she wasn't gon make it." Blue exhaled relieved by the news. "She wants to see you, Blue."

"Where's she at?" He asked, eagerly.

"She's at my house." Daniel said. "But, Effie Mae's children are there as well—and I can't have no mess in my home. And, especially in front of them children, they just like my own."

"I'm glad to hear that she got them back. I know how much she missed not having them." Blue stated. "I would never bring trouble to your home, Daniel. I know that's not what Effie Mae would want. And I love her too much to do anything to hurt her." Daniel could see Blue's love for Effie Mae in his eyes. He also realized that she remained the wife of his cousin.

"When can I come see her?"

"I'm sure Effie Mae want to see you as soon as possible."

"I don't open Blue's until around six, so if I can come at about two o'clock, would that be okay?"

"Yeah, I'll let Effie Mae know you coming."

"No!" Blue said, promptly. "If you don't mind, Daniel, I'd like to surprise Baby girl." His eyes briefly filled with tears. Daniel watched with surprise as he witnessed Blue's display of emotions over Effie Mae.

"You know Effie Mae's still my cousin's wife?"

"Yeah, I do. And I don't mean that man any disrespect, but if I wanted to stop loving Baby girl today, I couldn't."

"Just long as you know, her husband comes first!" Daniel glared at Blue momentarily then turned and walked away. Blue watched as he unlocked the door then exited the club. Overjoyed, with the news that he would soon be seeing the woman he loved, Blue leapt up hollered out in excitement.

"Yes! I'm going to see my baby!" He raced up the stairs leading to his apartment, his only wish being to see the surprised look in Effie Mae's eyes by his unannounced visit.

...

Effie Mae lay in bed brushing her hair after receiving her daily sponge bath by the volunteer Nurse, Ms. Freda. She looked in the hand held mirror, and stared at her face, still slightly disfigured. Effie Mae laid the mirror down onto the bed then retrieved her make-up bag from the nightstand. She removed a small circular box containing face powder and gently patted her face with the powder puff, attempting to cover her remaining bruises. Retrieving a tube of red lipstick from the bag, she skillfully spread it across her lips. She gazed at herself in the mirror and smiled then returned the items back onto the nightstand. Effie Mae hoped that Blue's visit would be today.

"Effie Mae?" Ms. Freda knocked then peeked her head inside the door. "You have a visitor." She smiled. "It's a man." She whispered. Effie Mae smiled. She knew for certain, that her gentleman caller was Blue.

"Send him in Ms. Freda."

"I sure will." Ms. Freda pulled the door up, leaving it cracked. Effie Mae watched in anticipation as the door began to open. J.R. poked his head in.

"Hey Effie Mae." He smiled. She looked at him in silence, surprised to see him there.

"Uh—J.R.? I'm surprised to see you here."

"Can I come in?" He asked, humbly.

"Yeah, this was once your room too." Effie Mae stated, humorously. J.R. quietly approached. He leaned in and kissed her lightly on the lips. Effie Mae glared at him, shocked by his actions.

"You still my wife."

"I'm surprised you still see me that way. I'm sure you know this . . ." She lightly rubbed her jaw. ". . . was done by a man. Somebody, I been with."

"How the children doing?" He asked, changing the subject.

"You tell me. Ms. Geraldine won't let me see my babies. She thinking I might scare them." She chuckled.

"It ain't that bad. You still look beautiful to me." He took a hold of Effie Mae's hand then gazed into her eyes, his lingering love for her, apparent. "Effie Mae, I'm sorry for taking the children like that. I was hurt and I was thinking with my heart and not with what I knew God wanted me to do."

"You know the funny thing is, J.R. the man that did this to me, told me a long time ago, that I didn't belong in my life with you." J.R. looked astonished by her seemingly close relationship with her attacker. "He was right. Momma, Ms. Sissy, Rev. Hill, they all knew that Effie Mae Reed didn't have no business marrying nobody." She thought for a moment. "But, you know what, J.R.; I eventually came to love my life with you." She lifted his hand and kissed it then stared into his eyes. "But by the time I realized it, I had made the worse mistake in my life." Neither said anything further. They simply looked at each other.

"Effie Mae." Ms. Freda stood just outside the door.

"Yes, Ms. Freda."

"There's another gentleman here to see you." She said with question.

"Another one?" Effie Mae laughed. "Send him on back here." She and J.R. awaited her mysterious visitor. Each looked in the direction of the door. In walked Blue. He held a bouquet of flowers in his hand.

"Blue!" Effie Mae said, thrilled.

"Hey Baby girl, how you feeling?" He asked with a love in his voice. J.R. looked at the unfamiliar man then stepped back and allowed him access to Effie Mae. Blue walked over and presented her with the flowers. A large smiled formed on her face as she removed them from his hand. Effie Mae gazed into his eyes as she raised the flowers to her nose, smelling them.

"Thank you Blue." She laid the bouquet onto the bed then opened her arms, requesting with her smile, that he enter. Blue sat down on the side of the bed and entered into her awaiting arms. He gently embraced her then romantically kissed her. J.R. watched, slightly shaken. The two lovers ended the kiss, but maintained their embrace.

"I've missed you Baby girl." He kissed her again. "I know Huck did this to you." He said, as he kissed her gently on the lips for a third time. "I'm sorry I didn't do more to protect you Effie Mae. But, I'm here now." They shared in another kiss. "Daniel told me that you got your children back. Now we can move to Pennsylvania like we talked about." Effie Mae glanced at J. R.

"Uh—Blue . . . this is J.R., my husband." Blue momentarily closed his eyes, disappointed to see J.R. at her side. He reluctantly released her from his arms then stood to greet, "*Effie Mae's husband.*" He turned around and extended his hand to his unexpected *rival*.

"How you doing J.R.?" The two men shook hands.

"I don't know after seeing all that."

"Man, I'm sorry. I didn't know . . ."

"How do you know my wife?" Effie Mae intervened.

"J.R., Blue's been taking care of me. He's a . . ." Blue interrupted.

"Truth is J.R., I love Effie Mae, and I would love to one day take her away from all of this. Baby girl, here — has stolen my heart." He turned to Effie Mae. She smiled. Daniel suddenly rushed into the room.

"What the hell's going on in here?" He looked at J.R. then to Blue. "Didn't I tell you that I didn't want that mess in my house?" He yelled.

"I'm sorry Daniel. I didn't know J.R. was gon be here. If I had known, I would've come at another time."

"Like I told you earlier, Effie Mae's husband comes first—that's his wife!"

"Okay. I can respect that. I'll leave." He looked at Effie Mae then to Daniel. "Can, I uh . . ."

"No!" Daniel shouted.

"It's okay Cousin Daniel. I know that Effie Mae's my wife, but when I walked out, I relinquished my right as her husband."

"You sure J.R.?" Daniel asked with uncertainty.

"Yeah, it's okay. I've been watching them going at it for the past fifteen minutes."

"What? You mean, they . . ." Daniel flashed Blue an angry look.

"It's okay." J.R. stated, calmly.

"Go ahead. Do what you got to do, then get out of my house!" Daniel snapped.

Blue returned to Effie Mae. She smiled as he approached. He sat on the bed and gently took her into his arms. They passionately kissed. Effie Mae held him tight. Daniel looked at J.R. He took note of his unease as he watched his wife sharing an intimate kiss with another man.

"Ahem!" Daniel cleared his throat as the kiss persisted.

Effie Mae and Blue released their mouths one from the other then exchanged smiles filled with undeniable love. They blushed.

"I love you Baby girl. Remember that." They stared briefly into each other's eyes and grinned. Blue kissed her lovingly on the cheek then rose from the bed.

"Bye."

"Bye Blue." Effie Mae beamed.

"Thank you Daniel." Blue said, humbly. He turned to leave then took a final look at J.R. The two men momentarily locked eyes then Blue walked away, exiting the room.

"What the hell was that?" Daniel asked as he looked in the direction of the doorway.

"Uh, Cousin Daniel, can I talk to my wife in private?" Daniel looked at J.R. then to Effie Mae and again to J.R.

"Go ahead, I guess that's between you and Effie Mae." Daniel shook his head as he left the room, purposely leaving the door open.

"Uh—the door Cousin Daniel."

"Oh, okay. I'll close it. What the hell was that? I told Blue . . ." Daniel said, continuing to talk to himself as he closed the door. J.R. walked over to Effie Mae and sat on the side of the bed.

"Blue? You love him?"

"He loves me." She avoided eye contact.

"That's not what I asked you." J.R. took a hold of her face and gently turned it towards him. "I asked you if you loved Blue."

"Tyrell. His name is Tyrell. If I knew what love was, J.R., I guess I could answer that question. Blue is just one of the many men that I've been with that told me he loved me." She said in a matter-of-fact tone. It's kind of hard to love somebody, J.R. when you can't even love yourself." He looked at her in amazement, surprised by her words.

Chapter Thirty

"Daniel, I'll be leaving for work in a few!" Ms. Geraldine yelled from the kitchen. "Dr. Brown called this morning, he said the nurse who was supposed to come over and help Effie Mae out today won't be here . . . she's sick with the flu or something."

"Now what? Somebody's got to bathe her." Daniel shouted from inside the bathroom. "I can't do it. That's a woman, Geraldine!"

"And I can't miss another day at Mrs. Winchester's. She's already complaining."

"What about me Geraldine? I've missed a few days myself."

"Yeah, Daniel, but you're a union worker."

"What's that suppose to mean?"

"It means I'm running late for work. I'll keep trying to see if I can find somebody to come over." Ms. Geraldine hurried out the kitchen door. "Bye, Daniel!" She shut the door then hurried towards the bus stop.

"Geraldine! Geraldine!" Daniel shouted, scurrying from the bathroom. He looked out the kitchen window as the bus drove away then strolled nervously through the dining room and into the hallway. He stopped just outside of Effie Mae's bedroom door and stood mute. He wondered how he would make it through the remainder of the day caring for her. Daniel slowly opened the door and went inside being seated in the chair next to the bed. Nervous, he again rose, walking quietly over to Effie Mae. His mind raced as he wondered what to do next.

"Effie Mae you woke?" Daniel asked, peeking over her shoulder as she lay on her right side. Effie Mae opened her eyes, turned over and looked at him.

"I am now, Mr. Daniel."

"Uh, the nurse that was supposed to come wash you up this morning got the flu. She ain't coming. So, uh—I guess I'll be taking care of you today."

"You? Where's Ms. Geraldine?"

"She just ran her butt out of here." He said. "But I'll be sitting right here, if you need anything. Just let me know."

"Mr. Daniel?"

"What you need Effie Mae?"

"The first thing, I need to do is get out of this bed and go to the bathroom."

"Oh, boy." Daniel's anxiety increased. "Okay. I'll wait outside the door and let you get out of the bed—make yourself decent."

"Looks like you gon be waiting a long time for that." Effie Mae teased. Daniel shook his head and lightly chuckled, amused by Effie Mae's truthful humor. "I haven't tried getting up on my own yet, but I'll see what I can do." Effie Mae gradually sat up. "The nurses usually help me, in and out of bed."

"Well you go ahead and give it a try. And if you can't do it, I'll be right outside the door. Is that gon be alright?"

"Sounds, just fine Mr. Daniel."

Daniel hurried from the room then peered in, through the half opened door. He watched as Effie Mae tried to stand, wearing only her sheer pink nightgown.

"You need some help Effie Mae?" He asked when he noticed her inability to lift herself from the bed.

"I guess I do. I thought I could do it by myself, but my body ain't letting me." Daniel reentered the room. He wrapped Effie Mae's arm around his neck then placed his hand onto her waist and lifted her from the bed. She stood to her feet.

"Thank you Mr. Daniel."

"Naw . . . it's alright." He said. "If, uh — you need me for anything else, just let me know."

He released her then left the room. Again, he stood directly outside the door and watched as Effie Mae tried to walk step-by-step towards the doorway — then stopped.

"Are you gon stand there and wait for me to fall, Mr. Daniel?" She joked.

"Well if you do, I'll be right here to pick you up." He laughed then opened the door and rushed in. Effie Mae suddenly lost her balance. Daniel swiftly caught her, breaking her fall. He placed her arm around his neck. The two stood face to face and glared into each other's eyes. She pulled his head forward and kissed him. Daniel responded. Their impromptu kiss abruptly ended, by a knock at the front door.

"Ms. Geraldine! Mr. Daniel!" A woman's voice called through the door. "Dr. Brown said you needed help?"

Chapter Thirty-One

Ms. Geraldine collected her thoughts on Effie Mae as she wrapped her thick, coarse hair around the pink hair rollers and prepared to retire for the evening. Daniel lay on the right side of the bed, covered only by a blue sheet. He replayed in his mind the kiss he and Effie Mae shared. He wondered if the knock on the door had not occurred, could have actually shared in intimacy with his cousin's wife. His mind told him no—but his body said, without doubt—yes. He tried unsuccessfully, to dismiss the thought, but the harder he tried, the more difficult it became.

"I'm sure glad to see that Effie Mae's doing better." Ms. Geraldine said. Daniel remained silent. "Daniel?"

"Huh." He replied.

"Did you hear me?" Ms. Geraldine shifted her eyes briefly to him, curious by his peculiar behavior.

"Uh, yeah, I heard you, Geraldine." He remained deep in thought.

"Daniel, are you feeling okay?"

"Uh . . . what did you say, Geraldine?"

"I said—that I was glad to see that Effie Mae was doing better."

"Yeah, I'm glad too." He reached over and pulled the quilted, floral bedspread over his head and prepared to go to sleep.

"Are you sure you're feeling okay, Daniel? I know that flu is going around."

Ms. Geraldine appeared mystified by his out of character behavior. "I hope you're not still thinking about sending Effie Mae back to Mississippi." Daniel avoided direct eye contact, when rolling over towards her to address her concerns—regarding Effie Mae.

"Let's not worry about that right now, Geraldine. Let's just concentrate on her getting better. Then we'll see." He rolled back over and covered his head with both the covers and a pillow.

A large lump formed in Ms. Geraldine's throat as she thought about Dr. Brown's prior warning. She looked at the blanket covered silhouette of her husband then turned off the light and lay down, resting her head on the pillow. Her concern for Effie Mae now shifted to her own insecurities.

...

Wearing a full length, pastel pink, cotton bathrobe, Effie Mae returned to her bedroom from the bathroom, after an hour of submerging herself in a tub of warm water, in an effort to relieve the minor discomforts that continued to linger in her once beaten body. She stood momentarily in front of the dresser mirror. Her exceptional beauty now regained. She ran her hand gently over her right cheek, still slightly bruised and swollen. Effie Mae vividly recalled the enraged look in

Huck's eyes as he beat her within inches of her life. She abruptly looked away.

In preparation for her scheduled office visit with Dr. Brown, after four months of recuperating, Effie Mae walked over to the open closet and looked inside. She noted the pinstriped skirt purchased by J.R. many years ago. She removed it from the hanger and laid it on top of the bed, then went in search of the silk blouse she'd worn with that skirt. Effie Mae opened the top dresser drawer and rambled inside, in searched of the blouse. She located it in the rear left corner. She removed it from the drawer and quickly took note of how wrinkled it was.

"This thing is too wrinkled—now where did I put that iron?" She asked herself as she tossed the blouse onto the bed. Preparing to slip into the skirt, she removed the full length bath robe, and stood wearing only her pink silk underwear.

Effie Mae turned in the direction of the bedroom door, when she sensed a presence on the other side. Daniel abruptly entered into the room.

"Are you ready Effie Mae?" His eyes explored every inch of her semi-naked body. He turned away then again looked, unable to resist. He walked over and eagerly took her into his arms. They stared into each other eyes. Neither spoke one word. Effie Mae leaned in, and the two simultaneously connected in a passionate kiss. Daniel lifted her up into his arms then carried her over to the bed. Forsaking the fact that Effie Mae was his cousin's wife, he willingly engaged in intimacy with her.

...

After an exhausting day of cooking, helping with homework and playing a game of *Old Maid* with the children, Ms. Geraldine put them to bed. She decided not to join Daniel out back as she'd always done. Physically drained, she retired to her room for the evening.

Effie Mae lay in bed sleepless, as she thought of the intimate moment between her and Daniel.

Outback, Daniel engaged in his usual nightly smoke. He replayed in his mind the intimacy he and Effie Mae had shared. Drawn by the memories, he put away his pipe and entered into the house. He walked past Effie Mae's bedroom and down the hall to the door of the bedroom he shared with his wife. He peeked inside hoping to find her already asleep.

"Geraldine. You sleep?" He whispered. "Geraldine." After receiving no reply, He quietly closed the door then looked in the direction of Effie Mae's room. He paced outside the door as he tried to talk himself out of repeating a family *taboo*. Weakened by lust, Daniel opened the door and entered; his plan being to return to his wife's bed, before sunrise. He pulled back the covers and climbed into Effie Mae's awaiting arms. They kissed, and again the two engaged in a night of intimacy. Unknown to Daniel, Millie Ann watched from the cracked bathroom door, as he entered into her Momma's bedroom.

Effie Mae lay in Daniel arms, as she'd done for the past several weeks. She appeared to have seemingly forgotten about his marriage to Ms. Geraldine and her being the estranged wife of his cousin.

Ms. Geraldine, like every morning, routinely prepared the children for school then saw them off, prior to leaving for work.

"Effie Mae! I'm leaving now." She called out from the kitchen. "Remember, if you run into any problems just call me at Ms. Winchester's.

"Okay, Ms. Geraldine." Effie Mae replied.

"I thought Daniel said he was staying home today. But, I don't see his car out here." She said, unsuspectingly. "I guess he must plan on coming home early. I'll see you when I get home!" She hurried out the door and headed for the bus stop.

"Bye, Ms. Geraldine." Effie Mae said then kissed Daniel gently on the lips.

"Bye, Ms. Geraldine." Daniel teased. "Effie Mae that's cold. In here talking about, "bye, Ms. Geraldine" and you in here laid up with her husband!" Effie Mae lifted the sheet and gestured as though she were getting out of bed.

"Then I guess maybe I should get out of the bed with—Ms. Geraldine's husband." She said, playfully. Daniel pulled her back and into his arms.

"And what about you Mr. Daniel? You just as bad as me."

"Tell me something Effie Mae."

"What's that Mr. Daniel?"

"That's it."

"What's it"

"Why you still calling me—Mr. Daniel?"

"That's what I always called you."

"Well stop! Call me Daniel." He kissed her on the lips.

"What? What do you think Ms. Geraldine's gon say, when she hears me calling you Daniel?"

"Don't call me that in front of Geraldine!"

"What if I forget?" Daniel thought about it for a moment.

"Well, just keep calling me Mr. Daniel." He again kissed her. "You know you got something of mines."

"What? I don't have nothing that belongs to you."

"Yes you do."

"What?"

"My heart."

"What? Your heart?"

"Yeah, Effie Mae, I think you done stole it." Daniel kissed her softly on the lips. "I'm serious. I done messed around and fell in love with you, girl"

"What about Ms. Geraldine?"

"What about Geraldine?"

"How you are gon lay here and say you love me, and you married to her?" Effie Mae sat up.

"Now, there you go complicating things." He pulled her back into his arms. "You let me worry about Geraldine."

"You know what Mr. Daniel, that's exactly what I'm gon do. Besides I have enough to worry about."

"Yeah—Geraldine catching us in here, messing around!" He chuckled. "I think we both should be worried about that."

"Mr. Daniel . . ."

"Uh-huh" He said kissing her on the neck and shoulders.

"I think I need to go see Dr. Brown."

"See Doc. Brown . . . I thought you were doing better?"

Effie Mae said nothing further.

That night, Ms. Geraldine lay sleepless. She reached over to cuddle with Daniel as she'd often done when being unable to sleep. Tonight, she found the space usually occupied by his warm body, now cold and vacant. She climbed out of bed, deciding to go in search of her missing husband. She walked down the hallway, right past Effie Mae's closed bedroom door.

Ms. Geraldine strolled through the dining room, and in the direction of the bathroom. She looked inside and noted that it was empty. She went to the backdoor and opened it, then poked her head out, expecting to discover Daniel seated on the back porch, smoking his pipe. Again, she saw no signs of him.

"Now, I wonder where he could be this time of night." Ms. Geraldine said to herself. She closed the door, and decided to go back to bed, ending her search.

She paused when she heard snoring coming from the living room. She turned and headed in that direction, certain she would find Daniel asleep on the couch. Her eyes widened when she discovered that the snoring belonged not to her husband, but Millie Ann, lying there asleep.

"Millie Ann?" Ms. Geraldine said, softly. Millie Ann opened her eyes and looked up. "Why are you in here, sleeping on the couch? Millie Ann remained silent. "Have you seen Daniel?" She nodded her head. "Well, where is he? I couldn't find him anywhere." Millie Ann got up and walked from the living room, through the kitchen and dining room, then stopped directly outside of her Momma's bedroom. She pointed at the door then scurried down the hallway. Ms. Geraldine watched in awe as Millie Ann entered into her own bedroom, quickly closing the door shut.

Ms. Geraldine apprehensively paced outside of Effie Mae's bedroom door, afraid to open it. Her mouth dried and her heart rapidly pounded, as the minutes passed. Determined to know the truth, she took a deep breath and turned the doorknob. She prayed that her fears would be unconfirmed.

Ms. Geraldine reluctantly opened the door and witnessed Daniel lying in bed asleep, cuddled, with his cousin's wife. She threw her hand over her lips as her mouth flung open. She felt as if the air were being sucked right out of her. Careful not to make a sound, she hastily turned away and retreated from the room, returning to her own, now broken bedroom. Ms. Geraldine lowered herself down onto the bed and painfully wept.

"Effie Mae." Daniel spoke just above a whisper as he pulled the cover from over her head.

"What time is it Mr. Daniel?" Effie Mae asked, as she rolled over onto her back. She looked into Daniel's face, and saw the extreme look of fear in his eyes.

"It's time for us to think on how we gon explain to Geraldine, what the hell I was doing in here in your bed all night."

"What?"

"I overslept! Geraldine knows I didn't come back to bed last night. She probably opened that door right there, and saw me and you in here naked as two jaybirds!"

"What are we gon do, Mr. Daniel?"

"Effie Mae, you gon have to leave!"

"What? Where am I gon go?"

"You can go back home to Mississippi. I'll come see you."

"And what about this child I'm carrying?

Daniel stared at her in silence, unprepared for the news. He became angered by what he viewed as Effie Mae's problem.

"What? You pregnant Effie Mae?" He looked up at the ceiling. "Damn!"

...

Ms. Geraldine left early from work the next morning at Mrs. Winchester insistence, when she noticed, that she wasn't quite herself. In addition, she had spent the first two hours on the job, crying uncontrollably.

Ms. Geraldine climbed off the bus and headed in the direction of her home. She stepped onto the front porch then approached the door. Her hand trembled as she inserted the key, turning the knob, quietly opening the door. She rubbed her hand across her eyes, wiping away the tears puddled inside then entered. Ms. Geraldine walked through the kitchen and dining room then headed directly to Effie Mae's bedroom certain, that she would find the two lovers, still in bed. She exhaled as she prepared to surprise her husband and his cousin's wife. Ms. Geraldine stood momentarily outside the door building up her nerves then burst inside the room.

Daniel and Effie Mae quickly sat up, their attention being diverted from the dilemma of her pregnancy, to the unexpected return of Ms. Geraldine. Daniel gazed at his wife through apologetic eyes. Effie Mae remained speechless.

"Why, Effie Mae? Why would you do this to me?" She yelled.

"I'm sorry Ms. Geraldine . . ." Ms. Geraldine cut her off.

"Like you sorry about what you done to J.R." She shook her head. "I let your poor excuse for anything back into my home, after you ran your husband off! I took care of your children like they were my own, while you were out there lost in the world and working as a whore! And, I took care of you, when somebody almost beat you half to death! I've been nothing but good to you Effie Mae." Tears streamed down Ms. Geraldine's face. "All I want you to do is tell me why? Why would you lay in here with my husband, in my house?" Ms. Geraldine's pain magnified. "Now you're sitting there glowing and pregnant . . . I know its Daniel's." Effie Mae began sobbing." Daniel looked at Ms. Geraldine with guilt then reached over and put his arm around Effie Mae.

"That's enough Geraldine!"

"Daniel you should have known better!" She shouted.

"You right Geraldine. I should've. So, I'm just as responsible as Effie Mae. I could've walked away, but I didn't." He shook his head in response to his weakness. "Right now, I feel as low as a man can feel. Effie Mae is my cousin's wife."

"Shut up Daniel!" Ms. Geraldine snapped. "I don't want to hear a damn thing you have to say! So if I were you, I would get up and disappear from this room while you still have legs to walk!" Daniel shook his head—no.

"I told you Geraldine! I'm not getting ready to leave out of here and let you beat up on Effie Mae. That ain't gon solve nothing." He stated. "I understand you hurt and upset, but that ain't gon change a thing. There's a child on the way and that's what matters now. I don't know how we gon do it, but for the sake of those children, we gon have to get along in here."

Ms. Geraldine's attention turned back to Effie Mae. "Well, I tell you one thing Effie Mae, it might be your womb that's carrying my husband seed—but the child you give birth to—is going to be mines." She pointed her finger at Effie Mae. "Because the day you bring that baby into this world, that will be the day, I claim it as my own—mines and my husband's." She looked at Daniel." And don't you try to stop me, Daniel!" She turned and prepared to leave the room then stopped. She gazed angrily at Effie Mae. "And after you give birth to my baby …" She glared at Daniel then again looked at Effie Mae. "You get the hell out of my house!" Daniel gazed at his wife with disbelief. "So if I were you, Effie Mae Smith, I'd be calling my Momma in Mississippi. Let her know that you're on your way back home. Explaining to her the reason why, that's gon be your burden to bear."

Ms. Geraldine stormed from the room, slamming the door shut behind her. Daniel continued to comfort Effie Mae as she sobbed, uncontrollably.

Chapter Thirty-Two

Effie Mae lay in bed accompanied by Lil' J.R. He reached over and rubbed her belly.

"Is it a baby in your stomach Momma?"

"Yep."

"When is it gon come out?"

"Any day now Lil' J.R."

"Is it a boy like me? Or a girl, like Sarah?"

"I don't know yet. We'll just have to wait for it to get here." Effie Mae chuckled.

Millie Ann suddenly rushed into the room, winded from running.

"Momma, Huck wants you!" Effie Mae looked at her, alarmed by the mention of Huck's name.

"What?" She sat up. "What you talking about, Millie Ann?"

"I was getting the mail and I heard somebody call my name. And when I looked up, I saw this man standing on the corner down the streets."

"What? Are you sure he called your name, Millie Ann?

"Yeah! Then he said—tell Effie Mae that Huck wants to see her." Effie Mae placed her hand under her belly as she prepared to get out of bed.

"Stay here and watch your brother. Don't go back outside. And don't let your sisters come out either." Effie Mae sat on side of the bed. "Help me get my shoes on." Millie Ann picked up her shoes from the floor then kneeled and slid a shoe on each foot. Effie Mae rushed from the bedroom and into the kitchen.

Ms. Geraldine and Daniel watched television in the living room with the other children. They looked quickly into the kitchen when they heard Effie Mae rummaging through a kitchen drawer. They watched as she grabbed a butcher knife then hurried in the direction of the front door.

"Effie Mae?" Daniel called out. "What's going on? Where you going?"

"I'm going out here to kill Huck! That's where I'm going!" She snatched open the kitchen door. "He out there . . . talking to my child!" She yelled. "Don't be talking to my daughter!" Effie Mae said to herself then darted out the house. Daniel and Ms. Geraldine hastily arose.

"What did she say?" Ms. Geraldine asked as she walked swiftly into the kitchen. She looked out the window and saw Huck standing a block away looking at the house. "Daniel, go get Effie Mae! I'm calling the police." Daniel rushed out after Effie Mae. She looked back and saw him behind her then stopped.

"Go back Mr. Daniel! This between me and Huck!" She placed her left hand under her belly, and carried the knife in her right hand.

"I can't let you do that, Effie Mae. He ain't worth it!" Daniel shouted. Huck smiled as he watched Effie Mae walking towards him. She stopped several feet away.

"What you want Huck?" She yelled.

"Girl, you pregnant again? Who's baby is it this time, Effie Mae? Blue? Or is it mines?" He laughed. "After I heard that you were still alive, you know I had to come see you."

"You stay away from my daughter!"

"Oh, you mean Millie Ann." You know I wouldn't do anything to your daughter, Effie Mae." He said with sincerity. "Come ride with me."

"Get away from here, Huck! Leave me alone!"

"Now, you know I can't do that. Come ride with me Effie Mae."

Daniel approached Effie Mae from behind, stopping only a few feet away. He gazed at Huck, as he cautiously kept Effie Mae in his sight.

"We've already called the police, Huck. So go ahead and leave!"

"Stay back Mr. Daniel!" Effie Mae shouted.

"Come on now Effie Mae. You know you're pregnant. I don't want anything to happen to you or our child." Daniel momentarily shook and lowered his head, when he realized he'd let it slip that Effie Mae's unborn child was his.

Huck looked at Daniel then to Effie Mae and laughed. "Girl, you something else. Daniel? What did your wife have to say about that, Daniel?" Huck continued laughing. "You pimping now, Daniel?" Huck teased as he gazed at Effie Mae then shifted his eyes back to Daniel. "Well, I didn't give you permission to pimp Effie Mae. She belongs to me." Huck stated, angrily.

"I don't belong to nobody!" Effie Mae yelled.

"Come ride with me Effie Mae. Girl, don't make me mad."

"Man, you see that she's pregnant. Leave her alone, Huck!" Daniel shouted.

"What you gon do Daniel? Huh?"

"I told you we've already called the police."

"Where they at? You see the police, Daniel?' Huck laughed to himself. "Here's what I want you to do." He paused. "I want you to turn around and take your old ass back in the house before I hurt you—Effie Mae and y'all baby." He threatened.

"I'm not afraid of you Huck!" Daniel said.

"Well, you should be. Shouldn't he, Effie Mae?"

"Go back in the house, Mr. Daniel. Please! I don't want you to get hurt. I need you and Ms. Geraldine to care for my babies, if something happens to me. Please, Mr. Daniel!" Her eyes pleaded.

"I can't leave you out here like that Effie Mae."

"I'll be alright. Huck ain't gon hurt me. We have a special connection. Ain't that right Huck?" She turned to him and smiled.

"You know that's right. Now, come and get in the car." Effie Mae looked at Daniel then moved towards Huck. She walked over to him and entered into his arms. He removed the knife from her hand then kissed her on the forehead. "That's my girl." He looked at Daniel. "I better not see one police either. So, you go back in the house and call them. Tell them you want to cancel that report." Daniel watched helplessly. Huck put his arm around Effie Mae and escorted her to the passenger side of his car. He opened the door and helped her inside as he kept his eye on Daniel. "Bye,

Daniel." He mocked then walked over to the driver's side and opened the door. He suddenly stopped. "Oh! And uh, congratulations Pops!" He laughed as he climbed into his car then drove off.

...

Seated in the living room of Buckeye's efficiency apartment, Huck put his arm around Effie Mae and repeatedly kissed her on the side of the face. Buckeye watched.

"How you been doing Effie Mae?" Buckeye asked. Effie Mae looked at him and rolled her eyes. Huck chuckled.

"How you think she's doing Buckeye? She pregnant—again."

"Huck man, is that your baby?"

"It should've been." He reached over to rub Effie Mae round belly. She flinched. "What you jumping for? I ain't gon hit you." He rubbed her belly. Naw, Buckeye, Effie Mae done sunk her teeth into old Daniel. Got his old ass strung out too!" He chuckled.

"Daniel? Ain't he some kin to Effie Mae?

"Naw, he's kin to her husband. Get this Buckeye. He brought his old ass outside ready to take me on, over Effie Mae." He laughed.

"He did?" Buckeye eyes widened.

"Yeah! Now you know I would've had hurt him, right?" Huck laughed and again kissed Effie Mae on the face. "But, Effie Mae saved him. Ain't that right?" He kissed her on the cheek.

"What you want Huck?" She asked.

"It's like you told old Daniel, we got a connection. We just need to figure out how it's gon ever be just me and you. We got too many players in the game."

"Hey! Don't Daniel have a wife, Huck?" Buckeye asked, in hindsight.

"Yeah, and she lives right there in the house. You know what I think Buckeye? I think old Daniel's pimping. Is he pimping, Effie Mae? How much you think he gon charge me for you?" He laughed.

"I need to go home and see about my babies."

"You'll go home when I say you can! You understand me Effie Mae?" Huck yelled.

Effie Mae cringed, afraid that he might hit her. "But now, you need to tell me how you survived that beatin' that I gave you?" He looked puzzled. "Girl, I know you were dead! Wasn't she dead Buckeye?"

"She looked like she was to me." Buckeye nodded.

"Buckeye wanted to throw your ass in the river. But, I wouldn't let him. Instead I thought we should just leave you outside where old Daniel could find you. Is that who found you Effie Mae?" He chuckled. "Girl, somebody upstairs was looking out for you." He said. Buckeye nodded. "But, I learned my lesson Effie Mae. I ain't gon hit you no more." He kissed her on the cheek. "Turn around." Effie Mae turned and looked at him. Huck kissed her passionately on the lips. "That's my girl. After you have that baby. You come see me." He kissed her again. "You hear me Effie Mae?" She remained silent. "You hear me?" He stated, firmly.

"Yeah Huck."

"You still messing with Blue?"

"Mr. Daniel won't let him come to the house."

"I bet he won't." Huck teased. "He wanted you all to his self!" The two men laughed.

Chapter Thirty-Three

Ms. Geraldine watched apprehensively as Ms. Ida prepared to detach Effie Mae and son by way of the umbilical cord. Seconds after Ms. Ida cut and clamped the cord, Ms. Geraldine seized the infant. She vaguely allowed Effie Mae to catch a glimpse of him. The midwife curiously observed the unusual exchange, confused by what had just taken place.

"Daniel Lee Jones Jr." Ms. Geraldine said. "That what I'm naming my son. I'm giving him the same name as his daddy, my husband, Daniel Lee Jones Sr." Ms. Ida gazed at her in shock, perplexed by her bizarre statement.

"Your son?" She asked.

"Yes! My son! And that's what you're going to put on the birth record, Ms. Ida."

"Now, Geraldine you know I can't do that. I brought this child in this world and it wasn't your womb that I pulled him from."

"Ms. Ida, this Jezebel laid down with my husband right here in this very bed—while I lay sleeping, and got pregnant with his child." Ms. Ida's mouth flung open. "The way I see it, this was the good Lord's way of giving me the child my womb was never blessed to receive. So, Ms. Ida, I'm going to ask you one last time, to write my husband's name on that birth record as the father and my name as the mother." Ms. Ida looked mysteriously at Ms. Geraldine then glanced at Effie Mae, who silently nodded her head in agreement.

"Now, I understand how you might feel that you deserve this child, but as a woman of God, I just wouldn't feel right, if I signed Effie Mae's child over to you and Daniel, no matter how he came about. It looks to me, like that's a matter you, Daniel and Effie Mae need to work out."

"Ms. Ida—here's what I want you to do." Ms. Geraldine ignored the words she'd just spoken. "I want you to go into my bedroom down the hall and look in my top dresser drawer. I want you to reach down on the right hand side, and take out that glass jar tucked away in the corner." Ms. Ida listened to the vivid instructions. "Inside of that jar is $578 that I've been saving for the last five years. All you have to do is sign my husband's name on that birth record as the father, and sign your name as the midwife. I won't even ask that you sign my name—you can leave that part blank." Ms. Ida's facial expression change as the offer tempted her. "And before the sun goes down this evening, this baby's going to have a mother listed on that birth record!" Ms. Geraldine concluded as she cuddled, Daniel and Effie Mae's, illegitimate son in her arms.

Ms. Ida glanced at Effie Mae then again to Ms. Geraldine.

"You said $578 in a glass jar in the top right hand corner in your dresser?" She repeated.

"That's what I said." Ms. Ida nervously hurried towards the closed bedroom door then stopped.

"I don't want to know! Whatever y'all decide to do—I don't want to know!" She opened the bedroom door and scurried from the room.

...

Effie Mae awakened through the night from the cry of her infant son. She wanted desperately to take him into her arms and nurse him as she had, with her other children. She knew that Ms. Geraldine purposely taunted her due to her continued hurt. The door swung open.

"D.J.'s hungry." Ms. Geraldine stated. She handed Effie Mae a breast pump and two four ounce bottles. Effie Mae took the items and laid them on the bed. "I'll be back in thirty minutes."

Ms. Geraldine turned and walked away then closed the door behind her. Effie Mae picked up a bottle and the pump then prepared to extract milk from her breast.

"Effie Mae." Daniel whispered as he removed the cover from over her head. Effie Mae turned over and reached for the breast pump.

"The baby needs more milk?" She asked, still half asleep.

"Effie Mae. It's Daniel." She opened her eyes in response to his voice, curious of his intent.

"Mr. Daniel? What you want? I'm still healing from . . ." He interrupted.

"I'm not in here for that!" He said. "I want to talk to you."

Effie Mae sat up. Daniel gazed at her and smiled. "What?"

"I was just thinking, that's all."

"Now, Mr. Daniel . . . ."

"Can't a man think?" He grinned. "I got something for you. Close your eyes and open your hand."

"Huh?

"See—there you go. Just do it girl!" Effie Mae closed her eyes and opened her hand. Daniel placed a photo in it. "Open your eyes." She opened her eyes and looked at the picture of her newborn son. "That's our boy, Effie Mae." She smiled as she examined the photo carefully.

"He looks just like you Mr. Daniel. He's beautiful." She rubbed her hand across the photograph.

"We didn't do half bad—did we?"

"Don't let Ms. Geraldine hear you saying that." Effie Mae chuckled as she continued admiring their son.

"You know Effie Mae. D. J. is almost a month old. I know Geraldine said you had to leave, but . . ." Effie Mae cut him off.

"I can stay?"

"Nope! Geraldine meant what she said. And it ain't nothing I can do to stop her. And I don't think I would, if I could."

"So, you want me out too?"

"Naw! I want you to stay! But now, what do you think would happen if you did?" He raised an eyebrow. "Girl, I ain't over you!" Effie Mae looked at him, surprised by his statement. She blushed. "When I said that I was in love with you . . . I meant that."

"What about Ms. Geraldine?"

"I love my wife. But I ain't ever been in love with her. Back when we got married, a man looked for a wife who he thought would be a good helpmate—cooking, cleaning, and caring for the children, somebody who would meet his basic needs. You loved her, but you didn't necessarily have to be—in love with her." He took a hold of Effie Mae's hand that held the photo, and placed it against his heart. "I guess, me never being in love with Geraldine, left my heart wide open. And when we got together, girl . . . you just walked right in."

But . . ." He cut her off.

"Yeah, I know. You my cousin's wife, but that don't matter. I couldn't have you anyway. I could never leave Geraldine. I couldn't hurt her like that." He paused. "I guess in my fantasy life, I would keep Geraldine as my wife—wife; and you would be the wife, that made me feel alive, feel like a man . . ." Effie Mae interrupted.

"I guess the thing about fantasies, Mr. Daniel is, they ain't real." Effie Mae stared into his eyes. He leaned in and kissed her. She gazed curiously into his eyes.

"That was just my way of saying goodbye. You gave me a son, and he'll always remind me of what we had." Daniel smiled. "What I'm trying to figure out now, is how I'm gon explain to J.R., how that happened."

"I think he know—how it happened." Effie Mae teased.

"You know what I mean."

"Yeah, I know. But let me tell him."

"I can't let you do that, Effie Mae."

"J.R. was once in love with me, I think I can make him understand how people can sometimes do things, that they later regret doing."

"I didn't say all that! I don't regret falling in love with you. I don't regret us having a son. The only thing I regret is the timing." He kissed Effie Mae again.

"Okay now, Mr. Daniel." That's enough." They laughed. "Mr. Daniel?"

"Yeah."

"You think you can let me see our son, and let me hold him?" Effie Mae's eyes pleaded.

"Ms. Beverly—Ms. Ida's sister, watches him for Geraldine. Let me talk to her." He winked.

"Thank you Mr. Daniel." Effie Mae took a hold of his hand and kissed it. He stared helplessly into her eyes.

"I guess I better get on out of here and go to work . . . ." He paused. "Before, I can't." Daniel gently kissed her on the lips then walked away.

Effie Mae removed the hangers containing her clothes from the closet and laid them on the bed. She retrieved her suitcases, also in the closet, and set them on the floor. She walked over to the dresser and opened the top drawer. Millie Ann entered the room as Effie Mae began removing her clothes.

"Are you leaving Momma?" Millie Ann asked as she wrapped her arms around her Momma's waist. "I don't want you to leave."

"Well, Millie Ann, this is Ms. Geraldine and Mr. Daniel's house. So, if they want me to leave, I have to go."

"Is it because of D.J.?" Effie Mae looked down at her, surprised by her question.

"What do you mean Millie Ann?"

"I know that D.J. is Mr. Daniel's baby." She began crying. "I'm sorry Momma."

"Sorry for what Millie Ann?" Effie Mae consoled her.

"I told Ms. Geraldine that Mr. Daniel was in the bed with you." Effie Mae placed her hands on Millie Ann shoulders and glared into her eyes.

"You did what? When?"

"One day when I was in the bathroom, I got ready to come out and I saw Mr. Daniel go in your room. I opened your door and I saw . . ." Effie Mae's gasped.

"Sit down on the floor with me Millie Ann." Effie Mae sat on the floor and positioned her back against the bed. Millie Ann slid down next to her. "What you saw me and Mr. Daniel doing was natural, but it was wrong. Do you understand what I'm saying?" Millie Ann shook her head—no. "What I'm trying to say is—it's natural for a man and woman to be together like me and Mr. Daniel were. But it was wrong because he's Ms. Geraldine's husband. Do you understand now?" Millie Ann nodded—yes.

"If it was wrong Momma, then why did you and Mr. Daniel do it?" Effie Mae laughed half-heartedly.

"I can't even answer that Millie Ann." She thought for a moment. "Can I wait until you get older to explain that to you?" Millie Ann nodded. "You know Millie Ann I'm finally learning that we can't always have what we want . . . ." Effie Mae hesitated. ". . . . just because we want it. Sometimes, if we think about how getting what we want, might hurt somebody else, or even ourselves, maybe we wouldn't want it at all."

"Can we go with you, Momma?" Millie Ann looked up at her.

"Not right now. I'm still trying to figure out where I'm gon go."

"What about Daddy?"

"Little girl, you sure do ask a lot of questions." Effie Mae chuckled. "I don't think that would work."

"Why? Don't you love, Daddy. He loves you."

"Well, Millie Ann, that's something else I'm gon have to talk to you about when you get older."

"What about Blue?" Effie Mae's mouth opened.

"Blue? What do you know about Blue?"

"I know he came to see you when you were sick."

"And how do you know that?"

"I heard daddy talking about it when we were over at his house."

"And, just what did your Daddy say?"

"He said that Blue made you happy."

"He did?" Effie Mae blushed as she thought about Blue.

"Who's Lil' J.R.'s Daddy?"

"What?" Effie Mae looked at her, puzzled by her insight. "Who told you that your daddy wasn't Lil' J.R.'s Daddy?"

"I heard Ms. Geraldine and Mr. Daniel talking about it."

"Well, you know what Millie Ann . . . it looks like I'm gon have to talk to your Daddy, Ms. Geraldine and Mr. Daniel about talking so much around you. But since you asked, I'm gon tell you." Effie Mae took a deep breath. "Nope—Lil' J.R. ain't your daddy's son. His daddy's name is Anthony." She smiled.

"Anthony? Who is that?" Millie Ann looked confused.

"Anthony is a man that once loved me so much, he asked me to marry him. But, his Momma and Daddy wouldn't let him."

"Why?"

"Well, that another one of those things I'm gon talk to you about when you get older, okay?"

"Okay."

"But, I want you to promise me something Millie Ann, if anybody . . . I don't care who it is, if they ever touch you down there or up here . . . ." Effie Mae pointed to those areas. "I want you to tell me right away! I don't care even if they say that they gon take you away from me. You tell me anyway! Let me handle it. You understand me Millie Ann?"

"Yeah."

"I mean it, Millie Ann!"

"Okay Momma." Effie Mae hugged her.

"Now, getting back to Anthony . . . ." She thought about her and Anthony's relationship and smiled. "I'm gon be taking Lil' J.R. real soon to go and see his Daddy."

"Oooh! Can me, Lena, Mahalia, Billie and Sarah, go see him too?"

"Yeah, I'd like that, Millie Ann." Effie Mae smiled. "I'm also gon take y'all to see your grandma Millie."

"Millie? That's my name." She said, excited.

"Yeah, me and your daddy named you after my Momma." She hesitated. "And, you might get to meet my baby sister, Annie Mae." Effie Mae's eyes filled with tears. They rolled down her cheeks. Millie Ann watched.

"Why are you crying Momma?" She reached up and wiped Effie Mae's tears.

"I've done so much wrong to so many people Millie Ann—and I don't know how to fix it. I don't even know if I can."

"I'll help you Momma." Millie Ann began crying.

J.R. entered into the room and observed Effie Mae and Millie Ann sitting on the floor crying.

"What's all them tears for?"

"Daddy!" Millie Ann leaped up and ran over and hugged him around his waist.

"Me and Millie Ann were just having a mother-daughter talk." Effie Mae wiped away her tears.

"You ready?"

"Ready for what, J.R.?" Effie Mae looked at him in question.

"Cousin Daniel didn't tell you?"

"Tell me what?"

"You coming to live with me."

"Yayyy!" Millie Ann clapped her hands. Effie Mae stared up at him from the floor in astonishment.

Chapter Thirty-Four

Effie Mae and J.R. convened in the kitchen eating a dinner of dressing, stuffed pork chops, cabbage, corn bread, and candied yams, cooked by Effie Mae. J.R. stared at her in silence amazed by the meal she'd prepared.

"What?" She said.

"You told me that you could cook, but until now, I doubted it ... since I'd never seen you do it." Effie Mae chuckled.

"I told you that you couldn't be Ms. Millie Reed's daughter and not know how to cook!" She paused. "Unless—you were Annie Mae Reed!" She laughed. J.R. continued his gaze.

"What?" She smiled.

"You been here for three weeks, and you ain't been out of the house once—and you ain't asked if Blue could come and see you. Are you and he . . . ." Effie Mae cut him off.

"I'm trying to put that life behind me." She laid her fork down. "I need to talk to you J.R."

"Okay." He said, curiously. "You ain't getting ready to tell me that one of them girls ain't mines either—are you?"

"No! Every last one of those girls is yours." She laughed. "But you close. I wanted to talk to you about Lil' J.R." She reached across the table and took a hold of his hand. "I'm so sorry about that."

"Effie Mae, you don't have to . . . ."

"Yeah, J.R., I do. You didn't deserve that." She released his hand, then walked around the table and sat next to him. He put his arm around her. She laid her head onto his chest. "I know who Lil' J. R.'s father is." He stared at her hoping that she would say that her son belonged to him. "He's Anthony's." J.R. swallowed the lump in his throat.

"You know it's funny, I always knew he wasn't my son, but I guess somewhere inside, I hoped he was."

"I'm sorry J.R." She looked up at him.

"Okay." He took a deep breath. "So tell me about Anthony ... my son's father?"

Effie Mae smiled as she reminisced.

"Anthony was the first boy to ask me to marry him. But, his Momma and Daddy wouldn't let him. And if you knew me back then, you wouldn't have let your son marry me either. As a matter of fact, there probably wasn't a family in all of Yazoo County, who would've let their son marry, Effie Mae Reed." J.R. glared at her in shock, taken back by her words.

"What?"

"I guess I probably was the only girl that had seen half the boys in the county with their pants down. And Effie Mae Reed was the talk of the town!" She chuckled. "Well, Anthony came to the house one day because he'd heard some of the other boys talking about me. I guess he wanted a piece of me too. But, Anthony was different." Effie Mae became deep in thought. "He never judged me. And he was always the perfect gentleman. And he loved me—for me. When I went back home, there he was smiling. Then he kissed me." J.R. shifted his eyes to her. "He told me he had a surprise for me, and asked me to come with him. I told him that I was married, but he begged me to come and see his surprise." She glanced up at J.R. "So, I went. This boy had bought me a house . . . us a house!" She quietly chuckled. "And he still wanted to marry me!" She laughed half-heartedly. "So, when he kissed me . . . ." She paused. "It was like I was seventeen year old Effie Mae Reed, again. So, we did what we always did when we got together." She said matter-of-factly.

"Ahem." J.R. cleared his throat. "Only this time—you got pregnant."

"Yeah, when I came back home to you, that's when I realized how much I really loved my life with you and our babies." She looked into his eyes and smiled. He kissed her on the forehead.

"Would you have ever told me Effie Mae if I hadn't read your diary?"

"I don't know J.R.? The Effie Mae, I was back then, probably not! But the Effie Mae, I am today. Yeah, she would have." He again kissed her on the forehead.

"Thank you for sharing that information with me."

"Lil' J.R. needs to know his daddy."

"Do you think that Anthony would want to know, that he fathered a son with another man's wife?"

"I don't know J.R."

"Well, if he does or doesn't—Lil' J.R. will always be my son. And I will always be Daddy to him."

"And that boy will always love you no matter what." She chuckled. "But, Anthony has a right to know that he has a son. I owe him that."

"How do you plan to do that?"

"I need to go back to home. Not just so that Anthony can see Lil' J.R., but I want Momma to see our babies. You know Momma has never seen our girls, except for Sarah. And she was just a baby like D.J." Effie Mae stopped.

"D.J.?" J.R. asked curiously. "That's the baby you just had? Millie Ann told me that you were pregnant, but when I asked her if Blue was the father, she wouldn't answer." Effie Mae gazed into his eyes, apprehensive about telling him the truth.

"I'll answer it. No. Blue's not D.J.'s daddy. And, if you want me to leave after I tell you who is, I'll have Blue come and get me."

"Why would I do that?"

"D.J. stands for . . . Daniel Jr."

"What the hell?" J.R. placed his hand briefly on his forehead then looked at her. "Effie Mae! Daniel? My Cousin?" He said, disappointed. "How much more can you hurt me? My cousin?" Why?" He stared at her. "Ms. Geraldine? That's why they made you move out, ain't it?" He shook his head in disbelief. "How could Daniel do this to me . . . to Geraldine? And you! How could you do that to Geraldine, Effie Mae? She was there for our children when you, when both of us were lost in ourselves."

"I'll go call Blue." Effie Mae prepared to stand.

"No! You don't have to leave." He took a hold of her arm. "Just tell me this—were you and he together when I was living there?"

"No! This happened when he was taking care of me after what happened to me."

"Was it a result your head injuries?"

"I wish I could say it was, but it wasn't. It was just Effie Mae Reed being Effie Mae Reed."

"And Cousin Daniel . . . being Cousin Daniel—but with my wife? You know he once told me that if you wasn't my wife, he'd have you for his self." J.R.'s anger increased. "Why didn't he tell me?"

"He wanted to, but I asked him to let me do it. I thought that it might be different coming from me."

"And you were right! Because, if he had told me . . . ." J.R. shook his head in fury.

"Am I your wife, J.R.? Or are we just still married?" She gazed into his eyes. "I guess we ain't lived as husband and wife in a long time." J.R. looked at her as he thought about her rational question. He said nothing further.

...

J.R. loaded his and Effie Mae's luggage into the trunk of his car.

"Are you sure about driving us J.R.? Because—if you don't want to make that ride, I can get Blue to drive us." She said from inside the car. J.R. got in and closed the door then stared at her.

"Effie Mae?"

"Huh?"

"Can I go just one day without hearing about Blue?" Effie Mae looked surprised by his request.

"If you take me to go see Blue, while you go pick my babies up from Ms. Geraldine's, I promise I won't say Blue's name once, for the entire trip."

"Take you to go see Blue?"

"Yeah, you know Ms. Geraldine don't want me anywhere near Mr. Daniel."

"I thought you said you were putting that life behind you?"

"I am. But, I haven't seen Blue in months.

"In months, Effie Mae?" He asked, skeptical.

"Okay. It ain't been months, but don't say nothing about it to Mr. Daniel. He didn't want Blue over at the house. But you know that wasn't gon happen."

"Effie Mae!"

"What? Blue wasn't gon stay away from me that long! Cause . . . Tyrell Jones loves him some Effie Mae . . . ."

"Effie Mae." J. R. interrupted.

"Huh?"

"Okay. I'll take you over to see Blue, while I go pick up the children. But, I'm coming right back, Effie Mae! So, you and Blue don't have time for nothing but a visit. You follow me?"

"Yeah, I follow you, J.R." He glared at her.

"Effie Mae."

"Okay J.R.! I'm gon be ready to go when you get back!"

"And if you ain't, we gon all be spending the entire weekend, at my house . . . me, you and the children. No Blue."

"Okay, J.R." He started the car and pulled off, headed on their way to Blue's Jazz Club.

Chapter Thirty-Five

Millie waited on the front porch for the arrival of Effie Mae, J.R. and their children. Rev. Hill and Sissy joined her.

"Millie. I ain't seen my brother since he came here looking for a—wife." She looked at Rev. Hill.

"Sissy."

"What Otis? I haven't said anything. Now have I Millie?" Millie remained silent, nervous about Effie Mae's return.

"But, you was getting ready to start. I heard it coming." Rev. Hill said.

"I promised you Otis, that I wasn't gon say anything about how Effie Mae did my poor brother, humiliating him like that, having another man's child . . . and I'm not!" She glanced over at Millie. "I'm sorry Millie." Rev. Hill raised an eyebrow.

"Sissy, if you get started, I'm telling you now. We gon get back in the car and I'm taking you home."

"Otis, you were the one, who thought it was a good idea for my baby brother to marry Effie Mae!" She shifted her eyes to Millie. "I'm sorry Millie."

"Let's go Sissy." Rev. Hill stood up.

"I'm not going anywhere until I see my baby brother and all them beautiful babies, he and Effie Mae, have. I even want to see that stray son of hers." She looked at Millie. "I'm sorry Millie.

"We gon see you on Sunday in church, Ms. Millie." Rev. Hill began walking off the porch.

J.R., Effie Mae and the children cruised down the road then pulled into the driveway.

"There here!" Sissy hurried from the porch and ran towards the car. "J.R.!" She rushed over to the driver's side and waited for him to open the door. Rev. Hill stepped back onto the porch. He and Millie watched as Effie Mae got out then opened the back door to let her many children out. A smile formed on Millie's face as she saw the faces of the grandchildren she'd never seen. She also took pleasure in seeing Effie Mae in the role of mother and wife. Sissy stared at Lil' J. R. as she hugged her baby brother. "He don't look like you . . . or Effie Mae." She whispered.

"Sissy, you said you wasn't gon say anything around the children—remember." J.R. said, whispering.

"What? All I said was that boy don't look like you or Effie Mae!" She turned around and looked into the glaring eyes of Rev. Hill. "Where's Sarah? The last time I saw her she was a newborn!"

"Hey Momma!" Effie Mae said as she walked onto porch. Her six children stood at the bottom of the stairs, unfamiliar with the woman their Momma referenced to as—Momma.

"How you doing, Rev. Hill?" Effie Mae greeted when approaching him on the porch.

"I'm doing just fine Effie Mae. It's good to see you again." He hugged her.

"Momma, I want you to meet your grandchildren." Effie Mae said with *motherly* pride. Millie held back her excitement as she awaited the introductions. "Come on over here, Millie Ann." Millie watched as fourteen year old, Millie Ann walked up the stairs and approached her. She reminded her of Effie Mae as a child.

"Hi Granny." Millie Ann hugged her then seated herself on the pink sofa that once sat in the living room.

"Lena, come on baby. Say hi to your Granny." Twelve year old Lena, resembling her Daddy walked over and embraced Millie. "What are you suppose to say Lena? Effie Mae asked.

"Hi Granny."

"Billie. You next." Eleven year old Billie looked much like Annie Mae. She stared at Millie with unfamiliarity then approached.

"Hi Granny." She hugged Millie then hurried back over to Effie Mae.

"Mahalia, come say Hi to your Grandma Millie." Ten year old Mahalia walked over to Millie and gave her a big hug.

"She looks like J.R. could've spit her out!" Rev. Hill said, laughing.

"Hi Granny." She scurried from the porch and ran over to her Daddy, taking a hold of his hand.

"Sarah. Come on baby girl." Eight and a half year old Sarah walked up to Millie and stared.

"My sister's name is Millie Ann." She said. "Is your name Millie Ann, too?"

"No. Sarah. Your Grandma Millie's name is, Millie Annabelle Reed." Effie Mae said. Sarah walked over to

Millie Ann and climbed onto her lap. "Say hi to your Granny and give her a hug."

"Hi Granny." Millie leaned down and hugged Sarah. Effie Mae turned to her son and smiled. "Come on Lil' J.R." Sissy turned to J.R., surprised. "Y'all still, calling him Lil' J.R.?"

"Why, not Sissy? He's still my boy."

"But . . . ." She began. Rev. Hill interrupted.

"Sissy? You want to stay here and enjoy your nieces and nephew or you ready to go."

"I'm gon stay right here where I am, Otis!"

Millie watched seven and a half year old Lil' J.R. as he walked up the stairs. She immediately saw his resemblance to Anthony. He walked past Effie Mae then over to Millie and hugged her around the hips.

"Hi Granny." He released his hold and rushed over to Effie Mae. Sissy gawked in silence.

"J.R., Effie Mae . . . y'all got a fine family!" Rev. Hill stated then turned to Millie.

"Ms. Millie let it work itself out." He too recognized Lil' J. R.'s resemblance to Anthony. "Well, Effie Mae, me and Sissy gon head on home, but we would love for you, J.R. and the children to come by the house before you leave. Sit down to dinner with us." He said, impressed by Effie Mae's impressive presentation.

"We sure will Rev. Hill." She replied.

"Come on Sissy. Let's head on home. J.R. and Effie Mae's gon bring the children by before they leave here."

"Well Millie, you know were here if you need us." Sissy said, shifting her eyes to Effie Mae.

"Uh, yeah Ms. Millie, if you need us for anything, you know we're just a phone call away." Rev. Hill glanced over at Effie Mae then again to Mille.

"I know you are Rev. Hill, Sissy. But, I'm sure with J.R. and Pete both here, everything's gon be alright." J.R. smiled, elated by him, Effie Mae and their children being together as a family.

...

Effie Mae relaxed on the front porch with her daughters. J. R and Lil' J.R. went to the store to pick up some additional groceries in preparation of Millie's home cooked, country supper. Inside the house, Millie began her dinner of boiled corn, fried chicken, mashed potatoes, mustard greens and corn bread.

Pete, Annie Mae and their children traveled down the road, on their way back from the Parker's family farm. A large smiled formed on Pete's face when he noticed Effie Mae seated on the front porch, surrounded by children. He pulled into the driveway and stopped. He shifted his eyes to Effie Mae then again to Annie Mae. Their many sons jumped from the bed of the truck and scattered towards the back of the house. Lil' Effie Mae, now eight and a half, sat between her parents. Effie Mae looked past Pete and over at Annie Mae, uncertain how she would be received, after her last visit home.

"I don't want no stuff out of you and Effie Mae!" Pete said as they remain seated in the truck. "That's your sister—your only sister!" He looked at Annie Mae. "You hear me Annie Mae?" He snapped.

"Yeah, I hear you Pete." She gazed in amazement at the nieces she'd never seen. "Look at all my beautiful nieces." Annie Mae smiled then her, Pete and Lil' Effie Mae got out of the truck.

"Hey, sister-in-law!" Pete said as he walked onto the porch, Lil' Effie Mae's hand enveloped inside of his.

Effie Mae stood, happy to see Pete. She smiled. "Is that Lil' Effie Mae?"

"Yeah, that's her." Pete looked down at her as she hid partially behind his leg. Effie Mae peeped around at her namesake and smiled.

"Come on round here and say hi to your Auntie." Lil' Effie Mae looked at her Auntie then slipped her hand from out of her Daddy's and darted into the house. "Lil' Effie Mae! Come back here girl!" Pete shook his head and laughed. "She ain't coming back." He turned his attention back to Effie Mae, apprehensive about hugging her.

"It's okay Pete! I'm sober."

"It's good to see you, Effie Mae." He hugged her.

"I owe you an apology, Pete. It's amazing how drinking scotch can make you do stuff you shame of." They ended their embraced.

"Don't worry about it Effie Mae. I'm just glad to see that you doing better." He turned to Annie Mae then again to Effie Mae. "You got Blue with you?'

"Nope. Me and J.R. drove down together."

"What? J. R.? Y'all back together or something?"

"Or something." She laughed then looked at Annie Mae. "Come on Annie Mae and give your big sister a hug." Annie Mae strolled over and wrapped her arms around her big sister then began crying.

"Aww, now there she go." Pete shook his head.

"I love you, Effie Mae."

"I know you do Annie Mae. And I love you too, Lil' girl. I'm sorry about how I acted the last time I was here." Tears rolled down Effie Mae's face. Pete watched, pleased by their reconciliation.

"You see all my babies?" Effie Mae said ending their embrace. The two sisters wiped away their tears.

"Yeah, I do! I can't imagine my big sister being Momma to all these kids?" Effie Mae laughed then turned to her daughters. The children looked at Annie Mae and Pete with unfamiliarity. Effie Mae pointed as she introduced her children. "This is Millie Ann, and this is Lena, and right here is Billie, this is Mahalia and this is my baby girl Sarah that you ain't seen since she was a baby."

Pete interrupted. "Do they sing? I see you named most of the girls after singers." He laughed.

"That's Sarah?" Annie Mae walked over and hugged her. "Did you know that I changed your diaper when you were a baby?"

"Uh-uh. Ms. Geraldine changed my diapers. She changed Lil' J.R.'s diapers too!" Sarah said, looking Annie Mae directly in the eye. "And . . . she changed D.J.'s diaper. Didn't she Millie Ann?" Annie Mae shifted her eyes to Effie Mae.

"D. J.? Effie Mae you got another baby?" She asked.

"That's Ms. Geraldine's baby." Millie Ann interrupted, trying to protect her Momma.

"No he's not! Momma had him in her stomach."

"Shut up Sarah! And get over here." Millie Ann said. Sarah walked over to Millie Ann and stood in front of her and waited to be picked up. Millie Ann lifted her onto her lap. Sarah said nothing further. Pete and Annie Mae looked in awe, puzzled by Sarah's words. Their attention diverted, when J.R. pulled into the driveway and stopped.

...

J.R. held Lil' J.R. on his lap as the family joined together for dinner. Pete gazed at Lil' J.R., attempting to see if he looked anything like Jimmy.

"How's things going in New York City, J.R.?" Pete asked as he ripped apart a chicken wing.

"Uh, fine. Everything's fine." J.R. said as he felt the strange vibe in the room. He glanced at Effie Mae.

"That's good! I'm glad to hear it." Pete said then shifted his eyes to Annie Mae.

"Effie Mae, child, you done had another baby?" Millie asked. Sarah seems to think you have." Effie Mae glimpsed at J.R. He cleared his throat.

"Did Sissy tell you that we almost lost Effie Mae a while back?" He said, changing the subject.

"What?" Millie shouted. Effie Mae looked at J.R. and subtly shook her head--no.

"Somebody beat my Momma up real bad. Mr. Daniel thought she was dead." Sarah said as she gnawed at her corn. "And we had to go over to Ms. Alberta's house and stay."

"Shut up Sarah!" Millie Ann said. Millie glared at J.R.

"I've always respected you J.R." She said. "From the first time I met you—you always seemed like a good man. But, don't sit here in my house and keep things about my daughter from me."

"Ms. Millie, all that stuff happened when Effie Mae and I were separated."

"Annie Mae, take the children in their rooms. They can finish eating in there. I need some answers from Effie Mae and J.R." Millie demanded.

"Uh-uh Momma! I didn't come down here for all this."

"Annie Mae. Do like I said!"

"Momma, if you want to talk to me, we can do it after dinner. Let my babies sit here and eat their food."

"I want you to . . . ." J.R. interrupted her.

"Uh, Ms. Millie . . . Effie Mae don't play when it comes to her babies. So, uh . . . if we can all just finish eating, I'm sure she'll tell you anything you want to know, after dinner."

"Yeah, Ms. Millie, why don't we do that?" Pete said. J.R. leaned over and kissed Effie Mae on the side of her face. Millie said nothing further as the room filled with the chatter of children's voices.

Millie congregated in the living room with her two daughters and son-in-laws. J. R. put his arm around Effie as they sat on the sofa and she prepared to answer Millie's questions. Pete relaxed in a chair and held Annie Mae on his lap.

"What you want to talk about Momma?" Effie Mae asked.

"The last time you were here, you were a mess! You were drunk, falling all over the place and trying to mess with Pete." Pete's mouth flung opened in response to her recollection of the event. J.R. looked at Pete in surprise then turned his attention to Effie Mae.

"Momma, I was drunk. I wasn't gon do nothing to Pete."

"And what about that boy's daddy? The minute I laid eyes on that child, I knew right then he belonged to Betsy Lewis' son!"

"Yeah Momma—he's Anthony's son." J.R. again kissed Effie Mae on the face, attempting to keep her calm. Pete seemed baffled by J.R.'s behavior, given the situation.

"Now, that's gon hurt Jimmy's heart. He thought for sure that boy was his." Pete said to Effie Mae. She glanced at him through regrettable eyes then turned to Millie.

"What else you want to know Momma?" J.R. intervened.

"Ms. Millie, me and Effie Mae done already talked about this, and we agreed to put it all behind us. That's the reason we came down here. I'm helping Effie Mae to find our son's father, so Lil' J.R. can meet him." Pete appeared stunned by J.R.'s dismissal of Effie Mae's infidelity. "But, Lil' J.R.'s gon always be my boy."

"Uh, I admire you for that J. R. Ain't too many men would handle the situation like you doing." Pete said.

"No . . . don't admire me, Pete. When I learned about my boy, I walked out on my family. And I lost a good woman." Pete shifted his eyes to Annie Mae and tried to avoid laughing.

"Uh, Ms. Millie . . . I'm gon let y'all finish this discussion. I need to go and lay down. I got to be at work early tomorrow." Pete said, feeling the need to distance himself from the *odd* conversation.

"Alright, son. You go ahead on, get some sleep." Millie said. Pete gave Annie Mae a quick kiss on the lips then lifted her from his lap and left the room. J.R. watched as Pete walked down the hallway then disappeared around the corner.

"I'll be in there in a minute Pete!" Annie Mae yelled as she positioned herself into the chair.

"Well, Momma if you don't have any more questions, me and J.R.'s gon leave here and go try to find Anthony." Effie Mae stood and prepared to depart.

"Yeah, Effie Mae—I do." She shifted her eyes to Annie Mae then again to Effie Mae. "Who is D.J.?" Effie Mae looked over at Annie Mae. J.R. rose from the sofa. "Uh, Ms. Millie, we traveled a long way, and if it's okay, we'd like to tend to what we came here to do. That trip's gon be just as long going back." He chuckled. "Come on children. It's time to go." J.R. yelled down the hallway. Millie silently gazed at Effie Mae.

...

"Turn right here J.R.!" Effie Mae said pointing to the house she remembered Anthony taking her to. He pulled into the driveway and stopped. J.R. glared through the windshield.

"Is he here?" J. R. asked, when seeing no car in the driveway or any signs of life in the home.

"Whose house is this Daddy?" Billie asked.

"Yeah, who lives here Momma? Your daddy?" Mahalia added.

"Y'all sit back and hush!" Effie Mae said, gazing through the back widow. "I see a lady standing across the street, let me go ask her." She opened the door and got out then headed in that direction.

"How you doing?" Effie Mae asked. The lady turned around.

"I'm doing fine. How you doing baby? What can I do for you?"

"I'm fine. Do you know the man that lives in that house over there?" Effie Mae pointed to Anthony's house.

"Oh, you mean Betsy Lewis' son, Anthony? Yes. I know Anthony. He's a fine young man, too!"

"Well, my name is Effie Mae Reed, and I'm a friend of Anthony's." The lady looked at her with curiosity.

"Effie Mae Reed? Millie Reed's gal?"

"Yes Ma'am."

"So, you're Effie Mae. You know I've spent many evenings talking to Anthony about you." She smiled. "That boy is crazy about you, too! He keeps thinking that one day he's gon marry you." She looked over at the car filled with children. "Who's that you got with you? Is all those youngins yours?"

"Yes Ma'am."

"That's a lot of youngins. Does Anthony know about that?"

"Yes Ma'am."

"He does? And he's still talking about marrying you?" She continued looking through the back window of the car as if counting heads. "Well, you know Anthony works in Jackson. He don't usually come home until the weekend. I reckon he should be here tomorrow." Her nosiness heightened. "Was there a message or something you wanted to leave with me, to give to Anthony? I'm sure he would love to know that you came looking for him."

"If you just let him know that I came by, that'll be just fine."

"Who's that driving you and all those youngins around?" The lady gaped at the car.

"Thank you Miss . . . ."

"Dawson. Ruby Dawson."

"Thank you Ms. Dawson."

"Uh-huh." She watched as Effie Mae walked away and got back inside the car.

"What did she say?" J.R. asked as Effie Mae closed the door.

"He won't be back until tomorrow. We can come back then." J.R. suddenly felt threatened by the thought of Effie Mae reuniting with Anthony.

"Okay! We can . . . come back tomorrow."

"J.R., I want to meet with Anthony by myself—me and Lil' J.R."

"Are you sure?"

"Yeah, ain't nothing gon happen" She teased.

"Are you sure?"

"Yeah, I'm sure." She smiled.

"Okay. If that's what you want Effie Mae. But, I'll be dropping you off and picking you up!"

"Okay J.R., that's fine. Now you acting like you my husband."

"I am." They laughed.

Effie Mae hurried from the door of the Cozi-T Motel that following morning with Lil' J.R. in her arms.

"Come on J.R.! I want to get over here early, before Anthony leaves the house or something." She said opening the car door, positioning Lil' J.R. in the middle, on the front seat, then quickly climbed in herself. Millie Ann exited the motel and rushed over to the car.

"Millie Ann, your Daddy gon be right back. He gon drop me and Lil J.R. off . . . and come right back.

"Okay Momma."

"I want you to go back in the room—watch your sisters. And don't come out!"

"Okay Momma."

"I mean that Millie Ann. Stay in there until your Daddy gets back!"

"I am."

"Okay." Effie Mae smiled as she closed the door. J.R. dashed from the motel and quickly climbed inside. He started the engine, backed out of the parking lot, and onto the road, then he, Effie Mae and Lil' J.R. headed down the road, on their way to Anthony's house.

J.R. drove slowly down the road as he approached Anthony's house. They saw a 1969 green two door, Chevelle Malibu, White top Convertible with white wall tires, parked in the driveway. Effie Mae's excitement heightened.

"Is that his car?" J.R. asked.

"I'm not sure. That's not the car he was driving the last time I saw him."

"Is he married?"

"I don't know J.R. He wasn't the last time I saw him.

"What if he's married?

"I'm not gon let that stop me from letting him know about Lil' J.R." Effie Mae said as she looked anxiously at the house. J.R. pulled into the driveway and stopped.

The front door opened. Effie Mae stared to see if it was Anthony. A man resembling him walked out onto the porch, wearing a red robe and plaid pajama pants. He gazed at the unfamiliar car in the driveway. Effie Mae watched to see if the gentleman with the neatly trimmed beard and mustache could possibly be him. All grown-up, his eyeglasses complimented his handsome face. Anthony walked down the steps and towards the car. An enormous smile formed on his face as he recognized Effie Mae. When seeing his *famous* smile, she knew for certain, that it was Anthony. She smiled then burst open the car door and rushed into his arms.

"Anthony!" She held him tight.

"Hey, Effie Mae." He kissed her on the lips. J.R. opened the door in response to Anthony's action. He got out, unintentionally, leaving Lil' J.R. inside.

"Uh, Effie Mae . . . I take it that, this must be Anthony?" J.R. noted his distinct features unique to Lil' J.R. He felt his nerves, seemingly sink down into the pit of his stomach. Anthony and Effie Mae ended their embrace.

"Daddy? Can I get out?" Lil' J.R. asked. J. R. rushed back to the car in response to his son's question.

"Is that your husband, Effie Mae?" Anthony asked as he watched J.R. take Lil' J.R. from the car.

"Yes . . . and No. I'll explain it to you later, Anthony." Lil' J.R. scurried over to Effie Mae and took a hold of her hand.

"Is that your son?" He looked at Lil' J.R.

"Yeah, that's my Ol' big headed boy." She chuckled.

"Did you want to come in?" Effie Mae looked at J.R.

"Take our babies over to Momma's house so they can eat."

"You sure?" He asked, reluctant to leave her alone with Anthony.

"I'll be alright, J.R."

"Uh, I can bring Effie Mae back home, when she's ready." Anthony stated, politely.

"I can come back and get her." J.R. said. His insecurity heightened.

"Anthony can bring me back J.R." Effie Mae said, smiling. J.R. hesitated then returned to the car. He stopped.

"Uh, Anthony—it was nice meeting you.

"You too, J.R." Anthony smiled then turned his attention back to Effie Mae. J.R. got back into the car and started the engine. He backed out of the driveway and drove slowly down the road. He watched through his rearview mirror as Anthony put his arm around Effie

Mae and walked her into the house. Lil' J.R. holding onto his Momma's hand.

"Are you hungry Effie Mae? I can get you something?"

"No. That's alright, Anthony."

"What about your little boy?"

"He gon be alright until we get back to Momma's."

"Come sit down with me." He smiled. Effie Mae sat next to him on the sofa. She positioned Lil' J.R. on her lap.

"You look so different Anthony."

"Huh?" He thought for a moment. "Oh—yeah, the beard and mustache, I guess I didn't have this the last time you saw me."

"That's what I want to talk to you about, Anthony." He stared at her then kissed her on the cheek.

"Stop kissing my Momma!" Lil' J.R. shouted.

"It's alright Lil' J.R., it's just because he's happy to see me." Effie Mae grinned. "You remember the last time I was here?" Anthony smiled. "Don't be smiling like that. I got my baby with me."

"You asked if I remembered."

"Well, anyway, I had this Ol' hard headed boy.

"He's not that bad is he?"

"He's just spoiled. But that's my baby."

"No I ain't." Lil' J.R. said. "I'm a big boy."

"Hush boy." Effie Mae put her hand over his mouth. He removed it. "But Lil' J.R.'s not my husband's son."

"He's not? Does your husband know that?"

"Yeah, he knows. That's why, when you ask me if he was my husband I said, I'd explain. We still married, but J.R. left me when he found out."

"I'm sorry to hear that Effie Mae."

"It's okay. We still friends. He just drove me and my babies down here to see Momma and Annie Mae and . . . you."

"Me? You came all this way to see me?"

"Yeah . . . and to bring your son down here, so you could meet him."

"My son?" He looked at Lil' J.R. "Effie Mae is that my son?"

"Yeah Anthony, that's your son." She said, smiling. "His name is Jimmy Anthony Rae. And he yours."

"But, how do you know, being married." Effie Mae took Lil' J.R. off her lap and stood him in front of her.

"Turn around Lil' J.R." He turned with his back facing Anthony. Effie Mae pulled his shirt up to his shoulder, revealing his unique birthmark. "That's how I know." Anthony's mouth opened wide. He looked at Lil' J.R.

"I've got a son, Effie Mae?"

"Yeah, you got a son, Anthony."

"Wow—wait until my parents find out that they have a grandson." He picked Lil' J.R. up and sat him in his lap. "I don't know what to say. We have a son." He leaned towards Effie Mae and kissed her on the lips.

"Stop kissing my Momma!" Lil' J.R. shouted then knocked the glasses off Anthony's face.

"Stop that Lil' J.R!" Effie Mae took him from Anthony and sat him back on her lap.

"Can we get married now, Effie Mae?" Anthony leaned down, and picked up his glasses then put them back on.

"Anthony." She blushed.

"I still love you, Effie Mae." He gazed into her eyes. "I asked you when we first met, if you would marry me . . . and you said yes."

"How can I marry you Anthony? My life is in New York, now?"

"Okay. I'll move to New York! I'd like to be in my son's life."

"Anthony! I can't answer that question right now."

"Will you promise me then, that you'll think about it?"

"Okay. I'll think about it."

"You mean that Effie Mae?"

"Yeah Anthony, I mean it." Anthony took a hold of her hand. He gave her a quick kiss on the lips.

"Stop!" Lil' J.R. yelled then swung at him. Anthony laughed then silently admired the son that he and Effie Mae *created.*

Chapter Thirty-Six

Effie Mae stood in the kitchen waiting for J.R. to return home from the church. Her attention was drawn to the door when she heard him unlock and open it. He entered and noticed the uneasy look on her face.

"Effie Mae? Everything okay?"

"I'm leaving J.R." He looked at her, puzzled by her decision.

"Uh—you moving back in with Daniel and Geraldine?"

"No. I'm moving in with Blue. He wants me there, and I want to be there."

"Blue. I was uh—hoping that we could . . . ." Effie Mae cut him off.

"Daniel should have never told you to come and get me." She looked into his eyes. "J.R., I can't be the wife that you want."

"Effie Mae, you are the wife I want."

"I enjoyed the time we spent together back home. I even love the way you stood up for me with Momma." She smiled. "And for a while J.R., it felt real. But, it ain't. It's just fantasy."

"Fantasy? Effie Mae, I want our life back!"

"That's just it J. R. . . . I don't. When Blue called me and asked if I would move back in with him, I never thought once about saying, no."

"I asked you Effie Mae, if you loved Blue. You never said yes."

"I don't know what I feel for Blue, J.R. I just know that being with him—I'm not trying to please Momma." She took a hold of J.R.'s hands then looked him directly in the face. "When I married you J.R., I was trying to get my Momma to love me again. Not because I loved you. In a way, I didn't choose you J.R., Momma did." J.R. was momentarily taken back by her candid words. "But Blue . . ." Effie Mae smiled. "I chose him. Do you understand what I'm trying to say, J.R.?"

"Yeah, Effie Mae . . . I guess I do. Does this mean that you want a divorce?"

"I ain't even thought that far ahead. I said I was moving in with Blue, not marrying him." She chuckled then momentarily gazed into his eyes. "Maybe, one day J.R. . . ." She paused. "I'll choose you for myself." She hugged him. "Now can you take me over to Blue's? J.R. light-heartedly laughed.

"Yes Effie Mae, I'll take you over to Blue's."

...

Blue finished his first set and hurried from the stage. He joined Effie Mae at her table. Angered by her drunken state, he motioned a waiter over to the table. The man came right away.

"I thought I told you not to bring Effie Mae anymore drinks."

"Nobody told me that."

"Well, now I'm telling you! Can't you see that she's already drunk?" Blue shouted.

"Okay." The man humped his shoulders and walked away. Blue turned his attention back to Effie Mae.

"You want me to help you upstairs Baby girl, so you can go to bed?"

"Come on Blue . . . take me to go see my babies." She slurred.

"You don't want Ms. Geraldine calling the Police on you again, Effie Mae. Why don't you wait until you've sobered up?" He reasoned. "Let me to talk to Daniel, first."

"Daniel! Those are my babies! How Ms. Geraldine gon tell me I can't see my own babies?"

"You hurt that woman, Baby girl. Right now, she's gon do everything she can to hurt you back. And drinking like this, it's just making things worse." He took a hold of her arm and attempted to lift her to her feet. Effie Mae snatched her arm away.

"Get your hands off me Blue!" She stated loudly. "So now it's my fault?" Blue gently kissed her on the cheek. "Okay, Baby girl. I'll take you over there in the morning. But you have to promise me that if I take you upstairs to bed, you gon stay there this time—okay? You know you gon need to get up early, if you want to see your kids before they leave for school."

"You mean that Blue? You gon take me to go see my babies?"

"Yeah Baby girl, I mean it. But you have to stay sleep this time, okay?"

"I knew you still loved me, Blue." Effie Mae said, delighted.

"Always, you know that." He again kissed her on the cheek then assisted her to her feet.

"That's my Blue. I knew I could count on you." He put her arm around his neck and caught her around the waist then walked her away from the table.

Huck and Buckeye entered. Huck watched as Effie Mae stumbled over to the stairs, being held up by Blue.

"See Buckeye, when I had her you never saw Effie Mae drunk like that. If Blue can't do no better than that, I'm gon have to take her back. I don't know why she wants Blue's ass, anyway." Buckeye nodded.

"Yeah Huck, she never looked like that when she was with you." The two men proceeded to the center of the room and seated themselves. Huck summoned Melvin, suited in a tuxedo, over to their table.

"How's things going tonight Melvin?"

"Busy night, what can I get you Mr. Huck?"

"When Blue gets back down here, let him know that I need to see him. And look here Melvin—make sure you let him know . . . I ain't asking."

"Yes Sir."

"And get me and Buckeye something to drink."

"Yes Sir." Melvin turned and walked away.

"What you gon do Huck?" Buckeye asked. Huck looked at him but said nothing. A few minutes later Melvin returned with a bottle of scotch. He placed it on the table then positioned a shot glass in front of both men. He filled each goblet to the rim. Huck caught glimpse of Blue as he returned from upstairs. He touched Melvin on the arm then motioned with his head, alerting him of Blue's return.

"Leave that bottle on the table Melvin." Huck said. Melvin nodded then walked away. He approached Blue and relayed the message. Blue looked over at Huck then headed in that direction. He approached then stood and waited as if requesting Huck's permission to sit.

"You wanted to see me, Huck?"

"Yeah, sit down Blue. It makes me nervous when a man stands over me. Make me think he might want to make a move on me. You ain't trying to make a move on me, are you Blue?" Huck looked at him and awaited his reply. Blue glanced over at Buckeye.

"Naw Huck." He said then seated himself to Huck's left.

"How you doing, Blue?"

"I'm . . . ." Huck cut him off.

"I know that wasn't Effie Mae I saw you taking upstairs?" Huck tossed the shot of scotch into his mouth.

"Uh . . . ." Huck interrupted.

"Because what I saw you dragging up those stairs looked like something, the vultures wouldn't even pick at." Huck picked up the bottle and poured himself another shot.

"I tried to tell her Huck!"

"You tried to do what? Is Effie Mae paying for them drinks, Blue? Or are you giving them to her?" Blue remained silent. "Would you want your Momma looking like that, Blue?"

"No. But . . ." Huck cut him off.

"Shut up Blue." Blue looked at Buckeye. "Here's what I want you to do, Blue. I want you to get Effie Mae cleaned up. You hear me?"

"Yeah Huck."

"Because if I see—or even hear about her looking like that again, I'm gon hurt you, Blue." He glared at Blue in anger. "I'm gon hurt you bad." Blue glanced briefly over to Buckeye. "And once she clean — you stay your ass away from her. I don't care what you got to tell her. But if I see you with Effie Mae again . . . show him what I'm gon do, Buckeye." Buckeye removed a match from behind his ear. He struck it on the bottom of his shoe then watched it burn.

"Now get your ass out of my face." Blue stood. He looked at Buckeye then turned and walked away. Huck watched him.

"Let's get out of here." Buckeye grabbed the bottle off the table then the two men got up and left.

Blue parked down the streets from Daniel and Ms. Geraldine's home. Effie Mae waited eagerly in the car to see her children.

"My babies should be coming out of the house in a minute, Blue." She watched intently.

"Effie Mae. I need to talk to you." He said. The front door opened. Effie Mae watched as the children came out wearing hats, scarves and boots. Millie Ann held Lil' J.R.'s hand as they walked down the streets. The other children followed.

"There they go Blue!" Effie Mae pulled the handle on the door and began opening it. Blue reached across her and again closed it.

"What you doing Effie Mae?" He yelled.

"I'm going and get my babies! Ms. Geraldine can't keep me from seeing my babies. Them my babies, Blue!" She yelled.

"Do you want her to call the police on you again? Because if you get out of this car, that's exactly what she's gon do."

"Let her call the police . . . I don't care!"

"You don't want that Baby girl." Blue took a hold her hand and held it to his lips then kissed it. "You got to get some help. As long as you drinking like that, the Social Worker said you can't have your kids back."

"I don't care 'bout what no Social Worker said, Blue! Those my babies!"

Effie Mae watched as Ms. Geraldine walked out onto the porch with D. J. cradled in her arms, watching as the children headed off to school.

"That's my baby she holding Blue!"

"I know, Baby girl."

"I'm gon go over there—right now, and take my baby out of her arms!" Effie Mae pulled the handle on the door. Blue reached over and gently removed her hand.

"Effie Mae, stop!" Blue said, agitated. She bursts into tears. He looked into her tear filled eyes. Blue felt helpless. "Let's go." He cuddled Effie Mae under his right arm and laid her head onto his chest. He kissed her gently on the forehead as he pulled away from the curve and drove off. Effie Mae continued to weep.

...

"What we doing here, Blue?" Effie Mae asked when he pulled up outside of J.R.'s house and parked. Blue remained silent. "Did you hear me Blue?"

"Effie Mae, I can't do this anymore."

"Do what anymore, Blue?"

"I'm walking away."

"I don't want you do walk away Blue. Is it my drinking? I'll stop Blue—I promise. Don't leave me Blue." She pleaded. He looked away.

"I don't love you any . . ." He stopped then again turned to her. "I love you Effie Mae." Effie Mae began crying then slid over next to him. She put her arms around his neck.

"Kiss me Blue." He looked into her eyes then passionately kissed her. He stopped. "I knew you loved me, Blue." She smiled. "Let's just go back home. I promise I'm gon stop drinking. You gon see."

"I can't Baby girl." He removed her arms from around his neck then opened the car door and got out.

"Get back in here, Blue!" He walked to the back of the car and unlocked the trunk. He removed her two suitcases and set them on the ground then looked towards the house. J.R. came out and walked over to the car. He opened the passenger side door.

"What you done—did, J.R.?" Effie Mae screamed.

"Come on Effie Mae." He said, softly.

"No! I'm going home with Blue! Tell him Blue." Blue closed the trunk and got back inside the car. You see J.R., Blue's taking me back home with him." Blue took her in his arms and tenderly kissed her. After ending the kiss, he momentarily stared into her eyes.

"I love you, Baby girl." He turned and looked away as J.R. reached inside and began pulling Effie Mae out.

"Let me go J.R.!"

"Come on Effie Mae." J.R. said, calmly.

"No! Take your hands off me, J.R.! I want Blue!" Unable to watch, Blue glared out of the driver's side window as J.R. gently removed Effie Mae from the car. Once outside, she sorrowfully lowered herself down onto her knees on the snow covered ground. "Don't leave me Blue!" She cried out. J.R. attempted to lift her from the ground as Blue again started the engine and prepared to leave. Tears rolled down Blue's face as he drove away, sobbing.

...

Effie Mae lay on the living room sofa watching television. She arose when she heard a knock at the kitchen door. She hurried to the door hoping that after two months, it would be Blue. She hastily opened the door.

"Hey, Effie Mae." Huck said, smiling. Effie Mae tried to push the door shut. Huck wedged his foot inside then forced it back open. "Is that how you treat people coming to see you girl?"

"What you want Huck?"

"Why I got to want something. Can't I just be coming to check on you?" Effie Mae walked back into the living room and sat down. Huck followed being seated next to her. She refused to look at him. "Oh, you mad?" Effie Mae remained silent. "Girl, I probably saved your life." He chuckled. She looked at him, curious by his words.

"I know you had something to do with Blue leaving me."

"What if I did? What you gon do?"

"Leave me alone Huck."

"I'm just looking out for you. Girl, I saw you a couple months ago down at Blue's." He laughed to himself. "You couldn't sell flowers at Ms. Norma's, much less . . ." She cut him off.

"I ain't going back to Ms. Norma's. So if that's why you here, you might as well go ahead and kill me now, because I'd rather be dead than to do that again."

"Look at you." He chuckled. "Is that what you want Effie Mae? Because, I can do that, if that's what you really want. And this time, I'm gon take Buckeye's advice and throw your ass in the river." He put his arm around her. "You don't love me no more Effie Mae?" He teased. "Look at you girl. Every time you get in trouble, Ol' Huck is there to bail you out." He placed his hand on the back of her head and pulled it towards him then kissed her. "I'm just asking for a little gratitude. That's all." He kissed her again. "Come on." He took a hold of her hand. "Where's the bedroom?" He paused when he heard the sound of the back door being unlocked. J.R. entered into the house.

"Effie Mae?" J.R. called out as he walked in the direction of the living room. He abruptly stopped when he saw Huck sitting with his arm around Effie Mae. "Uh, we have company?"

"You must be Effie Mae's husband?" Huck stood up.

"Yeah, and who are you?" J.R. looked at him in question.

"I'm an old friend of your wife's." J.R. glanced at Effie Mae. She ignored him. "I'll check you out another day, Effie Mae." Huck leaned down and tilted her head back then kissed her on the lips. He turned and looked into J.R.'s face, then walked away, exiting the home.

Effie Mae got up and walked away. She entered into her bedroom and slammed the door.

...

"Just let me speak to Blue!" Effie Mae yelled into the phone. Then don't tell him it's me, Melvin!" She waited on the phone until she heard his voice.

"This is Blue."

"Don't hang up Blue." He sat on the line unable to speak. "Please Blue. Just talk to me."

"How you doing Baby girl?" She smiled.

"Missing you." Blue cleared his throat. "Come see me Blue. I'm not drinking anymore"

"Effie Mae, you know I can't do that."

"Why? You scared of Huck? He came over here last week. I know he had something to do with you leaving me."

"I ain't no good for you Effie Mae."

"It's almost Christmas, Blue. And I want to get my babies something for Christmas.

"Effie Mae . . . ."

"Please Blue. After you take me shopping, I won't bother you again."

"You know you're not a bother to me."

"Then come pick me up."

"You know Huck's probably watching."

"I'll take the bus downtown. Pick me up down there then we can drive to Jersey City, and do some shopping. You still love me don't you, Blue?"

"You know I do, always." He said with a smile in his voice.

"I'll catch the early bus and meet you downtown at nine o'clock. Thank you Blue."

"Hey!"

"Huh?"

"I love you Baby girl."

"I know." She smiled. "Bye."

"Bye."

...

Effie Mae stepped off the bus and walked two blocks then went around a corner. She saw Blue parked and waiting. She hurriedly climbed inside the car. Blue pulled off then he and Effie Mae began their trip to Jersey City for a day of Christmas shopping. Effie Mae slid over under him and smiled. Blue put his arm around her then kissed her gently on the lips.

"I've missed you Baby girl." He kissed her again.

"I missed you too Blue. Can I come back and stay with you Blue?"

"If you do that Effie Mae, you may as well start grieving now. Because, Huck's gon kill me."

"He won't have to know."

"Once you start drinking again . . ." Effie Mae cut him off.

"Then, I won't start drinking again!"

"Baby girl, you have a problem. You start hanging around downstairs at Blue's and it won't be long before you drinking."

"Then, I won't go downstairs. I'll just stay upstairs and wait on you to get home."

"Let's just go get these toys for your kids."

"Okay, Blue." He kissed her lightly on the lips. Effie Mae smiled and laid her head on his chest as they continued their journey.

Chapter Thirty-Seven

Blue helped Effie Mae remove and carry the multitude of white, plastic bags filled with Christmas toys, from the car. She hurried down the sidewalk and onto the porch of Daniel and Ms. Geraldine's home. Blue followed behind. Daniel opened the door as she approached. He blocked the entrance.

"Merry Christmas, Mr. Daniel!" She said.

"Where you going Effie Mae?"

"I'm bringing my babies some Christmas gifts."

"Uh-uh. Did you ask Geraldine if that was okay?"

"Why should I have to ask Ms. Geraldine if I can bring my babies something for Christmas?"

"Well you should've. Geraldine, don't want you in here."

"Well, can you give this stuff to my babies?

"Geraldine said, no."

"When did you ask her Mr. Daniel? I just walked up to the door."

"Go ahead on and leave Effie Mae. We don't want to have to call the police."

"The police! What for? I ain't drunk!"

"Come on Effie Mae." Blue said. "If they don't want you here, let's just leave."

"Let them call the police! It's not a crime for me to bring my babies Christmas presents!"

"Let's go Baby girl." Blue took a hold of her arm.

"Let me go Blue!" She snatched her arm away. "I ain't leaving until I give my babies their stuff!"

"Take her away from here now, Blue. Geraldine's already called the police."

"She didn't have to do that man. Blue stated, raising his voice. Effie Mae's not drunk! She just wanted to give her kids these gifts she bought them for Christmas."

"She should've asked before she bought them."

"You wrong man. What you and your wife are doing, is just plain wrong." Blue shook his head in pity. "And especially you Daniel, you got a child with Effie Mae." Blue again took a hold of Effie Mae's arm. "Come on Baby girl. Let's go."

"Why can't I give my babies these gifts, Blue?" She began crying.

"Because Effie Mae, these people have hearts colder than hot ice." Blue gently guided her away from the front door and off the porch. He took the gifts and put them in the back seat then opened the front door and helped Effie Mae inside. He walked around to the other side and got in. Daniel watched as they drove away. Blue glared at him as he slowly rode past.

Ms. Geraldine looked out from the kitchen window as she held D.J. in her arms.

Chapter Thirty-Eight

It's New Years Eve. Effie Mae shared in continuous rounds of drinks with the party goers seated at her table, celebrating the holiday. Blue kept her in his sight as he played with the band. He paused, when Huck and Buckeye entered into the club and were seated near the entrance. Huck noticed Effie Mae sitting near the stage, heavily intoxicated. He gazed at Blue in rage.

"Buckeye! I want you to go up to that stage and tell Blue to get his ass over here now!"

"Okay Huck." Buckeye moved hastily towards the stage. Blue leaned forward and received the message then looked at Huck. He propped his horn against the wall and walked over to Huck's table.

"Huck, I tried to . . . ." Huck leapt up from his chair and put Blue in a headlock then held a knife to his throat.

"You tell me Blue, why I shouldn't cut your throat!"

"I told them not to serve Effie Mae, but . . . ." Huck cut him off.

"But my ass Blue! You own this damn club. You can't run your own club Blue?"

"Let him go Huck!" Buckeye said.

"You want to change places with him Buckeye?"

"Man you know Effie Mae's got a problem. Blue can't stop her from drinking!" Huck glared at Blue then released him.

"You owe Buckeye! He just saved your life Blue." Huck straightened his clothes. "Sit down Blue. You got sixty seconds to tell me what the hell happened." Blue sat down. Huck joined him. "Last time I saw Effie Mae she was sober."

"Daniel wouldn't let her give her kids the Christmas gifts she bought them!"

"Is that right? How would you know that Blue? I told you to stay your ass away from Effie Mae, didn't I?

"She called me and asked if I would take her to get some stuff for her kids for Christmas. I couldn't turn her down."

"Maybe you should've. Then maybe she wouldn't be over there now, so drunk—she don't know the time of day."

"So, when we got over there and Daniel . . . ." Huck interrupted.

"Daniel?"

"Yeah, he told her she couldn't see her kids. And then he said that his wife had called the police. After that, she's been down here every night. My bartender didn't give her anything to drink. But you know Effie Mae—she can always get people to do what she wants."

"Get you, Blue. She can always get you to do what she wants. That's why I told you to stay your ass away from her." Huck stared at him. "Now get over there and bring me Effie Mae, before I change my mind about cutting your throat." Blue stood. He hurried over to

Effie Mae's table. He touched her shoulder. She looked up at him.

"Hey Blue." She slurred. "Can I go home with you tonight?"

"Come on Effie Mae." Blue assisted her to her feet.

"Where we going, Blue?"

"Huck's here. He wants you to sit with him."

"Huck? Is he gon buy me some more to drink?"

"You got to ask him that." Blue escorted her over to Huck's table and helped her into a chair.

"Hey, Huck!"

"Hey, Effie Mae." He waved his hand for Blue to go.

"Blue said you wanted to buy me some more drinks." Huck stared angrily at Blue then looked at Effie Mae.

"Blue lied. I can't do that Effie Mae."

"Is it New Years yet?"

"Are you living with Blue again Effie Mae?"

"No! Did Blue say that? I live with J.R."

"Is that right? So where is J.R., Effie Mae? Do he know you in here drinking like this?"

"He at the church." She slurred.

"At church, huh? I'm taking you home girl."

"I ain't ready to go home!"

"Yeah, you ready." He stood and lifted Effie Mae to her feet. "Come on Buckeye." Huck gazed momentarily at Blue then escorted Effie Mae out the door.

...

J.R. entered into the house after the New Year had come in. He walked into the living room and saw Huck seated on the couch. Effie Mae cradled in his arms.

"Uh, is everything alright?" He asked.

"Do it look like everything is alright—preacher? Your wife is passed out drunk, and I bet you didn't even know she was out the house." Huck gawked at J.R. "What kind of man are you, preacher?"

"I don't know what you mean." Huck shook his head.

"What? You still mad at Effie Mae because she had your son by another man? Is that what it is—preacher!"

"Who told you that? And what business is that of yours?"

"It's my business, when I see Effie Mae hurting like this. See what you don't know preacher . . . . is that me and Effie Mae have a special connection. I understand her and she understands me. And that's something nobody can take away from us."

"Hurting? What makes you think my wife's hurting?"

"Your wife?" Huck laughed to himself. "Damn shame. Did you even know that, "your wife" tried to take her kids some toys for Christmas? And Daniel and his wife wouldn't let her near those kids!" Huck's fury heightened. "Naw! You didn't know that." J.R. looked at Effie Mae, clueless. "How long you gon keep punishing Effie Mae? And how long you gon let Daniel and his wife keep treating her like she's a stepmother? If you were a real man—preacher, you'd get your ass over there and get your own kids. What they doing with them anyway? I understand why Effie Mae might not be able to take care of them, but what's wrong with you—preacher?" J.R. remained silent. "If you can't do a better job of taking care of Effie Mae, I might just have to take her—and your kids away from you!" Huck gently laid Effie Mae onto the sofa then stood. He momentarily watched her as she slept. "Now you let Effie Mae know that I'll be back tomorrow. Tell her to get those toys ready. We're playing Santa Claus." Huck looked at J. R. then brushed past him. He walked briskly through the kitchen and exited out the back door, slamming it behind him.

...

Huck walked swiftly through the parking lot when seeing Daniel headed toward his car after work, preparing to unlock the door.

"Hey Daniel!" Huck called out then rushed him. He forced Daniel into a headlock and twisted his arm behind his back then slammed him up against the car. "I heard about what you done to Effie Mae! You like hurting women, Daniel?"

"I'm not the one that beat her half to death!"

"You see me beat Effie Mae, Daniel? Because I know she didn't tell you that!"

"She didn't have too!"

"Yeah, she did. Otherwise what you saying is just speculation. And I ain't gon have you going around town spreading your speculations about me, Daniel!"

"What you want Huck?"

"It ain't what I want. It's what Effie Mae wants. And what she wants Daniel—is to have Christmas with her kids and give them the presents she bought them." Daniel struggled to free himself. Huck applied more pressure. "And you know what Daniel, you and your wife's gon let her do just that. Because, if you don't I'm gon hurt you Daniel!"

"I'll call the police!"

"Call the police, huh? You love your wife Daniel? Well, you can call the police, but be prepared to start putting flowers on her grave—on Sundays, birthdays, Mother's Day, Christmas. You get what I'm saying, don't you Daniel?" Daniel stopped struggling. He said nothing further.

"You know what Daniel? I think you're a coward. You messed with that girl and got her pregnant, then you and your wife start treating her like she's the blame for you lusting after your cousin's wife." He looked at Daniel in disgust. "But, let me tell you what you gon do. I'm gon bring Effie Mae by there today. And not only are you and your wife, gon let her have Christmas with her kids, but you gon let her hold her son too; spend time with him. And if you even think about giving me, any kind of trouble, you gon find out just how dangerous I am, Daniel!" Huck released him, and began to walk away. He abruptly stopped then turned back around. He briefly gazed at Daniel. "Ms. Geraldine, right?" Daniel watched as Huck again turned and walked away.

...

Effie Mae and Huck pulled out front of the home of Daniel and Ms. Geraldine.

"You ready Effie Mae?"

"Yeah, thank you Huck." She smiled.

"Kiss me."

"What? What if Ms. Geraldine or Mr. Daniel's watching?"

"They can learn something. Come on now girl, kiss me." He stared and waited. Effie Mae leaned towards him. Huck took a hold of her chin with his thumb and index finger then slightly tilted her head. He gently kissed her on the lips. "Okay. Let's go." They reached over the seat and retrieved the white plastic bags filled with multiple, bright colored Christmas toys. Both carried three bags each as they walked up the stairs and onto the front porch. Ms. Geraldine swung open the door as they approached.

"Kids, your Momma's here! And it looks like she's brought lots of Christmas presents." She cheerfully welcomed Effie Mae and Huck into her home. The children hurried from the living room into the kitchen. Their eyes widened at their belated presents.

"Let's go back in the living room where y'all can sit down and open your gifts." Effie Mae said as she headed in that direction. Daniel and Ms. Geraldine gawked at Huck.

"Effie Mae, I know you want to see D.J." Ms. Geraldine said. "Daniel, why don't you go and get the baby so Effie Mae can spend some time with him." Daniel left the room and returned minutes later with D.J. He handed him to Effie Mae. Ms. Geraldine watched and smiled as she successfully hid her rage.

"Look how big he's gotten." Effie Mae smiled then kissed his cheeks. Lil' J.R. walked over and laid his head on her arm.

"I want to go with you, Momma."

"Your Daddy's gon be coming tomorrow to take you all to go live with him." Ms. Geraldine said. "Would you like that Lil' J.R.?" She asked.

"Is Momma gon be there too?" He asked.

"I sure am Lil' J.R." Effie Mae turned to Huck and smiled. She silently mouthed the words—thank you, as she continued to admire her newborn son.

Chapter Thirty-Nine

Effie Mae washed the breakfast dishes after seeing her children off to school. She stopped when she heard a knock at the door. She strolled over believing it to be Huck. She looked through the kitchen curtain and saw Anthony standing on the other side. Her mouth opened as she stared at him in awe. She unbolted the door then stood mute.

"Hey, Effie Mae." He smiled.

"Anthony." She gazed at him, unable to believe her eyes.

"Are you going to invite me in?"

"Yeah, uh . . . come on in Anthony." He entered into the house. Effie Mae closed the door and stared at him, surprised by his unexpected arrival.

"Do I get a hug, a kiss—something?" Effie Mae walked up to him and wrapped her arms around him. Anthony embraced her then romantically kissed her.

"How did you find me?" She asked ending their embrace.

"Oh! I asked Ms. Mille."

"And she told you? My Momma?"

"Yes! She gave me Daniel's number. I called him and spoke to a . . . Ms. Geraldine?"

"Yeah, Ms. Geraldine's . . . Mr. Daniel's wife." Effie Mae said with regret, as she thought of her brief affair with Daniel.

"She gave me the address to where you were staying and here I am!" Anthony looked around. "I like your house Effie Mae."

"This is J.R.'s house."

"Isn't that your husband?"

"That's Momma's husband." She laughed to herself.

"Huh?"

"That's a long story Anthony. But, anyway—right now, I'm staying with J.R. since I don't have any place else to live." Anthony smiled and gazed at her in silence.

"What?" She blushed.

"You're beautiful Effie Mae."

"You don't look half bad yourself Anthony." She touched his beard. "I can't get over you having a beard."

"Do you like it?"

"Yeah, I do. It makes you look so handsome." Anthony pulled her into his arms and kissed her.

"Did you think about my proposal?"

"I've had so much stuff going on in my life Anthony; I haven't had time to think about nothing."

"Then, I'll ask you again. Effie Mae . . . will you marry me?" She gazed into his eyes. She hesitated then smiled.

"Yes. Yes, Anthony, I will marry you." They again kissed. Anthony abruptly stopped. He reached inside his shirt pocket and took out a ring. A large smile formed on Effie Mae's face. He got down on one knee. "Wait!" Effie Mae looked at her wedding ring from J.R. still on her finger. She removed it then extended her hand to Anthony. He took a hold of it and slid the ring he'd given to her many years ago, onto her finger, then took her in his arms and passionately kissed her.

...

Anthony drove Effie Mae to Blue's Jazz Club and parked out front. She looked at him then took a deep breath.

"You need me to come in with you, Effie Mae?"

"I need to do this by myself."

"Okay. But I'll be right out here in the car if you need me."

"Thank you Anthony." Effie Mae's eyes filled with tears as Anthony gazed at her.

"Are you alright?"

"I don't know Anthony. But when I come out, just let me cry, okay?"

"Okay." He looked at her with concern. Effie Mae nervously gazed at Anthony as she opened the door and got out. She walked over to the Jazz Club and knocked. Blue came from upstairs in response to the sound. He looked out and saw Effie Mae. He smiled then opened the door.

"Hey Baby girl." He hugged then kissed her lightly on the lips. "Come on in."

"Hey Blue." She smiled as she entered.

"You must be trying to get me killed?" He looked around outside then quickly closed and locked the door.

"You know I wouldn't do that. Well, not intentionally." Effie Mae laughed then took a hold of his hand and held it to her cheek. "I'm leaving Blue."

"What? Where are you going?"

"I'm moving back home." She paused. "I'm getting married!"

"No!" He wrapped his arms around her.

"I always thought if I got married again, it would be to you Blue."

"If you want me to marry you, Baby girl, I will."

"Blue, if I married you—Huck would definitely hurt you, and me! You know he's always been jealous of our relationship." She chuckled as her eyes filled with tears.

"I'll take that chance, Baby girl!" Tears erupted from Blue's eyes.

"I ain't worth dying for Blue."

"You are to me. I love you Effie Mae. I don't want to lose you." Tears flowed down his face. Effie Mae reached up and wiped his tears with her hands as she too wept, uncontrollably.

After five minutes of tearful weeping, Blue lifted his shirt and wiped both his and Effie Mae's saturated faces as their tearful moment subsided.

"Look at us." He laughed half-heartedly. They stared lovingly at one another then closed their eyes and passionately kissed. They gradually opened their eyes as the kiss ended.

"Can I come and see you, Baby girl?"

"Yeah, I would like that Blue." She smiled. He cleared his throat.

"Are you gon tell me who the lucky man is?"

"Yeah, it's the first man who ever asked me to marry him, a man who I chose."

"Anthony?"

"Yeah." Effie Mae smiled. "It's Anthony. That boy came all the way up here from Mississippi to get me, Blue!" She said, excitedly.

"All the way from Mississippi?" Blue said, somewhat disappointed.

"I know! Ain't that crazy?" Effie Mae grinned.

"Promise me Baby girl, that you won't forget me."

"I ain't ever gon forget you, Blue." Effie Mae looked into his eyes then lightly kissed him.

"Will you promise me, if this marriage with Anthony don't work, you'll marry me?"

"Are you asking me to marry you Blue?" Effie Mae blushed.

"Yeah, Baby girl—I am." He smiled.

"Well, I promise you Blue, that if me and Anthony don't make it—I'm definitely gon marry you." Blue smiled then he and Effie Mae again kissed.

"Well, I guess I better go." She ended their embrace. "Anthony's outside waiting in the car. Effie Mae turned to leave.

"Hey!"

"Huh!"

"I love you Baby girl."

"I know." Effie Mae paused then turned back around. "I love you too, Blue." His eyes widened in response to her shocking words. His smile seemingly stretched across his face. "Bye Blue."

"Bye Baby girl." His eyes again filled with tears. Effie Mae unlocked the door then hurried away, crying.

Chapter Forty

Effie Mae, Anthony and her children watched cartoons in the living room. Anthony held Lil' J.R. on his lap.

"What's your favorite food Lil' J.R." Anthony asked.

"Um, chicken!" He nodded his head.

"Chicken. That's my favorite food too!"

Effie Mae delighted in their father-son, interaction. She suddenly heard J.R. unlock the back door as he prepared to enter into the house. Effie Mae went into the kitchen and waited for him. J.R. opened the door then noticed her gazing at him as he entered.

"Okay. What is it? The last time I saw that look on your face you were moving back in with Blue."

"That's over." Her eyes moistened.

"What? What's going on? Are you alright?" He asked. Anthony entered into the kitchen. Lil' J. R. held onto his hand. J.R. stared questionably at Anthony, shocked by his presence.

"Uh, Anthony when did you, uh — get to New York?" He asked bothered by Lil' J.R. holding onto

Anthony's hand. Effie Mae noticed the uneasy look in his eyes.

"Lil' J.R., go watch cartoons." He released Anthony's hand and ran into the living room.

Anthony extended his hand to J.R. The two men shook.

"I got here yesterday."

"Yesterday? Effie Mae didn't say anything about it." J.R. glanced at Effie Mae. "I guess you came to see Lil' J.R.?"

"Actually, I . . . ." Effie Mae cut him off.

"Let me talk to J.R., Anthony."

"Okay." Anthony returned to the living room. Lil' J.R. jumped onto his lap.

"We can talk in the bedroom J.R." They exited the kitchen, walked through the living room then entered into her bedroom.

"What's going on?" J.R. asked, worried. Effie Mae gently closed the door.

"J.R., Anthony is here to take me back home."

"Take you back—for a visit?"

"I'm leaving J.R." She said. "Anthony asked me to marry him. And I said yes." She held out her finger and showed him the engagement ring. J.R. took a deep breath.

"I wish I could say . . . I wish you well. But I'd be lying." He took a hold of her hands then gazed into her eyes. "I guess I was still hoping that we could work things out." Effie Mae laughed to herself. "What?" He asked, puzzled by her laughter.

"It's funny . . . "

"What?" J.R, asked, confused.

"Today—Blue asked me to marry him too. As many times as that man said he loved me, he waited until after I said, yes to somebody else."

"What did you say?"

"I said—yes." I promised Blue that if things didn't work out between me and Anthony, I'd come back and marry him." Her eyes moistened with tears. "You know what J.R.?" She paused. "I learned something today."

"What's that?" He asked.

"I learned that . . . I love Blue." J.R. looked perplexed

"Then why marry Anthony?"

"Anthony is good for me, J.R. He always has been. And, I realized that I've always loved him, even when I didn't know what love was." She half-heartedly laughed. "I even love you, J.R." He smiled, boyishly. "It's a different kind of love . . ." She emphasized. "But, we gon always be a family." Effie Mae wrapped her arms around his neck and kissed him. He kissed back as he thought how much he enjoyed the kiss. "Can I take my babies with me?" Effie Mae asked as the kiss ended. J.R.'s closed eyes abruptly opened. He cleared his throat.

"Effie Mae, you ain't never took care of the children by yourself."

"Anthony's gon help me. And I got Momma and Annie Mae." Her eyes pleaded. "J.R., I can't live without my babies."

"You sure you can handle all those children?"

"No, J.R., I ain't sure. But I want to try." He stared into her begging eyes, as he considered her request.

"Okay. But promise me Effie Mae, that if it becomes more than you can handle, or you start drinking again, that you gon call me right away, so I can come and get the children before things get too bad."

"Okay, I promise." She smiled. "Thank you J.R." She kissed him again.

"Would you say yes?"

"Huh?"

Would you say yes, if I asked you to marry me again?" J.R. teased, hoping that her answer would be—yes.

"You asking me to marry you, J.R.?" Effie Mae blushed.

"Yeah, Effie Mae . . . "He smiled. "I think I am."

"Yeah, boy . . . I'd marry you again. You, gon have to get in line this time, though." She teased. J.R's mouth flung open.

"Behind who?"

"Let me see. Anthony—Huck—Blue . . ." Effie Mae smiled when saying *Blue's* name.

"What? Huck? Huck asked you to marry him?" J.R asked, surprised.

"Yeah, he did." She chuckled. "Huck asked me to marry him a long time ago, but I chose to stay with you." He stared momentarily into her eyes.

"I want you to know Effie Mae that I never regretted marrying you." She smiled.

"Thank you for saying that, J.R." They exchanged a brief kiss.

Chapter Forty-One

Anthony pulled in front of Daniel and Ms. Geraldine's home and parked. He agreed to take Effie Mae to see her son, fathered by Daniel, before leaving town. Looking at her through sympathetic eyes, Anthony leaned over and kissed her.

"Thank you Anthony." Effie Mae said as she thought of their new life together.

"I guess you want me to wait in the car?"

"No, I want you to come see my baby!" She said, elated. Anthony got out and walked around the car then opened her door. Effie Mae beamed as she climbed out. Anthony took a hold of her hand, smiling as he closed it. They walked hand in hand on their way to Daniel and Ms. Geraldine's home. Daniel opened the door when he heard her knock. Effie Mae and Anthony entered.

"How you doing, Effie Mae?" Daniel looked at Anthony with curiosity as he closed the door behind them.

"I'm fine Mr. Daniel." She said, smiling.

"Who is this young man?"

"This is Anthony, Lil' J.R.'s Daddy." Daniel's mouth slightly opened. He remained momentarily speechless, stunned by Effie Mae's bold introduction.

"Uh, how are you doing Anthony?"

"Just fine Sir." Anthony extended his hand to him. The two men shook, each looked at the other with unease.

"I guess you here to see D.J?" Daniel glanced at Anthony wondering if he knew his sordid history with Effie Mae.

"Uh, yeah—Effie Mae told me all about you and her." Anthony stated in a matter-of-fact tone. Daniel shifted his eyes to Effie Mae then again to Anthony, uncomfortable that knowledge of he and Effie Mae's indiscretion had been shared.

"Uh, let me go and get D.J." Daniel left the kitchen to retrieve the infant. Effie Mae and Anthony went into the living room and sat down. Daniel met with the bitter eyes of Ms. Geraldine as he entered into their bedroom. He walked over and gently removed the child from her arms. She gawked at him in anger as he exited the room, on his way to place his son into the arms of its biological Momma.

A huge smile formed on Effie Mae's face when Daniel returned to the room and placed their infant son into her arms.

"You see my beautiful baby boy, Anthony?" She kissed him on the forehead.

"He looks like you Mr. Daniel." Anthony stated.

"Mr. Daniel . . . Effie Mae and I are getting married." Daniel's eyes widened. He glanced at Effie Mae then again looked to Anthony.

"Does J.R. know about that?" Daniel asked, turning his attention back to Effie Mae.

"Yeah, I told him yesterday." She said. Daniel briefly shifted his eyes to Anthony, uncomfortable by the news.

"Is he alright?"

"Yeah, we talked about it. He understands."

"And the children?" Daniel asked.

"J.R.'s gon let me take my babies home to live with me and Anthony."

"Oh!" Daniel looked disturbed. Well, uh . . . congratulations Anthony, Effie Mae."

"Thank you Mr. Daniel." Effie Mae said. "And thank you for letting me see my baby boy." Effie Mae beamed as she delighted in her moment of bonding with her infant son. Anthony shared equally in her joy. Daniel discreetly scrutinized Anthony. He saw him as a rival.

Chapter Forty-Two

Anthony stood at the trunk of his car and prepared for the journey home. He tossed two suitcases inside and waited for Effie Mae and J.R. to bring the rest.

Effie Mae and J.R. sorted through the multiple items of children's clothing, stuffing them inside the stiff, blue, wicker suitcases. Millie Ann entered into her Momma's bedroom.

"Momma?"

"Yeah, Millie Ann."

"Can I stay here with Daddy?"

"What?" Effie Mae stopped packing and looked at her.

"I want to stay here and help Daddy. He needs somebody to be here with him. I also want to help Ms. Geraldine take care of my baby brother, D.J." Effie Mae hugged her and smiled.

"Are you sure that's what you want to do, baby?"

"Yes Momma."

"Okay, Millie Ann. If that's what you want to do, it's fine. I'm gon miss you though." Effie Mae kissed her on the forehead. "Promise me that you gon call me, Millie Ann, anytime you want to talk."

"I will Momma."

"Make sure you have your Daddy bring you to come and see us, too." Effie Mae shifted her eyes to J.R.

"I will Momma." They hugged. Millie Ann walked over and hugged her Daddy around the waist.

"I love you Daddy."

"I love you too, Millie Ann." J.R. glanced over at Effie Mae. Then the proud parents smiled, impressed by their responsible young daughter's selflessness.

...

J.R. brought the last of the children's luggage out and gave them to Anthony to put in the trunk. Effie Mae sat in the car as the children played in the front yard. She turned and looked out the back window, when she heard a car pull up. Anthony looked with curiosity at the gentleman driving. He walked over to the open passenger side window of his car and looked in at Effie Mae.

"Do you know that gentleman?"

"Uh, yeah, Anthony—that's my friend Huck.

"Huck?"

"Huck." She smiled. "We share a lot of history, intimate history . . . so you might want to turn your head."

"Huh? Should I be worried?"

"No! You ain't Blue." She laughed then got out and walked back to Huck's car and got in.

"Hey Effie Mae." He smiled.

"Hey, Huck." She smiled.

"Yeah, I see you done added another player to the game."

"What?"

"Blue told me that you were going back home—getting married and all." He gazed into her eyes then looked through the windshield at Anthony. "So, that's your son's Daddy?"

"Yep! That's Anthony."

"Slide over here." He said. "I don't know if Anthony gon be alright with what I'm about to do—but if he ain't . . . ."

"Yeah, he's gon be alright. I explained our relationship to him—for the most part."

Effie Mae slid over. Huck took her in his arms and passionately kissed her.

"Now get in the back seat."

"Huck!"

"I'm just playing with you girl." He laughed. "Unless Anthony okay with that too?" He teased.

"I don't think no man would be okay with that."

"You know Effie Mae, me and you—we have something special. You ain't gon find that with nobody else but me." He kissed her lightly on the lips. "You know that, right?"

"Yeah, I know that, Huck." She grinned. "You know Huck; I want to thank you for what you done for me and my babies."

"Wrong is wrong! And what your husband, Daniel and his wife, were doing to you—that was wrong, Effie Mae."

"You know Huck, if I didn't know better; I'd think that you loved me."

"Girl, you know I love you."

"No. I'm serious."

"I wouldn't have done all that for you, if I didn't." He kissed her.

"Well, I guess I can tell you something, now that I'm leaving."

"What's that? You love me?"

"You know I do. But, that's not what I was gon say."

"Then what you gon say Effie Mae?"

"You know that night you came over to my apartment and kept my man from seeing me?"

"Yeah, I remember him trying to get something for nothing."

"My response to you, that ain't had nothing to do with Blue; Baby . . . that was all Huck!" She giggled. He blushed.

"How you gon tell me something like that Effie Mae, when you getting ready to move thousands of miles away." He slightly tilted his head. "Girl, you are something else." He quietly laughed.

"I know." Effie Mae said, smiling. She and Huck stared into each other's eyes, before he again romantically kissed her.

"Bye Huck." She smiled.

"Bye Effie Mae." He smiled. "I'm gon give you one year to fit into your life with Anthony, then girl I'm coming to get your ass."

"What?" She blushed.

"I mean that Effie Mae! One year." He again kissed her lightly on the lips. "Get on."

She chuckled then slid over. She opened the door and got out. The two momentarily gazed at each other as Huck prepared to leave. Effie Mae watched as he drove off, then again joined Anthony, who patiently assisted the children in getting into the car.

"So, that was Huck?"

"That was Huck." She said in a matter-of-fact, tone.

Effie Mae and Anthony loaded the last of items into the trunk. She noticed J.R. and Millie Ann as they came outside and watched from the front yard. Effie Mae looked briefly at Anthony then approached J.R. and Millie Ann.

"Well, J.R. this ain't goodbye. I expect you to call me and our babies as often as you want. And that goes for you too, Millie Ann." She paused. "You know J.R., you could always move back home."

"And you and Anthony could always move to New York."

"And deal with Huck. No! That's too much, even for Effie Mae Reed to deal with."

"Effie Mae Smith." J.R. corrected. "But I guess you never really were Effie Mae Smith."

He hugged and kissed her. "You take care, Effie Mae."

"You too J.R." She smiled.

"Bye, Momma!"

"Bye, Millie Ann. I love you baby."

"I know." Effie Mae and Millie Ann embraced.

Effie Mae walked back over to the car and prepared to get in. Anthony closed the trunk then hurried from the rear and opened her door. She climbed inside and sat next to Lil' J.R. seated between the two. Anthony turned to J.R. and Millie Ann then smiled. He closed Effie Mae's door and waved goodbye then walked hastily to the other side. He got in, joining Effie Mae and the children. J.R. and Millie Ann watched as Anthony started the car then drove away.

www.ingramcontent.com/pod-product-compliance
Lightning Source LLC
Chambersburg PA
CBHW071257110426
42743CB00042B/1084